# Comparing ISO 9000, Malcolm Baldrige, and the SEI CMM for Software

# Comparing ISO 9000, Malcolm Baldrige, and the SEI CMM for Software

## A Reference and Selection Guide

Michael O. Tingey

*IBM Corporation*

To join a Prentice Hall PTR
mailing list, point to:
http://www.prenhall.com/register

Prentice Hall PTR
Upper Saddle River, NJ 07458
http://www.prenhall.com

Library of Congress Cataloging-in-Publication Data

```
Tingey, Michael O.
    Comparing ISO 9000, Malcolm Baldrige, and the SEI CMM for
    software : a reference and selection guide / Michael O. Tingey.
      p.  cm.
    Includes index.
    ISBN 0-13-376260-2 (case)
    1. Quality control. 2. ISO 9000 Series Standards. 3. Total
    quality management. 4. Computer software—Quality control.
    I. Title.
    TS156.T575  1997
    658.5'62—dc20                                    96-28936
                                                     CIP
```

Editorial/production supervision: *BooksCraft, Inc., Indianapolis, IN*
Cover design director: *Jerry Votta*
Cover design: *Design Source*
Acquisitions editor: *Bernard Goodwin*
Manufacturing manager: *Alexis R. Heydt*

© 1997 by Prentice Hall PTR
Prentice-Hall, Inc.
A Simon & Schuster Company
Upper Saddle River, NJ 07458

The publisher offers discounts on this book when ordered in bulk quantities.
For more information, contact:

Corporate Sales Department
Prentice Hall PTR
One Lake Street
Upper Saddle River, NJ 07458
Phone: 800-382-3419  Fax: 201-236-7141
E-mail: corpsales@prenhall.com.

Opinions expressed in this document, as well as any errors and omissions, are strictly those of the author.
The contents of this book in no way reflect the official opinions or position of the IBM Corporation.

Printed in the United States of America

10  9  8  7  6  5  4  3  2

ISBN: 0-13-376260-2

Prentice-Hall International (UK) Limited, *London*
Prentice-Hall of Australia Pty. Limited, *Sydney*
Prentice-Hall Canada Inc., *Toronto*
Prentice-Hall Hispanoamericana, S.A., *Mexico*
Prentice-Hall of India Private Limited, *New Delhi*
Prentice-Hall of Japan, Inc., *Tokyo*
Simon & Schuster Asia Pte. Ltd., *Singapore*
Editora Prentice-Hall do Brasil, Ltda., *Rio de Janeiro*

# Contents

## Part I
## Introduction

# Part II
## Quality Management System Assessment Methodologies

# Part III
## Comparing QMS Assessment Methodologies

# Part IV
# Framework for Comparing QMS Assessment Methodologies

# Part V
# Appendixes

# List of Figures

# List of Tables

# Preface

This book is an in-depth study that compares three quality management system (QMS) assessment methods: Malcolm Baldrige National Quality Award (MB), International Organization for Standardization 9000 (ISO 9000), and the Software Engineering Institute (SEI) Capability Maturity Model (CMM) for Software.

Many companies are finding themselves in a position where they must assess their quality management system using more than one assessment model. This is causing an increase in the cost of conducting business, which can be minimized by understanding where these assessment models overlap and how they differ from one another.

This book also establishes a framework from which to compare QMS assessment methodologies in general. This outline provides assistance in deciding which methodology is best suited for an organization's QMS. It also provides a cross-reference among the various methodologies for specific aspects of a quality management system.

An overview and detailed analysis of each methodology is provided. Also included is a complete translation of all assessment methodology requirements into statements of activity. The following specific methodologies were used for the comparison:

- ✦ Software Engineering Institute Capability Maturity Model for Software (1993, latest published revision)
- ✦ ANSI/ASQC Q9001—1994, Quality Systems—Model for Quality Assurance in Design, Development, Production, Installation, and Servicing (American equivalent to ISO 9001, 1994). (1994, latest published revision)
- ✦ 1995 Malcolm Baldrige National Quality Award (published annually)

This book is divided into five parts and is structured so that each part can be used independently of the others. Using the subsequent paragraphs, people of differing experience levels can quickly find the material that is of the most importance to them. Those who are new to TQM and quality management systems can start with Part 1 and progress through the subsequent parts. Experienced practitioners can largely skip Parts 1 and 2 and focus on Parts 3, 4, and 5.

*Part I: Introduction* provides an introduction and a backdrop from which you can better understand the comparison. *Chapter 1* describes the two primary purposes of the book. *Chapter 2* introduces total quality management (TQM) and some of the various definitions of quality, identifying their common themes. *Chapter 3* further defines TQM by identifying the "Core Values and Concepts" underlying the ISO and MB quality management systems. *Chapter 4* provides the rationale for assessing the quality management system and the types of assessments.

*Part II: Quality Management System Assessment Methodologies* provides an overview for each of the three QMS assessment methodologies in *Chapters 5, 6, and 7* . *Chapter 8* briefly describes other QMS assessments.

*Part III: Comparing QMS Assessment Methodologies* is the core part of the book, comparing the three methodologies. *Chapter 9* gives a summary and overview of the comparison. *Chapter 10* provides a high-level view of where the methodologies intersect. *Chapters 11, 12, and 13* provide a detailed view as seen from each methodology's perspective and the corresponding requirements in the other two methodologies.

*Part IV: Framework for Comparing QMS Assessment Methodologies* provides the framework used for comparing the QMS methodologies. *Chapter 14* describes the approach used to compare the assessment methodologies. *Chapter 15* discusses conducting a system comparison in general and also identifies the assumptions used in the comparison. *Chapter 16* provides a high-level comparison using the QMS framework, which *Chapter 17* then summarizes.

*Part V* contains the appendixes. *Appendixes A, B, and C* provide the detailed requirements of MB, SEI, and ISO. *Appendixes D, E, F, G, H, and I* provide the detailed correlated requirements of MB, SEI, and ISO as seen from each methodology's perspective. *Appendix J* provides the detailed requirements of the SEI and ISO quality plans. *Appendixes K, L, and* M provide the QMS framework properties matrixes for MB, SEI, and ISO. *Appendix N* is the summary of properties matrixes.

## Keywords

Software Engineering Institute, SEI, Capability Maturity Model, CMM, International Organization for Standardization 9000, ISO, ISO 9000, ISO 9001, ISO 9004, Malcolm Baldrige National Quality Award, MB, MBNQA, Quality Management System, QMS, Total Quality Management, TQM, Market-Driven Quality, MDQ, Comparison, Assessment, Continuous Improvement, Quality Maturity, Process Reengineering, Reengineering, Framework, Methodology, Methodologies, Software Development Process

## Sources

Excerpts from the *Capability Maturity Model for Software, Version 1.1* (CMU-93-TR-24), and the *Key Practices of the Capability Maturity Model, Version 1.1* (CMU-93-TR-25), appear throughout this book with permission of the Software Engineering Institute, Carnegie Mellon University, Pittsburgh, PA 15213. Copyright © 1993 by Carnegie Mellon University.

Excerpts from the Q9001-1994 standards throughout this book appear with the permission of the American Society for Quality Control, 611 East Wisconsin, Ave., P.O. Box 3005, Milwaukee, WI 53201. Copyright © 1994, American Society for Quality Control. No part of these standards may be reproduced in any form, in an electronic retrieval system or otherwise, without the prior written permission of the copyright holder.

The author and publisher make no guarantee, either express or implied, with regard to the ISO 9000 registration.

Excerpts from the 1995 Malcolm Baldrige National Quality Control Award appear throughout this book.

The Malcolm Baldrige National Quality Award is published by the United States Department of Commerce and is considered public domain material.

# Acknowledgments

My thanks

To my wife Hilde, for her endless support and encouragement which made this book possible.

To my sons Michael and Russell, who gave me their time and patience to complete this project.

To Joe Ciccarino, for his time and advice in reviewing the original drafts of this work.

# I

---

# Introduction

*This section begins with a discussion of the two primary purposes of the book, followed by an introduction to quality and the notion of total quality management (TQM). We then explore TQM in much greater depth to give you a clearer understanding of what it entails. Finally, we discuss why you need to assess your quality management system and the different ways you can make the assessment.*

# Purpose

The purpose of this book is to compare three quality management system (QMS) assessment methodologies:

✧ Malcolm Baldrige National Quality Award (MB)
✧ International Organization for Standardization 9000 (ISO 9000)
✧ Software Engineering Institute (SEI) Capability Maturity Model (CMM) for Software

The competitiveness of corporations is becoming more and more important, due to the increase in global competition. An increase in the focus on improving quality has accompanied this growth. With the increased focus on quality improvement, many different models for determining the fitness of a business's QMS have emerged. The emergence of these different models has created a business problem. Many companies find themselves in a position where they must assess their business using more than one assessment model. Businesses select these models for different reasons. For some companies, using ISO 9000 and SEI CMM has become mandatory for doing business with other companies and governments. Other companies have recognized the need for quality improvement as an important element of long-term survival. Quality management system assessment is a costly and time-consuming process. It is therefore necessary, where at all possible, for companies to minimize this cost. One way to minimize cost is to understand where these assessment models overlap. This knowledge will assist in minimizing the number of procedures an organization must maintain in its QMS. The manner in which a company implements a quality management system can also have an impact on the costs associated with conducting assessments. This book compares three major assessment methodologies to help you understand where they overlap and how they differ from one another.

The second purpose of this book is to establish a framework for comparing QMS assessment methodologies. A framework is important because it provides a common point of reference from which to understand each methodology as it relates to another. Since each methodology was created with a different purpose in mind, it is necessary to derive a common context in which to compare the methodologies. This book will assist organizations by providing a basis for cross-referencing specific aspects of an organization's QMS with the various methodologies. This cross-reference, in turn, will help corporations understand how adding a second assessment methodology fits into an organization's current quality activities.

# Total Quality Management

Total quality management has become a very popular concept today as companies, schools, and governments increase their awareness of quality and what it means to their competitiveness. Quality has, of course, always been an important factor in many companies; however, more recently other types of "businesses" like governments and educational institutions are realizing the importance of quality. Another recent realization, even within business, is that quality does not apply just to that part of the business concerned with building products but that it applies to every part of the business. A definition for quality is "the extent to which products and services produced conform to customer requirements."[1] *Customer*, in this definition, means those internal and external to an organization.

Total quality management can be thought of as "a comprehensive set of management tools, management philosophies, and improvement methods including: customer orientation, the empowerment of employees, participative management, data-based decisions, continual improvement, a "process" orientation, and a set of quantitative tools for process improvement."[2]

A second definition of TQM is "a way to continuously improve performance at every level of operation, in every functional area of an organization, using all available

1. V. Daniel Hunt, *Managing for Quality: Integrating Quality and Business Strategy* (Business One Irwin, 1993), p. 33.
2. Robert A. Klein, "Achieve Total Quality Management," *Chemical Engineering Progress*, November 1991, p. 83.

human and capital resources. Improvement is addressed toward satisfying broad goals such as cost, quality, market share, schedule, and growth."[3]

A third definition comes from the U.S. Department of Defense: "TQM is both a philosophy and a set of guiding principles that represent the foundation of a continuously improving organization. TQM is the application of quantitative methods and human resources to improve the material and services supplied to an organization, all the processes within the organization, and the degree to which the needs of the customer are met, now and in the future. TQM integrates fundamental management techniques, existing improvement efforts, and technical tools under a disciplined approach focused on continuous improvement."[4]

There are many other definitions of quality management or total quality management. Each definition brings with it the individual's own view of a quality management system's key properties, based on personal experiences in the types of businesses with which the individual has been involved. These types of businesses can range from producing products, such as automobiles, computers, and aircraft, to providing services such as delivery, legal, and tax. Other businesses are a mixture of both product and service. For example, a restaurant provides half product and half service.[5] Despite this diversity of experience and the view of what a quality management system encompasses, there are some common threads. As seen in the preceding definitions, the focus on continuous improvement is common, as is the broad scope of improvement. The scope of improvement addresses all aspects of a business, not just the production of goods, the aspect with which quality has been traditionally connected.

3. Bruce Brocka and M. Suzanne Brocka, *Quality Management: Implementing the Best Ideas of the Masters* (Business One Irwin, 1992), p. 3.

4. Ibid., p. 4. Original U.S. Department of Defense reference not known.

5. International Organization for Standardization, *ISO 9004-2:1991, Quality Management and Quality System Elements—Part 2: Guidelines for Services* (American National Standards Institute, 1991), p. 1.

# Quality Management Systems

For most organizations, the implementation of total quality management involves the definition of a quality management system. A QMS is made up of various elements and a set of underlying principles. This chapter expands on the definitions of quality and total quality management by reviewing the guidelines or core values and concepts of ISO 9004-1 and the Malcolm Baldrige National Quality Award. Malcolm Baldrige's quality management system elements are also introduced. The expression "core values and concepts" comes from MB, which identifies these as a necessary "foundation for integrating customer and company performance requirements." ISO 9004-1 refers to these as "guidelines," but they are similar in concept to the Malcolm Baldrige core values and concepts because they are not intended as specific requirements but rather as an underlying philosophy or guide for a quality management system.

## ■ 3.1 ISO 9004, QUALITY MANAGEMENT SYSTEM GUIDELINES

A list of the core values and concepts for *ISO 9004-1-1994, Quality Management and Quality System Elements—Guidelines* follows. This section uses *ANSI/ASQC Q9004-1-1994,*[1] which is functionally equivalent to ISO 9004-1.

---

Note: This chapter quotes extensively from the ANSI/ASQC Q9000 standards series, which is the American equivalent of the ISO 9000 standards series.

1. American National Standards Institute (ANSI), *ANSI/ASQC Q9004-1-1994, Quality Management and Quality System Elements—Guidelines* (American Society for Quality Control [ASQC], 1994).

✧ Organizational goals

✧ Meeting customer/organization needs and expectations

✧ Risks, costs, and benefits

✧ Management responsibility

✧ Quality system elements

✧ Financial considerations of quality systems

✧ Quality in marketing

✧ Quality in specification and design

✧ Quality in purchasing

✧ Quality of processes

✧ Control of processes

✧ Product verification

✧ Control of inspection, measuring, and test equipment

✧ Control of nonconforming product

✧ Corrective action

✧ Postproduction activities

✧ Quality records

✧ Personnel

✧ Product safety

✧ Use of statistical methods

An abbreviated description of these elements follows.

## 3.1.1 ISO 9004, Core Values and Concepts

*Organizational Goals*

In order to meet its objectives, the organization should ensure that the technical, administrative, and human factors affecting the quality of its products will be under control, whether hardware, software, processed materials, or services. All such control should be oriented towards the reduction, elimination, and, most importantly, prevention of quality nonconformities.

A quality system should be developed and implemented for the purpose of accomplishing the objectives set out in the organization's quality policy.

Each element (or requirement) in a quality system varies in importance from one type of activity to another and from one product to another.

In order to achieve maximum effectiveness and to satisfy customer expectations, it is essential that the quality system be appropriate to the type of activity and to the product being offered.

### Meeting Customer/Organization Needs and Expectations

A quality system has two interrelated aspects, as follows.

✧ The customer's needs and expectations. "For the customer, there is a need for confidence in the ability of the organization to deliver the desired quality as well as the consistent maintenance of that quality."

✧ The organization's needs and interests. "For the organization, there is a business need to attain and to maintain the desired quality at an optimum cost; the fulfillment of this aspect is related to the planned and efficient utilization of the technological, human, and material resources available to the organization."

"Each of the above aspects of a quality system requires objective evidence in the form of information and data concerning the quality of the system and the quality of the organization's products."

### Benefits, Costs, and Risks

Benefit, cost, and risk considerations have great importance for both the organization and customer. These considerations are inherent aspects of most products. The possible effects and ramifications of these considerations are given in a to c.

a) Benefit considerations

For the customer, consideration has to be given to reduced costs, improved fitness for use, increased satisfaction, and growth in confidence.

For the organization, consideration has to be given to increased profitability and market share.

b) Cost considerations

For the customer, consideration has to be given to safety, acquisition cost, operating, maintenance, downtime and repair costs, and possible disposal costs.

For the organization, consideration has to be given to costs due to marketing and design deficiencies, including unsatisfactory product, rework, repair, replacement, reprocessing, loss of production, warranties, and field repair.

c) Risk considerations

For the customer, consideration has to be given to risks such as those pertaining to the health and safety of people, dissatisfaction with product, availability, marketing claims, and loss of confidence.

For the organization, consideration has to be given to risks related to deficient products which lead to loss of image or reputation, loss of market, complaints, claims, liability, and waste of human and financial resources.

An effective quality system should be designed to satisfy customer needs and expectations while serving to protect the organization's interests. A well-structured quality system is a valuable management resource in the optimization and control of quality in relation to benefit, cost, and risk considerations.

## Management Responsibility

"The responsibility for and commitment to a quality policy belongs to the highest level of management. Quality management encompasses all activities of the overall management function that determine the quality policy, objectives, and responsibilities, and implement them by means such as quality planning, quality control, quality assurance, and quality improvement within the quality system."

Management responsibility includes:

- ✧ Quality policy. "The management of an organization should define and document its quality policy."
- ✧ Quality objectives. "Management should document objectives and commitments pertaining to key elements of quality, such as fitness for use, performance, safety, and dependability."
- ✧ Quality system. "A quality system is the organizational structure, procedures, processes, and resources needed to implement quality management."

## Quality System Elements

Quality system principles include:

- ✧ Extent of application. "The quality system typically applies to, and interacts with, all activities pertinent to the quality of a product. It will involve all phases in the life-cycle of a product and processes, from initial identification of market needs to final satisfaction of requirements."
- ✧ Structure of the quality system.

    Input from the market should be used to improve new and existing products and to improve the quality system.
        Management is ultimately responsible for establishing the quality policy and for decisions concerning the initiation, development, implementation, and maintenance of the quality system.

- ✧ Documentation of the quality system.

    All the elements, requirements, and provisions adopted by an organization for its quality system should be documented in a systematic, orderly, and understandable manner in the form of policies and procedures.

The quality system should include adequate provision for the proper identification, distribution, collection, and maintenance of all quality documents.

✧ Auditing the quality system. "Audits should be planned and carried out to determine if the activities and related results of the organization's quality system comply with planned arrangements, and to determine the effectiveness of the quality system. All elements should be internally audited and evaluated on a regular basis, considering the status and importance of the activity to be audited. For this purpose, an appropriate audit program should be established and implemented by the organization's management."

✧ Review and evaluation of the quality system. "The organization's management should provide for independent review and evaluation of the quality system at defined intervals. The reviews of the quality policy and objectives should be carried out by top management, and the review of supporting activities should be carried out by management with executive responsibilities for quality and other appropriate members of management, utilizing competent independent personnel as decided on by the management."

✧ Quality improvement.

When implementing a quality system, the management of an organization should ensure that the system will facilitate and promote continuous improvement.

Quality improvement refers to the actions taken throughout the organization to increase the effectiveness and efficiency of activities and processes to provide added benefits to both the organization and its customers.

### Financial Considerations of Quality Systems

It is important that the effectiveness of a quality system be measured in financial terms. The impact of an effective quality system upon the organization's profit and loss statement can be highly significant, particularly by improvement of operations, resulting in reduced losses due to error and by making a contribution to customer satisfaction.

Such measurement and reporting can provide a means for identifying inefficient activities, and initiating internal improvement activities.

By reporting quality-system activities and effectiveness in financial terms, management will receive the results in a common business language from all departments.

Financial considerations of quality systems includes:

✧ Approaches to financial reporting of quality-system activities. "The approach(es) to financial reporting selected and used by particular organizations will be dependent upon their individual structures, their activities, and the maturity of their quality systems."

✧ Reporting. "The financial reporting of quality activities should be regularly provided to and monitored by management, and be related to other business measures such as 'sales,' 'turnover,' or 'added value'...."

### Quality in Marketing

Quality in marketing includes:

✧ Marketing requirements. "The marketing function should establish adequately defined and documented requirements for the quality of the product."

✧ Defining product specification. "The marketing function should provide the organization with a formal statement or outline of product requirements."

✧ Customer feedback information. "The marketing function should establish an information-monitoring and feedback system on a continuous basis."

### Quality in Specification and Design

Quality in specification and design includes:

✧ Contribution of specification and design to quality. "The specification and design function should provide for the translation of customer needs into technical specifications for materials, products, and processes."

✧ Design planning and objectives (defining the project). "Management should prepare plans that define the responsibility for each design and development activity inside and/or outside the organization, and ensure that all those who contribute to design are aware of their responsibilities in relation to the full scope of the project."

✧ Product testing and measurement. "The methods of measurement and test, and the acceptance criteria applied to evaluate the product and processes during both the design and production phases should be specified."

✧ Design review. "At the conclusion of each phase of design development, a formal documented, systematic, and critical review of the design results should be planned and conducted."

✧ Design qualification and validation. "The design process should provide periodic evaluation of the design at significant stages."

✧ Final design review and production release. "The final design should be reviewed and the results appropriately documented in specifications and drawings, which then form the design baseline."

✧ Market readiness review. "A determination should be made as to whether the organization has the capability to deliver the new or redesigned product."

✧ Design change control. "The quality system should include documented procedures for controlling the release, change, and use of documents that define the design input and the design baseline (output), and for authorizing the necessary work to be performed to implement changes and modifications that can affect product during its entire life-cycle, including changes in software and service instructions."

✧ Design requalification. "Periodic evaluation of product should be performed in order to ensure that the design is still valid."

✧ Configuration management in design. "This discipline may be initiated once the requirements have been defined, but is most useful during the design phase."

### *Quality in Purchasing*

"Purchases become part of the organization's product and directly affect the quality of its product."

Quality in purchasing includes:

✧ Requirements for specifications, drawings, and purchase documents. "The successful purchase of supplies begins with a clear definition of the requirements."

✧ Selection of acceptable subcontractors. "Each subcontractor should have a demonstrated capability to furnish product which meets all the requirements of the specifications, drawings, and purchase documents."

✧ Agreement on quality assurance. "The organization should develop a clear agreement with subcontractors for the assurance of product supplied."

✧ Agreement on verification methods. "A clear agreement should be developed with the subcontractor on the methods by which conformance to requirements will be verified."

✧ Provisions for settlement of disputes. "Systems and procedures should be established by which settlement of disputes regarding quality can be reached with subcontractors."

✧ Receiving inspection planning and control. "Appropriate measures should be established to ensure that received materials are properly controlled."

✧ Quality records related to purchasing. "Appropriate quality records related to product received should be maintained."

### *Quality of Processes*

Quality of processes includes:

✧ Planning for process control. "Planning of processes should ensure that these proceed under controlled conditions in the specified manner and sequence."

✧ Process capability. "Processes should be verified as being capable of producing product in accordance with specifications."

✧ Supplies, utilities, and environment. "Where important to product quality characteristics, auxiliary materials and utilities, such as water, compressed air, electric
power, and chemicals used for processing, should be controlled and verified periodically to ensure uniformity of effect on the process."

✧ Handling. "The handling of product requires proper planning, control, and a documented system for incoming, in-process, and final product; this applies not only during delivery but up to the time of being put into use."

### Control of Processes

"Product quality should be addressed in each phase of the life-cycle."
  Control of processes includes:

✧ Material control, traceability, and identification. "All materials and parts should
conform to specified requirements before being introduced into a process."

✧ Equipment control and maintenance. "All equipment, including fixed machinery,
jigs, fixtures, tooling, templates, patterns, and gauges, should be proved for accuracy
prior to use."

✧ Process-control management. "Processes which are important to product quality
should be planned, approved, monitored, and controlled."

✧ Documentation. "Documentation should be controlled as specified by the quality
system."

✧ Process change control. "Those responsible for authorization of process changes
should be clearly designated and, where necessary, customer approval should be
sought."

✧ Control of verification status. "Verification status of product output should be identified."

✧ Control of nonconforming product. "Provision should be made for the identification
and control of all nonconforming products and materials."

### Product Verification

Product verification includes:

✧ Incoming materials and parts. "The method used to ensure quality of purchased
materials, component parts and assemblies that are received into the production
facility will depend on the importance of the item to quality, the state of control and
information available from the subcontractor, and impact on costs."

✧ In-process verification. "Verifications, typically by inspections or tests, should be
considered at appropriate points in the process to verify conformity."

✧ Finished product verification. "To augment inspections and tests made during processing, two forms of verification of finished product are available."

## Control of Inspection, Measuring, and Test Equipment

Control of inspection, measuring, and test equipment includes:

✧ Measurement control. "Control should be maintained over all measuring systems used in the development, production, installation, and servicing of product to provide confidence in decisions or actions based on measurement data."

✧ Elements of control.

> The procedures for control of inspection, measuring, and test equipment and test methods should include, as appropriate:
>
> a)  suitable specification and selection, including range, accuracy, and robustness...
>
> b)  initial calibration prior to first use in order to validate the required accuracy...
>
> c)  periodic recall for adjustment, repair, and recalibration...
>
> d)  documentary evidence covering unique identification of...
>
> e)  traceability to reference standards of known accuracy and stability....

✧ Subcontractor measurement controls. "The control of measuring and test equipment and test methods may be extended to all subcontractors."

✧ Corrective action. "Where measuring processes are found to be out of control, or where inspection, measuring, and test equipment are found to be out of calibration, appropriate action is necessary."

✧ Outside testing. "The facilities of outside organizations may be used for inspection, measurement, testing, or calibration to avoid costly duplication or additional investment...."

## Control of Nonconforming Product

"The steps for dealing with nonconforming product should be established and maintained in documented procedures."

These steps include:

✧ Identification. "Suspected nonconforming items or lots should be immediately identified and the occurrence(s) recorded."

✧ Segregation. "The nonconforming items should be segregated, when practical, from the conforming items and adequately identified to prevent further unintended use of them until the appropriate disposition is decided."

✧ Review. "Nonconforming product should be subjected to review by designated persons to determine whether it can be accepted with or without repair by concession, repaired, reworked, regraded, or scrapped."

- Disposition. "Disposition of nonconforming product should be taken as soon as practicable."
- Action. "Action should be taken as soon as possible to prevent unintended use or installation of nonconforming product."
- Avoidance of recurrence. "Appropriate steps should be taken to avoid the recurrence of nonconformity."

## Corrective Action

"The implementation of corrective action begins with the detection of a quality-related problem and involves taking measures to eliminate or minimize the recurrence of the problem."

Corrective action includes:

- Assignment of responsibility. "The responsibility and authority for instituting corrective action should be defined and part of the quality system."
- Evaluation of importance. "The significance of a problem affecting quality should be evaluated in terms of its potential impact on such aspects as processing costs, quality-related costs, performance, dependability, safety, and customer satisfaction."
- Investigation of possible causes. "The relationship of cause and effect should be determined, with all potential causes considered."
- Analysis of problem. "In the analysis of a quality-related problem, the root cause or causes should be determined before corrective action is planned."
- Elimination of causes. "Appropriate steps should be taken to eliminate causes of actual or potential nonconformities."
- Process controls. "Sufficient controls of processes and procedures should be implemented to prevent recurrence of the problem."
- Permanent changes. "Permanent changes resulting from corrective action should be recorded in work instructions, production-process documentation, product specifications, and/or the quality-system documentation."

## Postproduction Activities

Postproduction activities include:

- Storage. "Appropriate storage methods should be specified to ensure shelf-life and to avoid deterioration."
- Delivery. "Provision for protection of the quality of product is important during all phases of delivery."
- Installation. "Installation procedures, including warning notices, should contribute to proper installations and should be documented."

✧ Servicing. "Special-purpose tools or equipment for handling and servicing products during or after installation should have their design and function validated, as for any new product."

✧ After sales. "Consideration should be given to the establishment of an early warning system for reporting instances of product failure or shortcomings, to ensure rapid corrective action."

✧ Market feedback. "A feedback system regarding performance in use should exist to monitor the quality characteristics of products throughout the life-cycle."

### Quality Records

"The organization should establish and maintain documented procedures as a means for identification, collection, indexing, access, filing, storage, maintenance, retrieval, and disposition of pertinent quality records."

Quality records includes:

✧ Quality records. "The quality system should require that sufficient records be maintained to demonstrate conformance to specified requirements and verify effective operation of the quality system."

✧ Quality records control. "The quality system should require that sufficient documentation be available to follow and demonstrate conformance to specified requirements and the effective operation of the quality system."

### Personnel

Personnel includes:

✧ Training. "The need for training of personnel should be identified, and documented procedures for providing that training should be established and maintained.

✧ Qualification. "The need to require and document qualifications of personnel performing certain specialized operations, processes, tests, or inspections should be evaluated and implemented where necessary, in particular for safety-related work."

✧ Motivation. "Motivation of personnel begins with their understanding of the tasks they are expected to perform and how those tasks support the overall activities."

### Product Safety

Consideration should be given to identifying safety aspects of products and processes with the aim of enhancing safety. Steps can include:

a)  identifying relevant safety standards in order to make the formulation of product specifications more effective;

b)  carrying out design evaluation tests and prototype (or model) testing for safety and documenting the test results;

c) analyzing instructions and warnings to the user, maintenance manuals, and labeling and promotional material in order to minimize misinterpretation, particularly regarding intended use and known hazards;

d) developing a means of traceability to facilitate product recall;

e) considering development of an emergency plan in case recall of a product becomes necessary.

## *Use of Statistical Methods*

Use of statistical methods includes:

✧ Applications. "Identification and correct application of modern statistical methods are important elements to control every phase of the organization's processes. Documented procedures should be established and maintained for selecting and applying statistical methods to: market analysis; product design; dependability specification, longevity, and durability prediction; process-control and process-capability studies; determination of quality levels in sampling plans; data analysis, performance assessment, and nonconformity analysis; process improvement; safety evaluation and risk analysis."

✧ Statistical techniques. "Specific statistical methods for establishing, controlling, and verifying activities include, but are not limited to, the following: design of experiments and factorial analysis; analysis of variance and regression analysis; tests of significance; quality-control charts and cusum techniques; statistical sampling."

# ■ 3.2 MALCOLM BALDRIGE QUALITY MANAGEMENT SYSTEM

Like ISO 9004-1, the Malcolm Baldrige National Quality Award identifies a set of core values and concepts that establish the basis for their primary QMS elements.

## 3.2.1 Malcolm Baldrige Core Values and Concepts

### *Customer-Driven Quality*

Quality is judged by customers. All product and service characteristics that contribute value to customers and lead to customer satisfaction and preference must be a key focus of a company's management system. Value, satisfaction, and preference may be influenced by many factors throughout the customer's overall purchase, ownership, and service experiences. These factors include the company's relationship with customers that helps build trust, confidence, and loyalty. This concept of quality includes not only the product and service characteristics that meet basic customer requirements, but it also includes those characteristics that enhance them and differentiate them from competing offerings. Such enhancement and differentiation may be based upon new offerings, combinations of product and service offerings, rapid response, or special relationships.

Customer-driven quality is thus a strategic concept. It is directed toward customer retention and market share gain. It demands constant sensitivity to emerging customer and market requirements, and measurement of the factors that drive customer satisfaction and retention. It also demands awareness of developments in technology and of competitor's offerings, and rapid and flexible response to customer and market requirements.

Success requires more than defect and error reduction, merely meeting specifications, and reducing complaints. Nevertheless, defect and error reduction and elimination of causes of dissatisfaction contribute significantly to the customers' view of quality and are thus also important parts of customer-driven quality. In addition, the company's success in recovering from defects and errors ("making things right for the customer") is crucial to building customer relationships and to customer retention.

## Leadership

A company's senior leaders need to set directions and create a customer orientation, clear and visible values, and high expectations. Reinforcement of the values and expectations requires personal commitment and involvement. The leaders' basic values and commitment need to include areas of public responsibility and corporate citizenship. The leaders need to take part in the creation of strategies, systems, and methods for achieving excellence and building capabilities. The systems and methods need to guide all activities and decisions of the company. The senior leaders need to commit to the development of the entire work force and should encourage participation and creativity by all employees. Through their personal involvement in activities, such as planning, communications, review of company performance, and recognition of employees' achievements, the senior leaders serve as role models, reinforcing the values and encouraging leadership and initiative throughout the company.

## Continuous Improvement and Learning

Achieving the highest levels of performance requires a well-executed approach to continuous improvement. The term "continuous improvement" refers to both incremental and "breakthrough" improvement. The approach to improvement needs to be "embedded" in the way the company functions. Embedded means: (1) improvement is part of the daily work of all work units; (2) improvement processes seek to eliminate problems at their source; and (3) improvement is driven by opportunities to do better, as well as by problems that must be corrected. Opportunities for improvement include: employee ideas; R&D; customer input; and benchmarking or other comparative performance information.

Improvements may be of several types: (1) enhancing value to customers through new and improved products and services; (2) reducing errors, defects, and waste; (3) improving responsiveness and cycle time performance; (4) improving productivity and effectiveness in the use of all resources; and (5) improving the company's performance and leadership position in fulfilling its public responsibilities and serving as a role model in corporate citizenship. Thus improvement is driven not only by the objective to provide better products and services, but also by the need to be responsive and efficient—both conferring additional marketplace advantages. To meet these objectives, continuous improvement must contain cycles of planning, execution, and evaluation. This requires a basis—preferably a quantitative basis—for assessing progress and for deriving information for future cycles of improvement. Such information should provide direct links between performance goals and internal operations.

## Employee Participation and Development

A company's success in improving performance depends increasingly on the skills and motivation of its work force. Employee success depends increasingly on having meaningful opportunities to learn and to practice new skills. Companies need to invest in the development of the work force through ongoing education, training, and opportunities for continuing growth. Such opportunities might include classroom and on-the-job training, job rotation, and pay for demonstrated skills. Structured on-the-job training offers a cost effective way to train and to better link training to work processes. Work force education and training programs may need to utilize advanced technologies, such as electronic support systems and "information highways." Increasingly, training, development, and work organizations need to be tailored to a more diverse work force and to more flexible, high performance work practices.

Major challenges in the area of work force development include: (1) integration of human resource management-selection, performance, recognition, training, and career advancement; and (2) aligning human resource management with business plans and strategic change processes. Addressing these challenges requires acquisition and use of employee-related data on skills, satisfaction, motivation, safety, and well-being. Such data need to be tied to indicators of company or unit performance, such as customer satisfaction, customer retention, and productivity. Through this approach, human resource management may be better integrated and aligned with business directions, using continuous improvement processes to refine integration and alignment.

## Fast Response

Success in competitive markets increasingly demands ever-shorter cycles for new or improved product and service introduction. Also, faster and more flexible response to customers is now a more critical requirement. Major improvement in response time often requires simplification of work organizations and work processes. To accomplish such improvement, the time performance of work processes should be among the key process measures. There are other important benefits derived from this focus: response time improvements often drive simultaneous improvements in organization, quality, and productivity. Hence it is beneficial to consider response time, quality and productivity objectives together.

## Design Quality and Prevention

Business management should place strong emphasis on design quality—problem and waste prevention achieved through building quality into products and services and into production and delivery processes. In general, costs of preventing problems at the design stage are much lower than costs of correcting problems which occur "downstream". Design quality includes the creation of fault-tolerant (robust) or failure-resistant processes and products.

A major issue in competition is the design-to-introduction ("product generation" ) cycle time. Meeting the demands of rapidly changing markets requires that companies carry out stage-to-stage coordination and integration ("concurrent engineering" ) of functions and activities from basic research to commercialization.

From the point of view of public responsibility, the design stage involves decisions regarding resource use and manufacturing processes. Such decisions affect process waste streams and the composition of municipal and industrial wastes. The growing demands for a cleaner environment mean that companies need to develop design strategies that include environmental factors.

Consistent with the theme of design quality and prevention, continuous improvement needs to emphasize interventions "upstream"—at early stages in processes. This approach yields the maximum overall benefits of improvements and corrections. Such upstream intervention also needs to take into account the company's suppliers.

## Long-Range View of the Future

Pursuit of market leadership requires a strong future orientation and a willingness to make long-term commitments to all stakeholders—customers, employees, suppliers, stockholders, the public and the community. Planning needs to anticipate many types of changes including those that may affect customers' expectations of products and services, technological developments, changing customer segments, evolving regulatory requirements, community/societal expectations, and thrusts by competitors. Plans, strategies, and resource allocations need to reflect these commitments and changes. A major part of the long-term commitment is developing employees and suppliers, fulfilling public responsibilities, and serving as a corporate citizenship role model.

## Management by Fact

A modern business management system needs to be built upon a framework of measurement, information, data, and analysis. Measurements must derive from the company's strategy and encompass all key processes and the outputs and results of those processes. Facts and data needed for performance improvement and assessment are of many types, including: customer, product and service performance, operations, market, competitive comparisons, supplier, employee-related, and cost and financial. Analysis refers to extracting larger meaning from data to support evaluation and decision making at various levels within the company. Such analysis may entail using data to reveal information—such as trends, projections, and cause and effect—that might not be evident without analysis. Facts, data, and analysis support a variety of company purposes, such as planning, reviewing company performance, improving operations, and comparing company performance with competitors' or with "best practices" benchmarks.

A major consideration in the use of data and analysis to improve performance involves the creation and use of performance measures or indicators. Performance measures or indicators are measurable characteristics of products, services, processes, and operations the company uses to track and improve performance. The measures or indicators should be selected to best represent the factors that lead to improved customer, operational, and financial performance. A system of measures or indicators tied to customer and/or company performance requirements represents a clear and objective basis for aligning all activities with the company's goals. Through the analysis of data from the tracking processes, the measures or indicators themselves may be evaluated and changed. For example, measures selected to track product and service quality may be judged by how well improvement in these measures correlates with improvement in customer satisfaction and customer retention.

## Partnership Development

Companies should seek to build internal and external partnerships to better accomplish their overall goals.

Internal partnerships might include those that promote labor-management cooperation, such as agreements with unions. Agreements might entail employee development, cross-training, or new work organizations, such as high performance work teams. Internal partnerships might also involve creating network relationships among company units to improve flexibility and responsiveness.

External partnerships may be with customers, suppliers, and educational organizations for a variety of purposes, including education and training. An increasingly important kind of external partnership is the strategic partnership or alliance. Such partnerships might offer a company entry into new markets or a basis for new products or services. A partnership might also permit the blending of a company's core competencies or leadership capabilities with complementary strengths and capabilities of partners, thereby enhancing overall capability, including speed and flexibility.

Partnerships should seek to develop longer-term objectives, thereby creating a basis for mutual investments. Partners should address the key requirements for success of the partnership, means of regular communication, approaches to evaluating progress, and means for adapting to changing conditions. In some cases, joint education and training initiatives could offer a cost-effective means to help ensure the success of an alliance.

## Corporate Responsibility and Citizenship

A company's management should stress corporate responsibility and citizenship. Corporate responsibility refers to basic expectations of the company—business ethics and protection of public health, safety, and the environment. Health, safety and environmental considerations need to take into account the company's operations as well as the life cycles of products and services. Companies need to address factors such as resource conservation and waste reduction at their source. Planning related to public health, safety, and the environment should anticipate adverse impacts that may arise in facilities management, production, distribution, transportation, use and disposal of products. Plans should seek to prevent problems, to provide a forthright company response if problems occur, and to make available information needed to maintain public awareness, safety, and confidence. Inclusion of public responsibility areas within a performance system means meeting all local, state, and federal laws and regulatory requirements. It also means treating these and related requirements as areas for continuous improvement "beyond mere compliance." This requires that appropriate measures of progress be created and used in managing performance.

Corporate citizenship refers to leadership and support—within reasonable limits of a company's resources—of publicly important purposes, including the above-mentioned areas of corporate responsibility. Such purposes might include education improvement, improving health care value, environmental excellence, resource conservation, community services, improving industry and business practices, and sharing of nonproprietary quality-related information. Leadership as a corporate citizen entails influencing other organizations, private and public, to partner for these purposes. For example, individual companies could lead efforts to help define the obligations of their industry to its communities.

## Results Orientation

A company's performance system needs to focus on results. Results ought to be guided by and balanced by the interests of all stakeholders—customers, employees, stockholders, suppliers and partners, the public, and the community. To meet the sometimes conflicting and changing aims that balance implies, company strategy needs to explicitly address all stakeholder requirements to ensure that actions and plans meet the differing needs and avoid adverse impact on the stakeholders. The use of a balanced composite of performance indicators offers an effective means to communicate requirements, to monitor actual performance, and to marshal support for improving results.

## 3.2.2 Malcolm Baldrige Quality Management System Elements

The Malcolm Baldrige National Quality Award outlines the elements of a quality management system within seven major categories.[2]

### Leadership

"The Leadership Category examines senior executives' personal leadership and involvement in creating and sustaining a customer focus, clear values and expectations, and a leadership system that promotes performance excellence. Also examined is how the values and expectations are integrated into the company's management system, including how the company addresses its public responsibilities and corporate citizenship."

### Information and Analysis

"The Information and Analysis Category examines the management and effectiveness of the use of data and information to support customer-driven performance excellence and marketplace success."

### Strategic Planning

"The Strategic Planning Category examines how the company sets strategic directions, and how it determines key plan requirements. Also examined is how the plan requirements are translated into an effective performance management system."

### Human Resource Development and Management

"The Human Resource Development and Management Category examines how the work force is enabled to develop and utilize its full potential, aligned with the company's performance objectives. Also examined are the company's efforts to build and maintain an environment conducive to performance excellence, full participation, and personal and organizational growth."

---

2. U.S. Department of Commerce, *The Malcolm Baldrige National Quality Award* (National Institute of Standards and Technology, 1995), p. 5.

### Process Management

"The Process Management Category examines the key aspects of process management, including customer focused design, product and service delivery processes, support services and supply management involving all work units, including research and development. The Category examines how key processes are designed, effectively managed, and improved to achieve higher performance."

### Business Results

"The Business Results Category examines the company's performance and improvement in key business areas—product and service quality, productivity and operational effectiveness, supply quality, and financial performance indicators linked to these areas. Also examined are performance levels relative to those of competitors."

### Customer Focus and Satisfaction

"The Customer Focus and Satisfaction Category examines the company's systems for customer learning and for building and maintaining customer relationships. Also examined are levels and trends in key measures of business success—customer satisfaction and retention, market share, and satisfaction relative to competitors."

## ■ 3.3 APPLYING QUALITY MANAGEMENT SYSTEM ELEMENTS TO AN ORGANIZATION

An organization's methods of implementing these elements define how an organization is going to manage TQM and how they will ensure the quality of the products that they provide. It is important to note that "each element (or requirement) in a quality management system varies in importance from one type of activity to another and from one product or service to another."[3] This variance in importance is based on factors such as the needs of the market, the nature of the product or service, and the customer's wants and needs. It is therefore necessary in a given type of business that the application of the elements be given careful consideration.

As with many systems, quality management systems need to be self-correcting. One of the most effective ways to accomplish this is by using system assessments. As will be seen later, the approach and form that these assessments assume vary with the individual assessment models.

---

3. American National Standards Institute (ANSI), *ANSI/ASQC Q9004-1-1994, Quality Management and Quality System Elements—Guidelines* (American Society for Quality Control [ASQC], 1994), p. 1.

# 4

# Assessment of Quality Management Systems

## ▪ 4.1 WHY ASSESSMENT?

One of the fundamental concepts of total quality management is the need for continuous improvement. Because of the complexity of quality management systems, all the requirements and correct measurements of the system cannot be known. There is also the dynamic nature to the system that is caused not just by the system itself but also by the needs of the customers of the system. It is therefore a key system requirement that a feedback mechanism be incorporated into the quality management system. This mechanism addresses not only the continuous improvement of product and services but also the continuous improvement of the quality management system itself.

Another aspect to assessment is becoming more and more important to those buying products or services. It involves the idea of ensuring that there are sufficient controls in place so that the chance of a defective product being released is greatly reduced. This need can be seen in life critical products such as medical devices, aircraft, and military equipment. ISO 9001, 9002, and 9003 define their scope as specifying "quality system requirements for use where a contract between two parties requires the demonstration of a supplier's capability to design and supply product." There is also a growing trend with commercial companies to require ISO 9000 registration for suppliers with which they do business. Part of TQM and one of Dr. W. Edwards Deming's 14 points is, "End the practice of awarding business on the basis of price tag. Instead, depend on meaningful measures of quality, along with price. Eliminate suppliers that can not qualify with statistical evidence of quality."[1] Businesses are using registration as a way of ensuring that their suppliers have a quality management system.

## ■ 4.2 TYPES OF ASSESSMENTS

Various types of assessments can be used. Assessments focus on different aspects of quality management systems. One aspect deals with specific contracts for the purchase of goods and services, such as with government procurement contracts. Another aspect focuses more on continuous improvement of the organization, such as the Malcolm Baldrige National Quality Award. The key difference between these two assessment models is that one is driven from outside the organization and the other is driven from within the organization. Assessments from outside the organization are generally contractual arrangements, as with government defense procurement. Many of these assessments are really audit models conducted by a second- or third-party assessor against a known standard such as ISO 9000 or the U.S. military quality procurement standards (MIL-Q). Assessments from within the organization are generally focused on continuous improvement, which is driven by the need to stay competitive. Some examples of these types of assessments are the Malcolm Baldrige National Quality Award, The Deming Prize, and The European Quality Award.

---

1. W. Edwards Deming, *Quality, Productivity, and Competitive Position* (Massachusetts Institute of Technology, Center for Advanced Engineering Study, 1982), p. 16.

P A R T

# II

---

# Quality Management System
# Assessment Methodologies

*Three quality management system assessment methodologies will be discussed in detail and others will be briefly described. The three assessment methodologies to be discussed in detail are:*

- ✧ *Malcolm Baldrige National Quality Award (MB)*
- ✧ *International Organization for Standardization 9001 (ISO 9001)*
- ✧ *Software Engineering Institute (SEI) Capability Maturity Model (CMM) for Software*

*These assessment methodologies represent the most popular and quantifiable assessments being used today in the United States. The SEI CMM is specialized in software, while the other two are generalized. These descriptions will include some background information, an outline of what the assessments are based on, and how the assessments are conducted.*

# 5

# 1995 Malcolm Baldrige National Quality Award

The Malcolm Baldrige National Quality Award was created by public law in 1987. The goal of this law is to promote the improvement of quality in the United States. The award was named in honor of the then Secretary of Commerce, who died while serving in office.

The Malcolm Baldrige National Quality Award is described as a framework, as illustrated in Figure 5.1.

The framework is made up of four basic elements:

✧ Driver. Senior executive leadership sets directions; creates values, goals, and systems; and guides the pursuit of customer value and company performance improvement.

✧ System. The system is composed of the set of well-defined and well-designed processes for meeting the company's customer and performance requirements.

✧ Measures of progress. Measures of progress provide a results-oriented basis for channeling actions to delivering ever-improving customer value and company performance.

✧ Goal. The basic aims of the system are the delivery of ever-improving value to customers and success in the marketplace.

The Malcolm Baldrige framework includes the criteria categories shown in Figure 5.1. Those criteria are made up of 7 categories, and within these 7 categories are 24 examination items. The examination items in turn expand into 54 areas to address. Each examination item is intended to focus the assessor on a major quality system requirement. The areas to address further break down these requirements with more specific details.

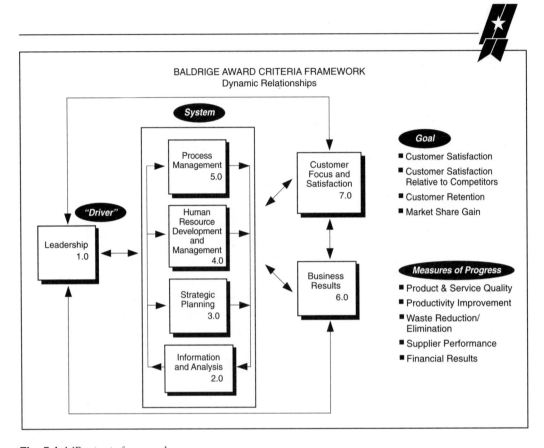

**Fig. 5.1** MB criteria framework.

Companies competing for the award describe their QMS by writing an application addressing all the examination criteria. All of the 24 examination items are assigned point values. The scoring is done by evaluation of the examination items based on three criteria:

✧ **Approach.** *Approach* refers to how the applicant addresses the item requirements— the *method*(s) used. The factors used to evaluate approaches include the following:

    ✗ appropriateness of the methods to the requirements

    ✗ effectiveness of use of methods. Degree to which the approach:

            is systematic, integrated, and consistently applied

            embodies evaluation/improvement cycles

            is based upon data and information that are objective and reliable

✗  evidence of innovation. This includes significant and effective adaptations of approaches used in other applications or types of businesses.

❖  **Deployment.** *Deployment* refers to the *extent* to which the applicant's approach is applied to all requirements of the item. The factors used to evaluate deployment include the following:

✗  use of the approach in addressing business and Item requirements

✗  use of the approach by all appropriate work units

❖  **Results.** *Results* refers to *outcomes* in achieving the purposes given in the item. The factors used to evaluate results include the following:

✗  current performance levels

✗  performance levels relative to appropriate comparisons and/or benchmarks

✗  rate, breadth, and importance of performance improvements

✗  demonstration of sustained improvement and/or sustained high-level performance

These criteria are used to establish a percentage that reflects the degree to which the item was satisfied. This percentage is multiplied by the available points for that item and a score is obtained. A listing of the 7 categories and 24 examination items, with their point values, is provided in Table 5.1. Details on each item can be found in Table A.1. The applications are reviewed and evaluated by members of the Board of Examiners in a four step process:

1. Independent review and evaluation by at least five members of the board.
2. Consensus scoring and evaluation for applications that score well in step 1.
3. Site visits to applicants that score well in step 2.
4. Judges' review and recommendations.

**Table 5.1** MB Examination Items and Point Values[a]

| Examination Categories/Items | Point Values |
|---|---|
| 1.0 Leadership | 90 |
|     1.1 Senior Executive Leadership (45 pts.) | |
|     1.2 Leadership System and Organization (25 pts.) | |
|     1.3 Public Responsibility and Corporate Citizenship (20 pts.) | |
| 2.0 Information and Analysis | 75 |
|     2.1 Management of Information and Data (20 pts.) | |
|     2.2 Competitive Comparisons and Benchmarking (15 pts.) | |
|     2.3 Analysis and Uses of Company-Level Data (40 pts.) | |

**Table 5.1** MB Examination Items and Point Values[a] (Continued)

| Examination Categories/Items | Point Values |
|---|---|
| 3.0 Strategic Planning | 55 |
| 3.1 Strategy Development (35 pts.) | |
| 3.2 Strategy Deployment (20 pts.) | |
| 4.0 Human Resource Development and Management | 140 |
| 4.1 Human Resource Planning and Evaluation (20 pts.) | |
| 4.2 High Performance Work Systems (45 pts.) | |
| 4.3 Employee Education, Training, and Development (50 pts.) | |
| 4.4 Employee Well-Being and Satisfaction (25 pts.) | |
| 5.0 Process Management | 140 |
| 5.1 Design and Introduction of Products and Services (40 pts.) | |
| 5.2 Process Management: Product and Service Production and Delivery (40 pts.) | |
| 5.3 Process Management: Support Service (30 pts.) | |
| 5.4 Management of Supplier Performance (30 pts.) | |
| 6.0 Business Results | 250 |
| 6.1 Product and Service Quality Results (75 pts.) | |
| 6.2 Company Operational and Financial Results (130 pts.) | |
| 6.3 Supplier Performance Results (45 pts.) | |
| 7.0 Customer Focus and Satisfaction | 250 |
| 7.1 Customer and Market Knowledge (30 pts.) | |
| 7.2 Customer Relationship Management (30 pts.) | |
| 7.3 Customer Satisfaction Determination (30 pts.) | |
| 7.4 Customer Satisfaction Results (100 pts.) | |
| 7.5 Customer Satisfaction Comparison (60 pts.) | |
| Total Points | 1000 |

[a]**Source:** U.S. Department of Commerce, *The Malcolm Baldrige National Quality Award* (National Institute of Standards and Technology, 1995), p. 20.

# 6

# 1994 ISO 9000

The International Organization for Standardization 9000 series consists of two types of standards. The first set are known as guidelines and are not "auditable" standards. These include the following:

- ✧ ISO 9000-1:1994, Quality Management and Quality Assurance Standards—Part 1: Guidelines for Selection and Use
- ✧ ISO 9000-2:1993, Quality Management and Quality Assurance Standards—Part 2: Generic Guidelines for the Application of ISO 9001, ISO 9002, and ISO 9003
- ✧ ISO 9000-3:1991, Quality Management and Quality Assurance Standards—Part 3: Guidelines for the Application of ISO 9001 to the Development, Supply, and Maintenance of Software
- ✧ ISO 9000-4:1993, Quality Management and Quality Assurance Standards—Part 4: Guide to Dependability Programme Management
- ✧ ISO 9004-1:1994, Quality Management and Quality System Elements—Part 1: Guidelines
- ✧ ISO 9004-2:1991, Quality Management and Quality System Elements—Part 2: Guidelines for Service
- ✧ ISO 9004-3:1993, Quality Management and Quality System Elements—Part 3: Guidelines for Processed Materials
- ✧ ISO 9004-4:1993, Quality Management and Quality System Elements—Part 4: Guidelines for Quality Improvement

The second type includes ISO 9001, ISO 9002, and ISO 9003, which are the standards to which an organization can be audited. Each of these three cover a different field of application:

- ❖ ISO 9001: 1994, Quality Systems—Model for Quality Assurance in Design, Development, Production, Installation, and Servicing
- ❖ ISO 9002: 1994, Quality Systems—Model for Quality Assurance in Production, Installation, and Servicing
- ❖ ISO 9003: 1994, Quality Systems—Model for Quality Assurance in Final Inspection and Test

The relationship of these models is illustrated in Figure 6.1. ISO 9001 is the broadest in scope of the three standards and will be discussed in detail. ISO 9002 and 9003 address the same basic elements as 9001, but to a lesser extent. ISO 9001 consists of 20 quality system requirements. Each of these 20 requirements is expanded into 46 subsections to provide more detail as required. An outline of the 20 requirements appears in Table 6.1. Details on each item can be found in Table B.1. The International Organization for Standardization operates a specialized information support unit, the ISO 9000 Forum, to provide facts to companies and organizations implementing ISO 9000.

ISO 9000 assessment is conducted as a registration process where a company becomes registered to one of the standards (9001, 9002, or 9003). The registration process consists of four major steps:

1. Preaudit (optional).
2. Audit (pass/fail).
3. Registration.
4. Surveillance audit (semiannual/on-going).

The registration process begins with a preaudit, which prepares the company for the actual audit. The preaudit is followed by a very detailed audit of the company's quality

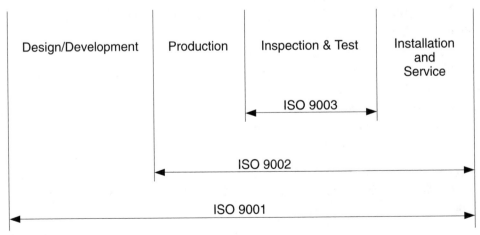

**Fig. 6.1** ISO 9001/9002/9003 relationship.

**Table 6.1** ISO 9001 Quality System Requirements [a]

4.1 Management Responsibility
    4.1.1 Quality Policy
    4.1.2 Organization
        4.1.2.1 Responsibility and Authority
        4.1.2.2 Resources
        4.1.2.3 Management Representative
    4.1.3 Management Review
4.2 Quality System
    4.2.1 General
    4.2.2 Quality-System Procedures
    4.2.3 Quality Planning
4.3 Contract Review
    4.3.1 General
    4.3.2 Review
    4.3.3 Amendment to Contract
    4.3.4 Records
4.4 Design Control
    4.4.1 General
    4.4.2 Design and Development Planning
    4.4.3 Organizational and Technical Interfaces
    4.4.4 Design Input
    4.4.5 Design Output
    4.4.6 Design Review
    4.4.7 Design Verification
    4.4.8 Design Validation
    4.4.9 Design Changes
4.5 Document and Data Control
    4.5.1 General
    4.5.2 Document and Data Approval and Issue
    4.5.3 Document and Data Changes
4.6 Purchasing
    4.6.1 General
    4.6.2 Evaluation of Sub-Contractors
    4.6.3 Purchasing Data
    4.6.4 Verification of Purchased Product
        4.6.4.1 Supplier Verification at Subcontractor's Premises
        4.6.4.2 Customer Verification of Subcontracted Product
4.7 Control of Customer-Supplied Product
4.8 Product Identification and Traceability
4.9 Process Control
4.10 Inspection and Testing
    4.10.1 General
    4.10.2 Receiving Inspection and Testing

**Table 6.1** ISO 9001 Quality System Requirements (Continued)[a]

| |
|---|
| 4.10.3 In-Process Inspection and Testing |
| 4.10.4 Final Inspection and Testing |
| 4.10.5 Inspection and Test Records |
| 4.11 Control of Inspection, Measuring, and Test Equipment |
|     4.11.1 General |
|     4.11.2 Control Procedure |
| 4.12 Inspection and Test Status |
| 4.13 Control of Nonconforming Product |
|     4.13.1 General |
|     4.13.2 Review and Disposition of Nonconforming Product |
| 4.14 Corrective and Preventative Action |
|     4.14.1 General |
|     4.14.2 Corrective Action |
|     4.14.3 Preventative Action |
| 4.15 Handling, Storage, Packaging, Preservation, and Delivery |
|     4.15.1 General |
|     4.15.2 Handling |
|     4.15.3 Storage |
|     4.15.4 Packaging |
|     4.15.5 Preservation |
|     4.15.6 Delivery |
| 4.16 Control of Quality Records |
| 4.17 Internal Quality Audits |
| 4.18 Training |
| 4.19 Servicing |
| 4.20 Statistical Techniques |
|     4.20.1 Identification of Need |
|     4.20.2 Procedures |

[a]**Source:** *ANSI/ASQC Q9001-1994, Quality Systems—Model for Quality Assurance in Design, Development, Production, Installation, and Servicing* (American National Standards Institute, 1994).

management system by a third-party auditor. Third-party audits are carried out by independent agencies that are accredited by standards organizations to conduct such audits. These audits verify compliance with the standard and, depending on the size of the organization, can last several weeks. If no major nonconformances are found during the audit, the company is recommended for registration. If any nonconformances are found, the company being audited must provide a corrective action plan to the registrar. The last step in the process is the continuous monitoring and verification of the quality management system. The surveillance audits are conducted by third-party auditors, usually twice yearly.

**7**

# 1993 SEI CMM for Software

The Software Engineering Institute is a federally funded research and development center operated by Carnegie Mellon University under contract and sponsorship of the U.S. Department of Defense. The SEI developed a framework for software process assessments called the Capability Maturity Model for Software. The CMM describes a process maturity framework of five maturity levels, as illustrated in Figure 7.1.

The maturity levels (except level 1) are broken down into 18 key process areas. Within the key process areas, there are 52 goals and 316 key practices. The goals (GO) summarize the key practices of a key process area. The key practices identify the top-level activities that contribute to satisfying the goals. SEI's 18 key process areas are organized by groupings of key practices, which are called common features. These common features[1] are:

- ✧ Commitment to Perform (CO). "Commitment to Perform describes the actions the organization must take to ensure that the process is established and will endure. Commitment to Perform typically involves establishing organizational policies and senior management sponsorship."
- ✧ Ability to Perform (AB). "Ability to Perform describes the preconditions that must exist in the project or organization to implement the software process competently. Ability to Perform typically involves resources, organizational structures, and training."

---

1. Software Engineering Institute, CMU/SEI-93-TR-25, *Key Practices of the Capability Maturity Model, Version 1.1* (Carnegie Mellon University, 1993), pp. O-27–O-28.

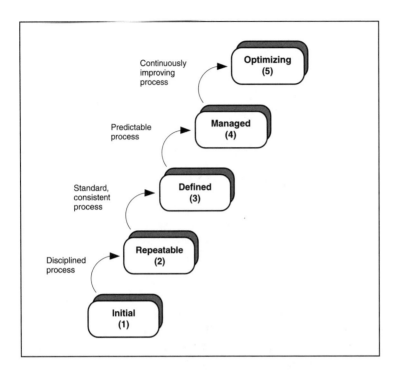

**Fig. 7.1** SEI five levels of software process maturity.

❖ Activities Performed (AC). "Activities Performed describes the roles and proce-
    dures necessary to implement a key process area. Activities Performed typically
    involves establishing plans and procedures, performing the work, tracking it, and
    taking corrective actions as necessary."

❖ Measurement and Analysis (ME). "Measurement and Analysis describes the need to
    measure the process and analyze the measurements. Measurement and Analysis typ-
    ically includes examples of the measurements that could be taken to determine the
    status and effectiveness of the Activities Performed."

❖ Verifying Implementation (VE). "Verifying Implementation describes the steps to
    ensure that the activities are performed in compliance with the process that has
    been established. Verifying Implementation typically encompasses reviews and
    audits by management and software quality assurance."

Table 7.1 outlines five maturity levels and their key process areas. Details on each
item can be found in Table C.1.

The CMM is used as a common framework for performing software process assessments and software capability evaluations.

A Software Process Assessment is an appraisal by a trained team of software professionals to determine the state of an organization's current software process, to determine the high-priority software process-related issues facing an organization, and to obtain the organizational support for software process improvement.[2]

A Software Capability Evaluation is an appraisal by a trained team of professionals to identify contractors who are qualified to perform the software work or to monitor the state of the software process used on an existing software effort.[3]

Both the assessment and evaluation methods use the same process to conduct appraisals:

1. Team selection
2. Maturity questionnaire
3. On-site visit
4. Findings

First, a team that has been trained in the concepts of the CMM and the assessment or evaluation method is selected. Then, representatives of the site to be appraised complete a maturity questionnaire. The assessment or evaluation team analyze the responses to the questionnaire next. This analysis identifies those areas of the CMM that require further investigation. The on-site visit is conducted typically over a five-day period. This visit consists of interviews and document reviews to determine if the key process areas have been satisfied. The results of this visit are documented in findings that identify the strengths and weaknesses of the organization's software process.[4]

**Table 7.1** SEI CMM Key Process Areas by Maturity Level[a]

### Level 1—Initial

"The software process is characterized as ad hoc, and occasionally even chaotic. Few processes are defined, and success depends on individual effort."

### Level 2—Repeatable

"Basic project management processes are established to track cost, schedule, and functionality. The necessary process discipline is in place to repeat earlier successes on projects with similar applications."

- Requirements Management (RM)
- Software Project Planning (PP)

2. Software Engineering Institute, *CMU/SEI-93-TR-24, Capability Maturity Model for Software, Version 1.1* (Carnegie Mellon University, 1993), p. xi.

3. Ibid.

4. Ibid., pp. 45–46.

**Table 7.1** SEI CMM Key Process Areas by Maturity Level[a] (Continued)

- Software Project Tracking and Oversight (PT)
- Software Subcontract Management (SM)
- Software Quality Assurance (QA)
- Software Configuration Management (CM)

### Level 3—Defined

"The software process for both management and engineering activities is documented, standardized, and integrated into a standard software process for the organization. All projects use an approved, tailored version of the organization's standard software process for developing and maintaining software."

- Organization Process Focus (PF)
- Organization Process Definition (PD)
- Training Program (TP)
- Integrated Software Management (IM)
- Software Product Engineering (PE)
- Intergroup Coordination (IC)
- Peer Reviews (PR)

### Level 4—Managed

"Detailed measures of the software process and product quality are collected. Both the software process and products are quantitatively understood and controlled."

- Quantitative Process Management (QP)
- Software Quality Management (QM)

### Level 5—Optimizing

"Continuous process improvement is enabled by quantitative feedback from the process and from piloting innovative ideas and technologies."

- Defect Prevention (DP)
- Technology Change Management (TM)
- Process Change Management (PC)

[a]**Source:** Software Engineering Institute, *CMU/SEI-93-TR-24, Capability Maturity Model for Software, Version 1.1* (Carnegie Mellon University, 1993), pp. 8–9, 31. Quoted passages found on pages 8 and 9.

# 8

# Other Quality Management System Assessments

There are many other quality management system assessment models. Most notable among these are the Deming Prize, the European Quality Award, and various government awards.

## ■ 8.1 DEMING PRIZE

The Deming Prize is named after W. Edwards Deming. Deming was regarded as one of the foremost leaders in quality management. In 1950, at the invitation of the Union of Japanese Scientists and Engineers, Deming went to Japan to lecture on statistical process control. The prize was "established in recognition and appreciation of W. Edwards Deming's achievements in the introduction and development of statistical quality control."[1] The Deming Prize uses ten major categories for its evaluation criteria.[2]

1. Policy
2. Management of Organization
3. Education
4. Information Gathering

---

1. Arthur R. Tenner and Irving J. DeToro, *Total Quality Management: Three Steps to Continuous Improvement* (Addison-Wesley Publishing Company, 1992), p. 235.
2. Ibid., pp. 238–239.

5. Analysis
6. Standardization
7. Control
8. Quality Assurance
9. Results
10. Future Planning

# ◼ 8.2 EUROPEAN QUALITY AWARD

The European Foundation for Quality Management (EFQM) was formed in 1988 by 14 leading Western European companies.[3] The EFQM started the European Quality Award in 1992. This award uses a format very similar to that of the Malcolm Baldrige award, except that they use nine categories instead of seven,[4] as shown in Table 8.1.

**Table 8.1** European Quality Award Categories[a]

1.0 Leadership (100 points)

2.0 Policy and Strategy (80 points)

3.0 People Management (90 points)

4.0 Resources (90 points)

5.0 Processes (140 points)

6.0 Customer Satisfaction (200 points)

7.0 People Satisfaction (90 points)

8.0 Impact on Society (60 points)

9.0 Business Results (150 points)

[a]**Source:** European Foundation for Quality Management (EFQM), *Self-Assessment Based on the European Model for Total Quality Management 1995.* 1995 Self-assessment Guidelines.

# ◼ 8.3 GOVERNMENT QUALITY AWARDS

There are a growing number of government quality awards. Quality awards similar to Malcolm Baldrige are being used in Mexico, Australia, and Canada. A growing number of

---

3. V. Daniel Hunt, *Managing for Quality: Integrating Quality and Business Strategy* (Business One Irwin, 1993), pp. 189–190.

4. Stephen George, *The Baldrige Quality System: The Do-It-Yourself Way to Transform Your Business* (John Wiley & Sons, 1992), pp. 263–264.

state quality awards are modeled after Malcolm Baldrige. Approximately 20 states are deploying these awards.[5] New York State's award is called the Excelsior Award and covers three sectors of "business": Public, Private, and Education. Awards were given beginning in 1992. The U.S. government has two awards for federal agencies—the Quality Improvement Prototype Award and the Presidential Award for Quality.

---

5. Ibid., p. 259.

# Comparing QMS Assessment Methodologies

*This section provides you with a methodology-specific view for comparing each of the three methodologies. It is structured so that it provides increasing levels of detail. This section begins with an overview of the three methodologies. Next a high-level comparison, which shows where the methodologies intersect, is provided. The high-level comparison is followed by three detailed "perspective-level" comparisons. The perspective chapters include reference charts and a detailed discussion of each methodology's comparison.[1]*

---

1. In comparisons with the SEI CMM, note that the SEI CMM common features are requirement "themes" that cut across the SEI CMM key process areas. A particular key process area may not show any direct requirement relationships but may have correlations through the common feature themes. Refer to Chapter 7, "1993 SEI CMM for Software" for a more detailed discussion of SEI's common features and key process areas. Details on key process area requirements included under the common feature themes are provided in Appendix C.

CHAPTER

# 9

# Comparison Overview

Each assessment model has a different motivation or intended purpose.

ISO emphasizes the basic elements of quality management and assesses with a very rigorous auditing model. An ISO 9000 registration effort is a very involved and detailed process. For most companies, it requires 12 months of preparation, depending on how good the quality system is at the outset. ISO auditors interview all levels of the organization, not just management. The initial registration audit is followed by periodic surveillance audits, usually twice per year. The driver behind ISO registration is that many governments and companies are now requiring their suppliers to have it.

The SEI CMM also emphasizes the basic elements of quality management; however, it does not employ an auditing model like ISO. It uses a detailed questionnaire followed up by interviews. The interviews focus on a small sampling of the organization. A CMM assessment is also an involved process, with a 12- to 18-month improvement cycle based on the findings of the assessment. SEI is used by the U.S. Department of Defense as one factor in determining suitable contractors. The SEI CMM is a software specific assessment.

The Malcolm Baldrige National Quality Award is a TQM model for a wide variety of businesses. Its creation was intended to raise the United States' awareness of quality and its importance to the nation. From a TQM perspective, MB provides the broadest model of a quality management system. It is less concerned with identifying the specific details of a given process. Instead, it relies on the knowledge of the examiners to judge whether the details are sufficient.

A good analogy of the relationship between MB, SEI, and ISO can be illustrated using the construction of a house. A house is viewed in many different ways by the people involved in its construction. The plumber looks at the house from a perspective of the water systems: the pipes, the hot water system, water delivery fixtures, water removal, etc. The electrician looks at the house from a perspective of the electrical systems: the wiring requirements, electrical distribution to each room, the lights, the outlets, etc. The framer looks at the house from a perspective of the basic structure of the house: the number of floors, location of entrances, wall construction, etc. The general contractor takes the perspective of managing the entire building of the house, dealing not only with schedule and cost, but also interfacing with the end customer, the home owner.

MB, SEI, and ISO are like these "system" builders in that they also take different views of the same object, the quality management system. SEI and ISO are focused on the infrastructure of the quality management system. They are most concerned with the basic structure of the system, much like the plumbers, electricians, and framers. In contrast, MB is more like the general contractor, less concerned with the specific details of each specialty and more focused on a broader set of issues, such as strategic planning and business results.

The best way to summarize the comparison is to address some common scenarios organizations may be facing today or in the future. The following scenarios will be discussed:

✧ An organization that has no formally defined QMS but that must seek ISO 9001 registration due to a mandate or competitive pressures

✧ An organization that is currently using the SEI CMM but whose customer will soon require ISO 9001

✧ An organization that is currently registered to ISO 9001, or has attained an SEI CMM maturity rating, but would like to advance their QMS toward a TQM approach

For the first organization, with no formally defined QMS, ISO 9001 is a great start. ISO 9001 will establish a basic quality management system and provide a great deal of discipline for this new quality system. This discipline takes the form of the initial registration effort as well as twice yearly follow-up audits to ensure that the organization is following the quality system that they defined. An important point here is that while ISO conducts audits to a specific set of requirements, it does not mandate a specific quality system. This means that an organization may need to focus on certain aspects of its QMS over others. The standard allows the organization to do this, thus allowing a great deal of flexibility in how they implement their quality management system. The requirements of ISO 9001 are basic to any quality system, regardless of the type of business. This is not to say that the organization won't require assistance in interpreting the requirements of the standard for their particular type of business. As an example, for organizations in the software industry, it is often difficult to interpret the requirements of ISO 9001, since it is written with a "hardware" orientation. It turns out, however, that every requirement in ISO 9001 does have a corollary in software. Interpreting ISO can be a daunting task due to its compact wording. Unfortunately, many ISO training classes focus strictly on auditing and do not discuss the standard in any detail. Consequently, many companies will benefit greatly by seeking outside assistance prior to engaging a third-party registrar.

The second organization, which has a quality management system, but has not necessarily addressed all the requirements of ISO 9001, should be in very good shape. An organization having a current SEI CMM level of 2 or greater meets many of the requirements of ISO 9001. This does not mean that ISO 9001 registration will be automatic. ISO has been described as a *say what you do then do what you say* type of assessment. The say-what-you-do part means that an audit of the system will first focus on a description of the quality system. The quality system is defined by ISO as "the organizational structure, procedures, processes, and resources needed to implement quality management."[1] The do-what-you-say part means that you will have to demonstrate with "objective evidence" that the system described does in fact exist, is working, and meets the requirements of the standard. One implication of the say-what-you-do-then-do-what-you-say approach is that if what is described goes beyond the requirements of ISO, it can be considered part of the scope of the audit, depending on its quality implications. A good example to illustrate this point is the Technology Change Management key process area of SEI. Technology Change Management is part of SEI's highest maturity level, Optimizing. The objective of this key process area is to improve "software quality, increase productivity, and decrease the cycle time for product quality."[2] Technology Change Management is not a direct requirement of ISO, but it can fall under the requirements of ISO when an organization establishes Technology Change Management to introduce new technologies, which can adversely affect the product quality. If Technology Change Management does fall under the scope of the ISO audit, all the applicable requirements of ISO must be satisfied.

The third organization has met the basic requirements of quality management through ISO 9001 registration or the SEI CMM but feels that there are some business improvements that can best be addressed by adding some TQM concepts to their quality management system. The best assessment for addressing TQM concepts is MB. It should be pointed out that Malcolm Baldrige assumes a certain level of quality "maturity." It does not delve into the details of the quality management system in the same way as ISO or SEI. The idea of a quality maturity is not a new one; Crosby's Quality Management Maturity Grid identifies five stages of maturity: Uncertainty, Awakening, Enlightenment,

---

1. American National Standards Institute (ANSI), *ANSI/ASQC Q9004-1-1994, Quality Management and Quality System Elements—Guidelines* (American Society for Quality Control (ASQC), 1994), p. 31.

2. Software Engineering Institute, *CMU/SEI-93-TR-25, Key Practices of the Capability Maturity Model, Version 1.1* (Carnegie Mellon University, 1993), p. 54.

Wisdom, and Certainty.[3] The idea of quality management maturity is important because conceptually it can be related to the behavior of an organization much as we relate maturity to the behavior of individuals. Since people are a key element of any QMS, this is an important concept. Malcolm Baldrige can help this third organization because it has reached a certain quality maturity; it can help in many business areas such as information and analysis, strategic planning, or customer focus and satisfaction. Malcolm Baldrige is perhaps better described as a business management methodology than as a quality management system, because it is really designed to focus management, especially senior management, on strategic business issues. Much of this focus is on the examination of results and customer satisfaction. Like the other two methodologies, Malcolm Baldrige is not a trivial assessment, nor is the business improvement cycle after the assessment. One of the central themes in Baldrige is the notion of continuous improvement. Baldrige focuses over 30% of its requirements on continuous improvement. Baldrige really is saying, "tell me what your business is, tell me how you go about it, tell me how you have been doing, then, most importantly, tell me what are you doing to improve." First-time users of Baldrige find that it asks many straightforward, but not easy to answer, questions.

An organization may benefit from using one assessment method over another at a certain point in time. As an example, a business at a maturity level of "awakening" may find more value in attempting ISO 9001 registration than in applying for the Malcolm Baldrige National Quality Award.

Before choosing a methodology, an organization should first determine the current condition of its quality management system. Any of the three methodologies discussed here can be used as a self-assessment vehicle. Next, an organization should determine where it would like to be in the future. This can be done by considering the core values and concepts used by Malcolm Baldrige, such as the long-range view of the future discussed on page 21. Only after these first two steps have been taken should an organization choose an assessment methodology. Lastly, it should be pointed out that the selection of a certain assessment methodology is not a final decision. In the vein of continuous improvement, the selection process should be repeated periodically to gauge progress and review an organization's goals.

---

3. Philip B. Crosby, *Quality is Free: The Art of Making Quality Certain* (McGraw-Hill Book Company, 1979), pp. 32–33.

# 10

# High-Level Comparison

This comparison provides a high-level view of where the three methodologies overlap and where they do not. A graphic summary of the comparison of the three methodologies is provided in Figure 10.1.

Starting with the Malcolm Baldrige view, we will review each methodology for three attributes:

- ✧ Where the other two methodologies have correlation
- ✧ Where the other two methodologies *do not* have correlation
- ✧ Where the other two methodologies are different in their correlations

## ■ 10.1 MALCOLM BALDRIGE CORRELATIONS

Categories where SEI and ISO correlate with Malcolm Baldrige follow:

- ✧ 1.1 Senior Executive Leadership
- ✧ 1.2 Leadership System and Organization
- ✧ 2.3 Analysis and Use of Company-Level Data
- ✧ 4.3 Employee Education, Training, and Development
- ✧ 5.1 Design and Introduction of Products and Services
- ✧ 5.2 Process Management: Product and Service Production and Delivery
- ✧ 5.4 Management of Supplier Performance
- ✧ 7.1 Customer and Market Knowledge

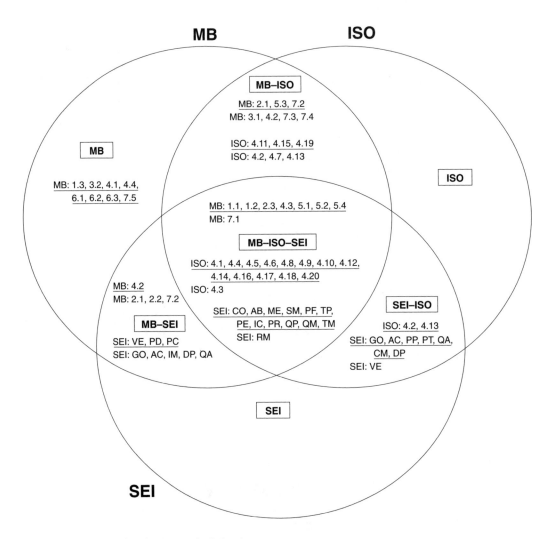

**Fig. 10.1** SEI CMM/MB/ISO 9001 high-level comparison.

*Correlation Key*

underlined = strong correlation

not underlined = some correlation

**Note:** The correlations presented here are summarized and represent the dominant correlation strength. This means that there may be specific correlations that differ from this generalized diagram.

**Note:** In comparisons with the SEI CMM, note that the SEI CMM common features are requirement themes that cut across the SEI CMM key process areas. A particular key process area may not show any direct requirement relationships, but may have correlations through the common feature themes. Refer to Chapter 7, "1993 SEI CMM for Software," for a more detailed discussion of SEI's common features and key process areas. Details on key process area requirements included under the common feature themes are provided in Appendix C.

SEI and ISO correlate to many of Baldrige's categories but are especially focused on detailed Process Management. They also touch on many other MB categories but do so at a different level of detail. SEI and ISO are written at a lower level than MB and provide detailed requirements for Process Management.

Categories where SEI and ISO *do not* correlate with Malcolm Baldrige follow:

- ✦ 1.3 Public Responsibility and Corporate Citizenship
- ✦ 3.2 Strategy Deployment
- ✦ 4.1 Human Resource Planning and Evaluation
- ✦ 4.4 Employee Well-Being and Satisfaction
- ✦ 6.1 Product and Service Quality Results
- ✦ 6.2 Company Operational and Financial Results
- ✦ 6.3 Supplier Performance Results
- ✦ 7.5 Customer Satisfaction Comparison

It is interesting to note where SEI and ISO have no correlation with Malcolm Baldrige. The missing elements in SEI and ISO highlight a real difference in philosophy with Baldrige. Public Responsibility and Corporate Citizenship, Strategic Planning, Human Resource Development and Management, and Business Results represent a significant portion of Malcolm Baldrige. This is in contrast to SEI and ISO, which devote an overwhelming portion of their requirements to process. The Malcolm Baldrige National Quality Award, as a TQM assessment, is really designed to focus management, especially senior management, on the issues of running a business. SEI and ISO are focused on the operational running of the production side of a business. SEI is even more focused than ISO and addresses software production.

Categories where SEI and ISO are different in their correlations with Malcolm Baldrige follow:

### SEI Correlations with Baldrige

- ✓ 2.1 Management of Information and Data
- ✦ 2.2 Competitive Comparisons and Benchmarking
- ✦ 4.2 High Performance Work Systems
- ✦ 7.2 Customer Relationship Management

### ISO Correlations with Baldrige

- ✦ 2.1 Management of Information and Data
- ✦ 3.1 Strategy Development

✧  4.2 High Performance Work Systems

✧  5.3 Process Management: Support Services

✧  7.2 Customer Relationship Management

✧  7.3 Customer Satisfaction Determination

✧  7.4 Customer Satisfaction Results

In 2.1 Management of Information and Data and 7.2 Customer Relationship Management, SEI and ISO differ in the strength of correlation. SEI has *some* correlation when compared to ISO, which has a *strong* correlation. ISO has a *strong* correlation with 5.3 Process Management: Support Services, where support services are included within the scope of the registration. ISO has *some* correlation with 4.2 High Performance Work Systems when compared to SEI, which has a *strong* correlation. The rest of SEI and ISO requirements have *some* correlation with Malcolm Baldrige.

## ■ 10.2 ISO 9001 CORRELATIONS

Categories where MB and SEI correlate with ISO follow:

✧  4.1 Management Responsibility

✧  4.3 Contract Review

✧  4.4 Design Control

✧  4.5 Document and Data Control

✧  4.6 Purchasing

✧  4.8 Product Identification and Traceability

✧  4.9 Process Control

✧  4.10 Inspection and Testing

✧  4.12 Inspection and Test Status

✧  4.14 Corrective and Preventative Action

✧  4.16 Control of Quality Records

✧  4.17 Internal Quality Audits

✧  4.18 Training

✧  4.20 Statistical Techniques

These ISO requirements focus on a core set of processes, to which both SEI and MB have a *strong* correlation. ISO provides a good model for process management.

There are no categories where MB and SEI *do not* correlate with ISO. MB and SEI have some correlation with all ISO requirements.

Categories where MB and SEI are different in their correlations when compared with ISO follow:

### MB Correlations with ISO

- ✧ 4.2 Quality System
- ✧ 4.7 Control of Customer-Supplied Product
- ✧ 4.11 Control of Inspection, Measuring, and Test Equipment
- ✧ 4.13 Control of Nonconforming Product
- ✧ 4.15 Handling, Storage, Packaging, Preservation, and Delivery
- ✧ 4.19 Servicing

### SEI Correlations with ISO

- ✧ 4.2 Quality System
- ✧ 4.13 Control of Nonconforming Product

MB and SEI have varying degrees of correlation with ISO. SEI has a *strong* correlation to 4.2 Quality System, and 4.13 Control of Nonconforming Product, whereas MB has *some* correlation. ISO has a *strong* correlation to 4.15 Handling, Storage, Packaging, Preservation, and Delivery and 4.19 Servicing, whereas SEI has no correlation. In many cases, SEI is more specific in its requirements than ISO in that it provides the user with more specific details. However, SEI's goals provide the user with a higher-level perspective on the key process area, which allows for satisfaction of the goals through implementations other than those specified in the key practices.

## ■ 10.3  SEI CMM CORRELATIONS

Categories where MB and ISO correlate with SEI follow:

- ✧ Requirements Management (RM)
- ✧ Commitment to Perform (CO)
- ✧ Ability to Perform (AB)
- ✧ Measurement and Analysis (ME)
- ✧ Software Subcontract Management (SM)
- ✧ Organization Process Focus (PF)
- ✧ Training Program (TP)

- ✧ Software Product Engineering (PE)
- ✧ Intergroup Coordination (IC)
- ✧ Peer Reviews (PR)
- ✧ Quantitative Process Management (QP)
- ✧ Software Quality Management (QM)
- ✧ Technology Change Management (TM)

ISO and MB have a *strong* correlation with SEI in all key process areas except for Requirements Management (RM) Three of the correlation areas—Commitment to Perform (CO), Ability to Perform (AB), and Measurement and Analysis (ME)—follow the SEI common feature theme. These correlations span all SEI's maturity levels.

There are no categories where MB and ISO *do not* correlate with SEI. MB and ISO have some correlation with all SEI requirements. SEI is an interesting methodology, because it covers such a wide range of requirements areas. It correlates with all areas in the other two methodologies in varying degrees. In every one of SEI's 18 key process areas, there is some correlation to some aspect of the other methodologies. This observation highlights an interesting difference between SEI and the other two assessments. SEI can be thought of in two dimensions, the first being the "verticals," the 18 key process areas, and the other being the "horizontals," the Goals (GO) and common feature themes. The common features—Commitment to Perform (CO), Ability to Perform (AB), Activities Performed (AC), Measurement and Analysis (ME), and Verifying Implementation (VE)—represent themes that cross all the key process areas. This is a unique approach, which the other assessments do not use. SEI's Goals (GO) are written at a higher level than the SEI key practices. This higher level is comparable to the level at which the Malcolm Baldrige National Quality Award is written.

Categories where MB and ISO are different in their correlations with SEI follow:

### MB Correlations with SEI

- ✧ Goals (GO)
- ✧ Activities Performed (AC)
- ✧ Verifying Implementation (VE)
- ✧ Software Quality Assurance (QA)
- ✧ Organization Process Definition (PD)
- ✧ Integrated Software Management (IM)
- ✧ Defect Prevention (DP)
- ✧ Process Change Management (PC)

*ISO Correlations with SEI*

❖ Goals (GO)
❖ Activities Performed (AC)
❖ Verifying Implementation (VE)
❖ Software Project Planning (PP)
❖ Software Project Tracking and Oversight (PT)
❖ Software Quality Assurance (QA)
❖ Software Configuration Management (CM)
❖ Defect Prevention (DP)

ISO and MB differ in their strength of correlation in Goals (GO), Activities Performed (AC), Software Quality Assurance (QA), and Defect Prevention (DP). ISO has a predominately *strong* correlation when compared to MB, which has *some* correlation. For Verifying Implementation (VE), ISO and MB also differ in their strength of correlation, with MB having a *strong* correlation and ISO having *some* correlation.

# 11

# Comparison from a Malcolm Baldrige Perspective

This chapter covers the 24 examination items of the Malcolm Baldrige National Quality Award. Each of these items is addressed in two subsections—ISO-associated statements and SEI-associated statements. Each subsection discusses the other methodology's associated statements and why they are associated. In discussing the association between statements, the terms "some correlation" and "strong correlation" are used. These terms are intended to give you a feel for the association and its significance. A summary of the correlations is provided in Figures 11.1 and 11.2. A detailed mapping of the correlations is provided in Appendix D and Appendix E.

## ■ 11.1 MALCOLM BALDRIGE, 1.0 LEADERSHIP[1]

"The Leadership Category examines senior executives' personal leadership and involvement in creating and sustaining a customer focus, clear values and expectations, and a leadership system that promotes performance excellence. Also examined is how the values and expectations are integrated into the company's management system, including how the company addresses its public responsibilities and corporate citizenship."

---

1. U.S. Department of Commerce, *The Malcolm Baldrige National Quality Award* (National Institute of Standards and Technology, 1995), p. 21.

**Figure 11.1** Malcolm Baldrige mapping to ISO 9001.

| Malcolm Baldrige | ISO 9001 | | | | | | | | | | | | | | | | | | | |
|---|---|---|---|---|---|---|---|---|---|---|---|---|---|---|---|---|---|---|---|---|
| | A | B | C | D | E | F | G | H | I | J | K | L | M | N | O | P | Q | R | S | T |
| 1.1 Senior Executive Leadership | ● | | | | | | | | | | | | | | | | | | | |
| 1.2 Leadership System and Organization | ● | | | | | | | | | | | | | | | | | | | |
| 1.3 Public Responsibility and Corporate Citizenship | | | | | | | | | | | | | | | | | | | | |
| 2.1 Management of Information and Data | | | | ● | ● | | | | ● | | | | | ● | | | | | | ● |
| 2.2 Competitive Comparisons and Benchmarking | | | | | | | | | | | | | | | | | | | | |
| 2.3 Analysis and Use of Company-Level Data | | | | | | | | | | | | | | ● | | | | | | ● |
| 3.1 Strategy Development | | | ○ | | | | | | | | | | | | | | | | | |
| 3.2 Strategy Deployment | | | | | | | | | | | | | | | | | | | | |
| 4.1 Human Resource Planning and Evaluation | | | | | | | | | | | | | | | | | | | | |
| 4.2 High Performance Work Systems | | | | ○ | | | | | | | | | | | | | | | | |
| 4.3 Employee Education, Training, and Development | | | | | | | | | | | | | | | | | | ● | | |
| 4.4 Employee Well-Being and Satisfaction | | | | | | | | | | | | | | | | | | | | |
| 5.1 Design and Introduction of Products and Services | | | | ● | ○ | | | | ● | | | | ● | ● | | | | ● | | |
| 5.2 Process Management: Product and Service Production and Delivery | | | ● | ● | ● | ● | ○ | ○ | ● | ● | ● | ○ | ● | ● | ○ | ○ | ● | | ● | ● |
| 5.3 Process Management: Support Services | | | | | | | | ● | | | | | ● | | | | | | | |
| 5.4 Management of Supplier Performance | | | | | ● | ○ | ● | | ● | | | | ○ | ● | | | | | | |
| 6.1 Product and Service Quality Results | | | | | | | | | | | | | | | | | | | | |
| 6.2 Company Operational and Financial Results | | | | | | | | | | | | | | | | | | | | |
| 6.3 Supplier Performance Results | | | | | | | | | | | | | | | | | | | | |
| 7.1 Customer and Market Knowledge | | | ○ | | | | | | | | | | | | | | | | | |
| 7.2 Customer Relationship Management | | | ○ | | ● | | | | | | | | ● | | | | | | | |
| 7.3 Customer Satisfaction Determination | | | | | | | | | | | | | | | | | | | ○ | |
| 7.4 Customer Satisfaction Results | | | | | | | | | | | | | | | | | | | ○ | |
| 7.5 Customer Satisfaction Comparison | | | | | | | | | | | | | | | | | | | | |

Malcolm Baldrige mapping to ISO 9001 key .

---

**Note:**

○ = Some correlation

● = Strong correlation

A  = 4.1 Management Responsibility
B  = 4.2 Quality System
C  = 4.3 Contract Review
D  = 4.4 Design Control
E  = 4.5 Document and Data Control
F  = 4.6 Purchasing
G  = 4.7 Control of Customer-Supplied Product
H  = 4.8 Product Identification and Traceability
I  = 4.9 Process Control
J  = 4.10 Inspection and Testing
K  = 4.11 Control of Inspection, Measuring, and Test Equipment
L  = 4.12 Inspection and Test Status
M  = 4.13 Control of Nonconforming Product
N  = 4.14 Corrective and Preventative Action
O  = 4.15 Handling, Storage, Packaging, Preservation, and Delivery
P  = 4.16 Control of Quality Records
Q  = 4.17 Internal Quality Audits
R  = 4.18 Training
S  = 4.19 Servicing
T  = 4.20 Statistical Techniques

---

# ▉ 11.2 MALCOLM BALDRIGE, 1.1 SENIOR EXECUTIVE LEADERSHIP

## 11.2.1 Malcolm Baldrige, Senior Executive Leadership; ISO-Associated Statements

Malcolm Baldrige, 1.1 Senior Executive Leadership, is associated with the ISO elements in 4.1 Management Responsibility.

Malcolm Baldrige defines *senior executives* as "the applicant's highest official and those reporting directly to that official." ISO refers to "management with executive responsibilities" but does not explicitly define this phrase; however, it is referring to an organization's highest official.

In general, ISO is very specific about management responsibilities and refers to "management with executive responsibilities" in three instances: 4.1.1 Quality Policy, 4.1.2.3 Management Representative, and 4.1.3 Management Review.

**Figure 11.2** Malcolm Baldrige mapping to SEI CMM.

| Malcolm Baldrige | SEI CMM | | | | | | | | | | | | | | | | | | | | | | | |
|---|---|---|---|---|---|---|---|---|---|---|---|---|---|---|---|---|---|---|---|---|---|---|---|---|
| | A | B | C | D | E | F | G | H | I | J | K | L | M | N | O | P | Q | R | S | T | U | V | W | X |
| 1.1 Senior Executive Leadership | ○ | ● | ● | | | ● | | | | | | | | | | | | | | | | | | |
| 1.2 Leadership System and Organization | | | | | | ● | | | | | | | | | | | | | | | | | | |
| 1.3 Public Responsibility and Corporate Citizenship | | | | | | | | | | | | | | | | | | | | | | | | |
| 2.1 Management of Information and Data | ○ | | ○ | ○ | ○ | | | | | | | | | | | | | | | | | | | |
| 2.2 Competitive Comparisons and Benchmarking | | | | | | | | | | | | | ○ | ○ | | | | | | | | | ○ | ○ |
| 2.3 Analysis and Use of Company-Level Data | | | | ● | | | ○ | | | | | | | | | ○ | | ● | ● | ○ | | | | |
| 3.1 Strategy Development | | | | | | | | | | | | | | | | | | | | | | | | |
| 3.2 Strategy Deployment | | | | | | | | | | | | | | | | | | | | | | | | |
| 4.1 Human Resource Planning and Evaluation | | | | | | | | | | | | | | | | | | | | | | | | |
| 4.2 High Performance Work Systems | | | | | | | | | | | | | | | | | | ● | | | | | | |
| 4.3 Employee Education, Training, and Development | | | ● | | | | | | | | | | | ● | | | | | | | | | | |
| 4.4 Employee Well-Being and Satisfaction | | | | | | | | | | | | | | | | | | | | | | | | |
| 5.1 Design and Introduction of Products and Services | | | | | | | ● | | | | | | | | | | ● | ● | ● | | ● | | | |
| 5.2 Process Management: Product and Service Production and Delivery | ● | | | | ● | ● | | | | | | | ● | ● | | | | | | | | | ● | ● |
| 5.3 Process Management: Support Services | | | | | | | | | | | | | | | | | | | | | | | | |
| 5.4 Management of Supplier Performance | | | | | | | | | ● | | | | | | | | | | | | | | | |
| 6.1 Product and Service Quality Results | | | | | | | | | | | | | | | | | | | | | | | | |
| 6.2 Company Operational and Financial Results | | | | | | | | | | | | | | | | | | | | | | | | |
| 6.3 Supplier Performance Results | | | | | | | | | | | | | | | | | | | | | | | | |
| 7.1 Customer and Market Knowledge | | | | | | | ○ | | | | | | | | | | | | | | | | | |
| 7.2 Customer Relationship Management | | | | | | | | | | ○ | | | | | | ○ | | ○ | | | | | | |
| 7.3 Customer Satisfaction Determination | | | | | | | | | | | | | | | | | | | | | | | | |

**Figure 11.2** Malcolm Baldrige mapping to SEI CMM. (Continued)

| Malcolm Baldrige | SEI CMM | | | | | | | | | | | | | | | | | | | | | | | |
|---|---|---|---|---|---|---|---|---|---|---|---|---|---|---|---|---|---|---|---|---|---|---|---|---|
| | A | B | C | D | E | F | G | H | I | J | K | L | M | N | O | P | Q | R | S | T | U | V | W | X |
| 7.4 Customer Satisfaction Results | | | | | | | | | | | | | | | | | | | | | | | | |
| 7.5 Customer Satisfaction Comparison | | | | | | | | | | | | | | | | | | | | | | | | |

Malcolm Baldrige mapping to SEI CMM Key.[a]

**Note:**

○ = Some correlation

● = Strong correlation

A  = Goals (GO)
B  = Commitment to Perform (CO)
C  = Ability to Perform (AB)
D  = Activities Performed (AC)
E  = Measurement and Analysis (ME)
F  = Verifying Implementation (VE)
G  = Requirements Management (RM)
H  = Software Project Planning (PP)
I   = Software Project Tracking and Oversight (PT)
J   = Software Subcontract Management (SM)
K  = Software Quality Assurance (QA)
L  = Software Configuration Management (CM)
M = Organization Process Focus (PF)
N  = Organization Process Definition (PD)
O  = Training Program (TP)
P  = Integrated Software Management (IM)
Q  = Software Product Engineering (PE)
R  = Intergroup Coordination (IC)
S  – Peer Reviews (PR)
T  = Quantitative Process Management (QP)
U  = Software Quality Management (QM)
V  = Defect Prevention (DP)
W = Technology Change Management (TM)
X  = Process Change Management (PC)

[a]**Note:** In comparisons with the SEI CMM, note that the SEI CMM common features are requirement themes that cut across the SEI CMM key process areas. A particular key process area may not show any direct requirement relationships, but may have correlations through the common feature themes. Refer to Chapter 7, "1993 SEI CMM for Software" for a more detailed discussion of SEI's common features and key process areas. Details on key process area requirements included under the common feature themes are provided in Appendix C.

ISO's 4.1.1 Quality Policy requires "management with executive responsibilities" to "define and document its policy for quality." This has a strong correlation with Baldrige's "senior executives" requirement for "creating and reinforcing values and expectations" as well as "setting directions and performance excellence goals."

ISO's 4.1.2.1 Responsibility and Authority requires "defining and documenting the responsibility, authority, and the interrelation of personnel who manage, perform, and verify work affecting quality." While this is not identified as a sole executive responsibility, it does have some correlation with the Malcolm Baldrige requirement for "setting directions and performance excellence goals through strategic and business planning."

ISO's 4.1.2.2 Resources requirement looks for "providing adequate resources, including the assignment of trained personnel, for management." This has a strong correlation with the Malcolm Baldrige "developing and maintaining a leadership system for performance excellence" requirement.

ISO's 4.1.2.3 Management Representative requires the assignment of a specific individual by executive management to ensure "that a quality system is established, implemented, and maintained." This is a very explicit requirement of ISO and is much more specific than Malcolm Baldrige. This, however, does have some correlation with the Malcolm Baldrige "developing and maintaining a leadership system for performance excellence" requirement.

ISO's 4.1.3 Management Review requires "reviewing the quality system at defined intervals sufficient to ensure its continuing suitability and effectiveness." This requirement is focused on the findings of internal audits of the quality management system, as defined by the ISO 9001 standard. This is again a very explicit requirement of ISO and is much more specific than Malcolm Baldrige. This has a strong correlation with the Malcolm Baldrige requirement for "reviewing overall company performance, including customer-related and operational performance."

As you can see, in this first Malcolm Baldrige examination item, there is a great deal of difference in the breadth and depth of the requirements between the two methodologies. Baldrige has statements that include phrases like "performance excellence goals" and "operational performance." They indicate Baldrige's focus on a much broader set of requirements than ISO. This set can include things like financial indicators, cycle time, productivity, safety, absenteeism, and turnover. ISO, in contrast, is very specific about the scope of its requirements.

## 11.2.2 Malcolm Baldrige, Senior Executive Leadership; SEI-Associated Statements

Malcolm Baldrige, 1.1 Senior Executive Leadership, has a strong correlation with SEI elements in just about all of its 18 key process areas. The majority of these requirements follow the SEI common feature known as Verifying Implementation (VE).

Malcolm Baldrige defines *senior executives* as "the applicant's highest official and those reporting directly to that official." SEI defines *senior manager* as "a management role at a high enough level in an organization that the primary focus is the long-term vitality of the organization, rather than short-term project and contractual concerns and pressures. In general, a senior manager for engineering would have responsibility for multiple projects."

Many of SEI's key practices require reviews "with senior management." These reviews address the Malcolm Baldrige requirement for "reviewing overall company performance, including customer-related and operational performance."

SEI also has several key practices that fall under the SEI common feature Commitment to Perform (CO). These key practices look for senior management to "sponsor" and "oversee" specific practices under the Technology Change Management (TM) and Organization Process Focus (PF) key process areas. These have a strong correlation with the Malcolm Baldrige requirement for "providing effective leadership and direction in building and improving company competitiveness, performance, and capabilities" and "creating and reinforcing values and expectations throughout the company's leadership system."

SEI has one key practice that falls under its Goals (GO) common thread (QA.GO.4), which requires senior management to act as an escalation point for unresolvable issues. This has some correlation with the Malcolm Baldrige requirement for "setting directions through leadership and personal involvement."

SEI also has one key practice that falls under its Ability to Perform (AB) common feature (PC.AB.4), which requires senior management to receive training in software process improvement. This has a strong correlation with the Malcolm Baldrige requirement for "developing and maintaining a leadership system for performance excellence."

## ■ 11.3 MALCOLM BALDRIGE, 1.2 LEADERSHIP SYSTEM AND ORGANIZATION

### 11.3.1 Malcolm Baldrige, Leadership System and Organization; ISO-Associated Statements

Malcolm Baldrige, 1.2 Leadership System and Organization, is associated with the ISO elements in 4.1 Management Responsibility. In general, ISO is very specific about management responsibilities.

ISO's 4.1.1 Quality Policy requires management to "define and document its policy for quality" and "ensure that this policy is understood, implemented and maintained at all levels of the organization." This has a strong correlation with Baldrige's requirement for "communicating and reinforcing the values, expectations, and directions of the company throughout the entire work force."

ISO's 4.1.2.1 Responsibility and Authority requires "defining and documenting the responsibility, authority, and the interrelation of personnel who manage, perform, and verify work affecting quality." This has a strong correlation with the Malcolm Baldrige requirement for "integrating the company's customer focus and performance expectations into the company's leadership system and organization."

ISO's 4.1.2.2 Resources requirement looks for "providing adequate resources, including the assignment of trained personnel, for management." This has some correlation with the Malcolm Baldrige requirement for "integrating the company's customer focus and performance expectations into the company's leadership system and organization."

ISO's 4.1.3 Management Review requires "reviewing the quality system at defined intervals sufficient to ensure its continuing suitability and effectiveness." This requirement is focused on the findings of internal audits of the quality management system, as defined by the ISO 9001 standard. This is a very explicit requirement of ISO and is much more specific than Malcolm Baldrige. This has a strong correlation with the Malcolm Baldrige requirement for "reviewing overall company and work unit performance."

Again, there is a great deal of difference in the breadth and depth of the requirements between the two methodologies. Baldrige has statements that include phrases like "performance expectations" and "high performance objectives." These indicate Baldrige's focus on a much broader set of requirements than ISO.

### 11.3.2 Malcolm Baldrige, Leadership System and Organization; SEI-Associated Statements

Malcolm Baldrige, 1.2 Leadership System and Organization, has a strong correlation with the SEI elements in just about all of its 18 key process areas. The majority of these requirements follow the SEI Common Feature known as Verifying Implementation (VE).

Many of SEI's key practices require reviews "with senior management" and "with the project manager." These reviews have a strong correlation with the Malcolm Baldrige requirement for "reviewing overall company and work unit performance."

## ■ 11.4 MALCOLM BALDRIGE, 1.3 PUBLIC RESPONSIBILITY AND CORPORATE CITIZENSHIP

### 11.4.1 Malcolm Baldrige, Public Responsibility and Corporate Citizenship; ISO-Associated Statements

There are no associated elements in ISO.

## 11.4.2  Malcolm Baldrige, Public Responsibility and Corporate Citizenship; SEI-Associated Statements

There are no associated elements in SEI.

# ◼ 11.5  MALCOLM BALDRIGE, 2.0 INFORMATION AND ANALYSIS[2]

"The Information and Analysis Category examines the management and effectiveness of the use of data and information to support customer-driven performance excellence and marketplace success."

# ◼ 11.6  MALCOLM BALDRIGE, 2.1 MANAGEMENT OF INFORMATION AND DATA

## 11.6.1  Malcolm Baldrige, Management of Information and Data; ISO-Associated Statements

Malcolm Baldrige, 2.1 Management of Information and Data, is associated with the ISO elements in 4.5 Document and Data Control, 4.6 Purchasing, 4.10 Inspection and Testing, 4.16 Control of Quality Records, and 4.20 Statistical Techniques. The ISO-related elements are generally focused on managing specific types of documents, data, and records.

All the ISO-related items have a strong correlation with the Malcolm Baldrige general requirement for "selecting and managing information and data used for planning, management, and evaluation of overall performance by the company."

ISO covers very specific ways that documents, data, and records must be controlled and managed. This includes the requirement for documented procedures. ISO does not address the Malcolm Baldrige areas of "selecting and managing information and data needed to drive improvement of overall company performance" and "evaluating and improving the selection, analysis, and integration of information and data, aligning them with the company's business priorities."

## 11.6.2  Malcolm Baldrige, Management of Information and Data; SEI-Associated Statements

Malcolm Baldrige, 2.1 Management of Information and Data, is not addressed by one specific area of SEI but rather has some correlation with the SEI elements in most of the 18

---

2. Ibid., p. 23.

key process areas. The majority of SEI's associated statements are in the common features of Activities Performed (AC) and Measurement and Analysis (ME). These key practices are specific to the process area they address, and involve the recording of data and the measurement of activities. One key practice (PD.GO.2), which is one of the Goals (GO) in Organization Process Definition (PD), requires "collecting, reviewing and making available information." Another key practice (QP.AB.2), which is an Ability to Perform (AB) common feature in Quantitative Process Management (QP), requires "establishing support for collecting, recording, and analyzing data for selected process and product measures."

## ■ 11.7 MALCOLM BALDRIGE, 2.2 COMPETITIVE COMPARISONS AND BENCHMARKING

### 11.7.1 Malcolm Baldrige, Competitive Comparisons and Benchmarking; ISO-Associated Statements

There are no associated elements in ISO.

### 11.7.2 Malcolm Baldrige, Competitive Comparisons and Benchmarking; SEI-Associated Statements

One of the Malcolm Baldrige core values and concepts is Continuous Improvement and Learning. Continuous Improvement and Learning discusses the need for "a well-executed approach to continuous improvement." They define *continuous improvement* as "both incremental and breakthrough improvement." Incremental improvement is one philosophy that basically says that the best way to continuous improvement is to put a process in place and then continually refine that process. Breakthrough improvement or reengineering, as it is perhaps more commonly referred to, espouses the philosophy that the best way to continuous improvement is to reexamine periodically the basic goals and intent of a process and totally reinvent how it is done. Both philosophies have their problems, however. The incremental approach is best where you have a technology base that is not changing rapidly. A good example of where incremental improvement is not good is the case of the slide rule company. The rapid advance of inexpensive electronic components made it possible to build inexpensive scientific calculators. This development put slide rule makers out of business virtually overnight. The breakthrough/reengineering approach is better where you have a rapidly changing technology base. This approach is not without its problems, too. It usually involves a great deal of risk due to the fact that, as with any new process, there are many unknowns, and therefore all the problems cannot be foreseen. This risk is a function of the complexity of the process(es) involved.

SEI puts a large emphasis on improvement throughout its key practices, and particularly within the Organization Process Focus (PF), Organization Process Definition (PD), and Process Change Management (PC) key process areas. This emphasis provides a means of internal benchmarking across the various projects that comprise the organization and has some correlation to Malcolm Baldrige. This internal benchmarking supports the incremental improvement philosophy. SEI makes no direct reference to conducting external benchmarks, but it does have some correlation to the Malcolm Baldrige requirement in its Technology Change Management (TM) process area. SEI defines technologies as tools, methods, and processes.

# ■ 11.8 MALCOLM BALDRIGE, 2.3 ANALYSIS AND USE OF COMPANY-LEVEL DATA

## 11.8.1 Malcolm Baldrige, Analysis and Use of Company-Level Data; ISO-Associated Statements

Malcolm Baldrige, 2.3 Analysis and Use of Company-Level Data, is associated with the ISO element 4.14.3 Preventative Action. This ISO element covers a wide range of information sources to "detect, analyze, and eliminate potential causes of nonconformities." This has a strong correlation to the Malcolm Baldrige requirement for "using analysis to gain an understanding of operational performance." ISO's 4.20.2 Procedures requirement has a strong correlation to Malcolm Baldrige by addressing the requirement for "analyzing data related to quality, customers, and operational performance...to support company-level review, action, and planning."

## 11.8.2 Malcolm Baldrige, Analysis and Use of Company-Level Data; SEI-Associated Statements

Malcolm Baldrige, 2.3 Analysis and Use of Company-Level Data, has a strong correlation with the SEI elements in Quantitative Process Management (QP) and Software Quality Management (QM) and with the Measurement and Analysis (ME) common feature. There are also associated SEI elements in Requirements Management (RM), Software Product Engineering (PE), and Defect Prevention (DP) key process areas. Quantitative Process Management (QP) is focused on controlling process performance quantitatively. Software Quality Management (QM) is focused on developing a "quantitative understanding of the quality" of the product. Quantitative Process Management (QP) has a strong correlation with MB and defines an infrastructure for addressing the Malcolm Baldrige requirement for "integrating and analyzing information and data from all parts of the company to support reviews, business decisions, and planning." The Measurement and Analysis (ME) common feature focuses on "measurements that could be taken to determine the status and effectiveness of the Activities Performed (AC)." This has a strong correlation to the MB requirement for "using analysis to gain an understanding of operational performance and company capabilities." The Requirements Management (RM) practice (RM.AB.1) for establishing "responsibility for analyzing system requirements and allocating them to hardware, software, and other system components" addresses the MB requirement for "using analysis to gain an understanding of customers...." There are associated practices in the Requirements Management (RM), Software Product Engineering (PE), and Defect Prevention (DP) key process areas that have some correlation to the MB requirement for "using analysis to gain an understanding of operational performance and company capabilities."

# ■ 11.9 MALCOLM BALDRIGE, 3.0 STRATEGIC PLANNING[3]

"The Strategic Planning Category examines how the company sets strategic directions, and how it determines key plan requirements. Also examined is how the plan requirements are translated into an effective performance management system."

# ■ 11.10 MALCOLM BALDRIGE, 3.1 STRATEGY DEVELOPMENT

## 11.10.1 Malcolm Baldrige, Strategy Development; ISO-Associated Statements

Malcolm Baldrige, Strategy Development, has some correlation with ISO's element 4.2 Quality System. Malcolm Baldrige's general requirement requires "planning overall performance and competitive leadership for short term and longer term." ISO addresses this through its "defining and documenting how the requirements for quality will be met" requirement. Malcolm Baldrige is much broader in its scope than ISO.

## 11.10.2 Malcolm Baldrige, Strategy Development; SEI-Associated Statements

There are no associated elements in SEI.

---

3. Ibid., p. 25.

# ▪ 11.11 MALCOLM BALDRIGE, 3.2 STRATEGY DEPLOYMENT

## 11.11.1 Malcolm Baldrige, Strategy Deployment; ISO-Associated Statements

There are no associated elements in ISO.

## 11.11.2 Malcolm Baldrige, Strategy Deployment; SEI-Associated Statements

There are no associated elements in SEI.

# ▪ 11.12 MALCOLM BALDRIGE, 4.0 HUMAN RESOURCE DEVELOPMENT AND MANAGEMENT[4]

"The Human Resource Development and Management Category examines how the work force is enabled to develop and utilize its full potential, aligned with the company's performance objectives. Also examined are the company's efforts to build and maintain an environment conducive to performance excellence, full participation, and personal and organizational growth."

# ▪ 11.13 MALCOLM BALDRIGE, 4.1 HUMAN RESOURCE PLANNING AND EVALUATION

## 11.13.1 Malcolm Baldrige, Human Resource Planning and Evaluation; ISO-Associated Statements

There are no associated elements in ISO.

## 11.13.2 Malcolm Baldrige, Human Resource Planning and Evaluation; SEI-Associated Statements

There are no associated elements in SEI.

---

4. Ibid., p. 27.

# ■ 11.14 MALCOLM BALDRIGE, 4.2 HIGH PERFORMANCE WORK SYSTEMS

### 11.14.1 Malcolm Baldrige, High Performance Work Systems; ISO-Associated Statements

Malcolm Baldrige's High Performance Work Systems 4.2.a(3), "ensuring effective communications across functions...," has some correlation to ISO's 4.4.3 Organizational and Technical Interfaces requirement.

### 11.14.2 Malcolm Baldrige, High Performance Work Systems; SEI-Associated Statements

Malcolm Baldrige's High Performance Work Systems 4.2.a(3), "ensuring effective communications across functions...," has a strong correlation to SEI's Intergroup Coordination (IC) requirement.

# ■ 11.15 MALCOLM BALDRIGE, 4.3 EMPLOYEE EDUCATION, TRAINING, AND DEVELOPMENT

### 11.15.1 Malcolm Baldrige, Employee Education, Training, and Development; ISO-Associated Statements

Malcolm Baldrige, 4.3 Employee Education, Training, and Development, is associated with the ISO elements in 4.18 Training. ISO devotes one of its 20 clauses to the topic of training. ISO's 4.18 Training has a strong correlation to Malcolm Baldrige's requirement for "addressing key performance objectives, including those related to enhancing high performance work units, with education and training." ISO is very narrowly focused in relation to MB. Malcolm Baldrige goes well beyond just training and addresses the need for the development of employees as a key resource.

### 11.15.2 Malcolm Baldrige, Employee Education, Training, and Development; SEI-Associated Statements

Malcolm Baldrige, 4.3 Employee Education, Training, and Development, is associated with the SEI practices in Training Program (TP) and the Ability to Perform (AB) common feature. These practices have a strong correlation with Malcolm Baldrige. SEI devotes one of its 18 key process areas to training. In addition, it devotes many practices specifically to training. The Training Program (TP) process area is focused on the group that will perform the training function for the organization. The Ability to Perform (AB) practices are specific to the process area and identify the particular needs of that process area.

## ■ 11.16 MALCOLM BALDRIGE, 4.4 EMPLOYEE WELL-BEING AND SATISFACTION

### 11.16.1 Malcolm Baldrige, Employee Well-Being and Satisfaction; ISO-Associated Statements

There are no associated elements in ISO.

### 11.16.2 Malcolm Baldrige, Employee Well-Being and Satisfaction; SEI-Associated Statements

There are no associated elements in SEI.

## ■ 11.17 MALCOLM BALDRIGE, 5.0 PROCESS MANAGEMENT[5]

"The Process Management Category examines the key aspects of process management, including customer-focused design, product and service delivery processes, support services and supply management involving all work units, including research and development. The Category examines how key processes are designed, effectively managed, and improved to achieve higher performance."

## ■ 11.18 MALCOLM BALDRIGE, 5.1 DESIGN AND INTRODUCTION OF PRODUCTS AND SERVICES

### 11.18.1 Malcolm Baldrige, Design and Introduction of Products and Services; ISO-Associated Statements

Malcolm Baldrige, 5.1 Design and Introduction of Products and Services, is associated with the ISO elements in 6 of ISO's 20 clauses: 4.4 Design Control; 4.5 Document and Data Control; 4.10 Inspection and Testing; 4.14 Corrective and Preventative Action; 4.15 Handling, Storage, Packaging, Preservation, and Delivery; and 4.19 Servicing.

---

5. Ibid., p. 30.

ISO 4.4 Design Control covers the design process very thoroughly with requirements for planning, organizational and technical interfaces, design input, design output, design review, design verification, design validation, and design changes. These requirements have a strong correlation to the Malcolm Baldrige requirements but are at a much more specific and defined level. An example of this is the Malcolm Baldrige statement "translating product and service design requirements into efficient and effective production/delivery processes, including an appropriate measurement plan." Malcolm Baldrige is not specific about what constitutes an "efficient and effective" process. ISO, on the other hand, is very specific about the elements a process should be made up of. Malcolm Baldrige covers the basic elements of a design process: translating customer requirements into design requirements, translating design requirements into processes, and reviewing and/or testing the "product" of the process. ISO takes these basic requirements and details them to a much greater and more specific extent. Malcolm Baldrige has one requirement that looks for "evaluating and improving designs and design processes." This follows one of Baldrige's key themes of continuous improvement. ISO does not explicitly address the theme of continuous improvement.

ISO 4.5 Document and Data Control has some correlation to the Malcolm Baldrige requirement for "efficient and effective" processes.

ISO 4.10 Inspection and Testing has a strong correlation to the Malcolm Baldrige requirement for "reviewing and/or testing product, service, and production/delivery process designs in detail to ensure trouble-free launch."

ISO 4.14.3 Preventative Action has a strong correlation to the Malcolm Baldrige requirement for "evaluating and improving designs and design processes so that introductions of new or modified products and services progressively improve in quality and cycle time."

ISO 4.15 Handling, Storage, Packaging, Preservation, and Delivery has a strong correlation to the Malcolm Baldrige requirement for "efficient and effective" processes. It is also very specific about the "mechanics" of the process and what it expects to find.

ISO 4.19 Servicing has a strong correlation to the Malcolm Baldrige requirement for "efficient and effective" processes.

Overall, there is a strong correlation between the Malcolm Baldrige requirements and these ISO elements; however, ISO is much more specific and detailed in its requirements.

## 11.18.2 Malcolm Baldrige, Design and Introduction of Products and Services; SEI-Associated Statements

Malcolm Baldrige, 5.1 Design and Introduction of Products and Services, is associated with the SEI elements in the Requirements Management (RM), Software Product Engineering (PE), Intergroup Coordination (IC), Peer Reviews (PR), and Software Quality Management (QM) key process areas.

Requirements Management (RM) has a strong correlation to the Malcolm Baldrige requirement for "translating customer requirements into product and service design requirements."

Software Product Engineering (PE) has a strong correlation to the Malcolm Baldrige requirement for "translating product and service design requirements into efficient and effective production/delivery processes, including an appropriate measurement plan."

Intergroup Coordination (IC) has a strong correlation to the Malcolm Baldrige requirement for "addressing all requirements associated with products, services, and production/delivery processes early in design by appropriate company units, suppliers, and partners to ensure integration, coordination, and capability."

Peer Reviews (PR) has a strong correlation to the Malcolm Baldrige requirement for "reviewing and/or testing product, service, and production/delivery process designs in detail to ensure trouble-free launch."

Software Quality Management (QM) has a strong correlation to the Malcolm Baldrige requirement for "designing key production/delivery processes to meet both key product and service quality requirements and company operational performance requirements."

## ■ 11.19 MALCOLM BALDRIGE, 5.2 PROCESS MANAGEMENT: PRODUCT AND SERVICE PRODUCTION AND DELIVERY

### 11.19.1 Malcolm Baldrige, Process Management: Product and Service Production and Delivery; ISO-Associated Statements

Malcolm Baldrige, 5.2 Process Management: Product and Service Production and Delivery, is associated with the ISO elements in 16 of ISO's 20 clauses. 4.4 Design Control; 4.5 Document and Data Control; 4.6 Purchasing; 4.9 Process Control; 4.10 Inspection and Testing; 4.11 Control of Inspection, Measuring, and Test Equipment; 4.12 Inspection and Test Status; 4.14 Corrective and Preventative Action; 4.17 Internal Quality Audits; 4.19 Servicing; and 4.20 Statistical Techniques have a strong correlation. 4.7 Control of Customer-Supplied Product; 4.8 Product Identification and Traceability; 4.13 Control of Nonconforming Product; 4.15 Handling, Storage, Packaging, Preservation, and Delivery; and 4.16 Control of Quality Records have some correlation. A large number of ISO clauses address this Malcolm Baldrige requirement, which is focused on the maintenance of process performance as well as the on-going evaluation and improvement of processes. These ISO clauses are generally looking for establishing and maintaining procedures to control or ensure some aspect of process quality and operational performance. These clauses have correlation to the Malcolm Baldrige requirement for describing "the key processes and their principal requirements." Malcolm Baldrige is, of course, looking for applicants to describe their specific processes. ISO abstracts this to a more generic process level, since it is intended to apply to many types of businesses. ISO 9001 leans toward the requirements of a hardware manufacturing type of business. This is understandable given ISO 9000's roots in defense hardware procurement. ISO does, however, provide guidelines (to the standards) for businesses such as *software* (ISO 9000-3:1991, Quality Management and Quality Assurance Standards—Part 3: Guidelines for the Application of ISO 9001 to the Development, Supply and Maintenance of Software), *services* (ISO 9004-2:1991, Quality Management and Quality System Elements—Part 2: Guidelines for Services), and *processed materials* (ISO 9004-3:1993, Quality Management and Quality System Elements—Part 3: Guidelines for Processed Materials).

Many of the ISO clauses such as 4.9 Process Control; 4.10 Inspection and Testing; 4.11 Control of Inspection, Measuring, and Test Equipment; 4.12 Inspection and Test Status; 4.17 Internal Quality Audits; and 4.20 Statistical Techniques have a strong correlation to the Malcolm Baldrige requirement for "maintaining process performance by use of the measurement plan and measurements and/or observations." Malcolm Baldrige requires that the measurement plan identify "what is to be measured, how and when measurements are to be made, and performance levels or standards to ensure that the results of measurements provide information to guide, monitor, control, or improve the process."

In referring to the maintenance of processes, Malcolm Baldrige clarifies this in the Areas to Address notes as "using measurements and/or observations to decide whether or not corrective action is needed." ISO's 4.14.2 Corrective Action clause has a strong correlation with this requirement.

ISO clause 4.14.3 Preventative Action has a strong correlation with the Malcolm Baldrige requirement for "evaluating and improving processes to achieve better operational performance, including cycle time." As stated previously, ISO is much more specific and detailed in its requirements. However, ISO has no requirements to improve cycle time.

## 11.19.2 Malcolm Baldrige, Process Management: Product and Service Production and Delivery; SEI-Associated Statements

Malcolm Baldrige, 5.2 Process Management: Product and Service Production and Delivery, is associated with the SEI elements in Requirements Management (RM), Software Project Planning (PP), Software Project Tracking and Oversight (PT), Software Quality Assurance (QA), Software Configuration Management (CM), Organization Process Focus (PF), Organization Process Definition (PD), Integrated Software Management (IM), Defect Prevention (DP), Technology Change Management (TM), and Process Change Management (PC).

These SEI elements have a strong correlation to the Malcolm Baldrige requirement for "maintaining process performance by use of the measurement plan and measurements and/or observations." As stated earlier, Malcolm Baldrige requires that the measurement plan identify "what is to be measured, how and when measurements are to be made, and performance levels or standards to ensure that the results of measurements provide information to guide, monitor, control, or improve the process." This requirement has a strong correlation in SEI process areas of Requirements Management (RM), Software Project Planning (PP), Software Project Tracking and Oversight (PT), Software Quality Assurance (QA), Software Configuration Management (CM), Integrated Software Management (IM), Defect Prevention (DP), and Technology Change Management (TM) through the common features of Measurement and Analysis (ME) and Verifying Implementation (VE). The Measurement and Analysis (ME) common feature practices are used to determine the status of specific activities. The Verifying Implementation (VE) common feature practices identify management reviews. In addition, Verifying Implementation (VE) practices also identify audit practices, which are conducted by an independent group (e.g., the software quality assurance group). The process areas of Software Project Tracking and Oversight (PT), Software Quality Assurance (QA), Software Configuration Management (CM), and Integrated Software Management (IM) further address the Malcolm Baldrige "measurement" requirement and provide strong correlation through their Goals (GO) statements. SEI also has a strong correlation to the Malcolm Baldrige "measurement" requirement through its key process areas of Organization Process Focus (PF), Organization Process Definition (PD), Technology Change Management (TM), and Process Change Management (PC). These key process areas have a strong correlation to the Malcolm Baldrige requirement for "evaluating and improving processes to achieve better operational performance, including cycle time; using process analysis, using benchmarking, using alternative technology, considering information from customers of the processes—within and outside the company."

# ■ 11.20 MALCOLM BALDRIGE, 5.3 PROCESS MANAGEMENT: SUPPORT SERVICES

### 11.20.1 Malcolm Baldrige, Process Management: Support Services; ISO-Associated Statements

In general, Process Management: Support Services are not considered part of ISO 9001. Third-party registration to ISO 9001, 9002, or 9003 involves the definition of a scope of the organization's registration. In many cases, an organization produces a product, and the scope of the registration is limited to the processes that have a direct influence on the quality of the product. Therefore, "support services" would be outside the scope of the registration, and not audited. Malcolm Baldrige gives examples of support services such as finance and accounting, sales, marketing, public relations, information services, supplies, personnel, legal services, secretarial, and other administrative services. An organization, however, can include support services in the scope of their registration. An example would be including secretarial services. In this case, the support services identified as under the scope of the registration would also be under the same requirements of the ISO standard as all the other processes.

If support services are included under the scope of the registration, then ISO's 4.9 Process Control has a strong correlation to this Malcolm Baldrige requirement. ISO requires that processes be "carried out under controlled conditions" and defines what controlled conditions must include. Malcolm Baldrige specifies how processes should be maintained "by use of the measurement plan and measurements and/or observations." Malcolm Baldrige's 5.3.c Area to Address goes beyond ISO's requirements and looks for "evaluating and improving processes to achieve better operational performance."

If support services are included under the scope of the registration, then ISO's 4.14 Corrective and Preventative Action has a strong correlation with the Malcolm Baldrige requirement for "evaluating and improving processes to achieve better operational performance, including cycle time." ISO is much more specific and detailed in its requirements.

### 11.20.2 Malcolm Baldrige, Process Management: Support Services; SEI-Associated Statements

There are no associated elements in SEI.

## ■ 11.21 MALCOLM BALDRIGE, 5.4 MANAGEMENT OF SUPPLIER PERFORMANCE

### 11.21.1 Malcolm Baldrige, Management of Supplier Performance; ISO-Associated Statements

Malcolm Baldrige, 5.4 Management of Supplier Performance, is associated with the following ISO elements: 4.6 Purchasing, 4.7 Control of Customer-Supplied Product, 4.8 Product Identification and Traceability, 4.10 Inspection and Testing, 4.13 Control of Nonconforming Product, and 4.14 Corrective and Preventative Action. Malcolm Baldrige defines *supplier* as "other-company providers of goods and services."

ISO clause 4.6.1 General has a strong correlation with the Malcolm Baldrige requirement for "assuring that materials, components, and services furnished by other businesses meet the company's performance requirements."

ISO clause 4.6.2 Evaluation of Sub-Contractors has some correlation with the Malcolm Baldrige requirement for "principal requirements for key supplier, the measures and/or indicators associated with these requirements, and the expected performance levels."

ISO clause 4.6.3 Purchasing Data has a strong correlation with the Malcolm Baldrige requirement for "communicating the company's requirements to suppliers."

ISO clause 4.6.4 Verification of Purchased Product has a strong correlation with the Malcolm Baldrige requirement for "assuring that materials, components, and services furnished by other businesses meet the company's performance requirements."

ISO clause 4.7 Control of Customer-Supplied Product has some correlation with the Malcolm Baldrige requirement for "assuring that materials, components, and services furnished by other businesses meet the company's performance requirements."

ISO clause 4.8 Product Identification and Traceability has a strong correlation with the Malcolm Baldrige requirement for "determining whether or not the company's requirements are met by suppliers."

ISO clause 4.10 Inspection and Testing has a strong correlation with the Malcolm Baldrige requirement for "assuring that materials, components, and services furnished by other businesses meet the company's performance requirements."

ISO clause 4.13 Control of Nonconforming Product has some correlation with the Malcolm Baldrige requirement for "assuring that materials, components, and services furnished by other businesses meet the company's performance requirements."

ISO clause 4.14 Corrective and Preventative Action has a strong correlation with the Malcolm Baldrige requirement for "evaluating and improving the company's management of supplier relationships and performance."

### 11.21.2 Malcolm Baldrige, Management of Supplier Performance; SEI-Associated Statements

Malcolm Baldrige, 5.4 Management of Supplier Performance, is associated with the SEI elements in Software Subcontract Management (SM). SEI provides a comprehensive set of practices, which have a strong correlation with the Malcolm Baldrige requirements for "assuring that materials, components, and services furnished by other businesses meet the company's performance requirements" and "communicating the company's requirements to suppliers."

# ■ 11.22  MALCOLM BALDRIGE, 6.0 BUSINESS RESULTS[6]

"The Business Results Category examines the company's performance and improvement in key business areas—product and service quality, productivity and operational effective-

---

6. Ibid., p. 34.

ness, supply quality, and financial performance indicators linked to these areas. Also examined are performance levels relative to those of competitors."

One of the Malcolm Baldrige key themes is an emphasis on business results. Part of Baldrige's core values and concepts includes Results Orientation. This core item emphasizes that a company must continually focus on the results and balance those results across the different stakeholders. Examples of stakeholders are customers, employees, stockholders, suppliers and partners, the public, and the community. This section represents a fundamental difference in philosophy among Malcolm Baldrige, ISO, and SEI. Malcolm Baldrige is focused at a much wider "business" view of a quality system. ISO and SEI are focused at a much more detailed and granular level of a quality management system. Baldrige sections Product and Service Quality Results, Company Operational and Financial Results, and Supplier Performance Results act as a linkage point for discussing the other sections in Malcolm Baldrige. As an example, item 6.1 discusses the results of the requirements stated in items 7.1 and 5.1.

## ■ 11.23 MALCOLM BALDRIGE, 6.1 PRODUCT AND SERVICE QUALITY RESULTS

### 11.23.1 Malcolm Baldrige, Product and Service Quality Results; ISO-Associated Statements

There are no associated elements in ISO.

### 11.23.2 Malcolm Baldrige, Product and Service Quality Results; SEI-Associated Statements

There are no associated elements in SEI.

## ■ 11.24 MALCOLM BALDRIGE, 6.2 COMPANY OPERATIONAL AND FINANCIAL RESULTS

### 11.24.1 Malcolm Baldrige, Company Operational and Financial Results; ISO-Associated Statements

There are no associated elements in ISO.

### 11.24.2 Malcolm Baldrige, Company Operational and Financial Results; SEI-Associated Statements

There are no associated elements in SEI.

## ■ 11.25 MALCOLM BALDRIGE, 6.3 SUPPLIER PERFORMANCE RESULTS

### 11.25.1 Malcolm Baldrige, Supplier Performance Results; ISO-Associated Statements

There are no associated elements in ISO.

### 11.25.2 Malcolm Baldrige, Supplier Performance Results; SEI-Associated Statements

There are no associated elements in SEI.

## ■ 11.26 MALCOLM BALDRIGE, 7.0 CUSTOMER FOCUS AND SATISFACTION[7]

"The Customer Focus and Satisfaction Category examines the company's systems for customer learning and for building and maintaining customer relationships. Also examined are levels and trends in key measures of business success—customer satisfaction and retention, market share, and satisfaction relative to competitors."

## ■ 11.27 MALCOLM BALDRIGE, 7.1 CUSTOMER AND MARKET KNOWLEDGE

### 11.27.1 Malcolm Baldrige, Customer and Market Knowledge; ISO-Associated Statements

Malcolm Baldrige, 7.1 Customer and Market Knowledge, is associated with the ISO elements in 4.3 Contract Review. In this clause, ISO is focused on a single contract situation and having a specific "contract" or agreement in place. This has some correlation to Mal-

---

7. Ibid., p. 36.

colm Baldrige. Malcolm Baldrige can apply to the specific contractual situation but, more generally, is aimed at the situation where a product is being created for a "market." In creating products for a market, there is a different set of issues and problems than those encountered in a specific contract situation. This Malcolm Baldrige requirement generally falls outside the scope of ISO.

### 11.27.2  Malcolm Baldrige, Customer and Market Knowledge; SEI-Associated Statements

Malcolm Baldrige, 7.1 Customer and Market Knowledge, is associated with the SEI elements in Requirements Management (RM). Like ISO, SEI is focused on a single contract situation and having a specific "contract" or agreement in place. This has some correlation to Malcolm Baldrige. Malcolm Baldrige can apply to the specific contractual situations but, more generally, is aimed at the situation where a product is being created for a "market." In creating products for a market, there is a different set of issues and problems than those encountered in a specific contract situation. This Malcolm Baldrige requirement generally falls outside the scope of SEI.

## ■ 11.28  MALCOLM BALDRIGE, 7.2 CUSTOMER RELATIONSHIP MANAGEMENT

### 11.28.1  Malcolm Baldrige, Customer Relationship Management; ISO-Associated Statements

Malcolm Baldrige, 7.2 Customer Relationship Management, is associated with the ISO elements in 4.3 Contract Review, 4.6 Purchasing, and 4.14 Corrective and Preventative Action.

ISO 4.3 Contract Review has some correlation with the Malcolm Baldrige requirement for "providing effective management of the company's responses and follow ups with customers to preserve and build relationships and to increase knowledge about specific customers and about general customer expectations."

ISO 4.6.4.2 Customer Verification of Subcontracted Product has a strong correlation with the Malcolm Baldrige requirement for "providing information and easy access to enable customers to seek information and assistance, to comment, and to complain."

ISO 4.14 Corrective and Preventative Action has a strong correlation with the Malcolm Baldrige requirement for "evaluating and improving the company's customer relationship management."

## 11.28.2  Malcolm Baldrige, Customer Relationship Management; SEI-Associated Statements

Malcolm Baldrige, 7.2 Customer Relationship Management, is associated with the SEI elements in Software Quality Assurance (QA), Integrated Software Management (IM), and Intergroup Coordination (IC). These SEI practices have some correlation with the Malcolm Baldrige requirement for "providing effective management of the company's responses and follow ups with customers to preserve and build relationships and to increase knowledge about specific customers and about general customer expectations." Malcolm Baldrige is much broader and is focused on organizations that are marketing to more than just a single customer.

## ■ 11.29  MALCOLM BALDRIGE, 7.3 CUSTOMER SATISFACTION DETERMINATION

This Malcolm Baldrige requirement is also much broader than ISO and SEI and is focused on organizations that are marketing to more than just a single customer. In creating products for a market, there is a different set of issues and problems than that encountered in a specific contract situation.

## 11.29.1  Malcolm Baldrige, Customer Satisfaction Determination; ISO-Associated Statements

ISO has some correlation to this requirement in its 4.19 Servicing clause, by requiring "procedures for performing, verifying, and reporting that the servicing meets the specified requirements...." Malcolm Baldrige is much broader in its requirements than ISO, because it looks at such issues as customer repurchase intentions and customer satisfaction relative to competitors.

## 11.29.2  Malcolm Baldrige, Customer Satisfaction Determination; SEI-Associated Statements

There are no associated elements in SEI.

# ■ 11.30 Malcolm Baldrige, 7.4 Customer Satisfaction Results

This Malcolm Baldrige requirement is also much broader than ISO and SEI and is focused on organizations that are marketing to more than just a single customer.

## 11.30.1 Malcolm Baldrige, Customer Satisfaction Results; ISO-Associated Statements

ISO has some correlation to this requirement in its 4.19 Servicing clause, by requiring "procedures for performing, verifying, and reporting that the servicing meets the specified requirements...." Baldrige Customer Satisfaction Determination and Customer Satisfaction Results are strongly focused on customer satisfaction. For many businesses, just meeting requirements is not always enough for attaining customer satisfaction.

## 11.30.2 Malcolm Baldrige, Customer Satisfaction Results; SEI-Associated Statements

There are no associated elements in SEI.

# ■ 11.31 Malcolm Baldrige, 7.5 Customer Satisfaction Comparison

This MB requirement is also much broader than ISO and SEI and is focused on organizations that are marketing to more than just a single customer.

## 11.31.1 Malcolm Baldrige, Customer Satisfaction Comparison; ISO-Associated Statements

There are no associated elements in ISO.

## 11.31.2 Malcolm Baldrige, Customer Satisfaction Comparison; SEI-Associated Statements

There are no associated elements in SEI.

# 12

# Comparison from an ISO 9001 Perspective

This chapter covers the 20 quality-system requirements of ISO 9001. Each of these requirements is addressed in two subsections—MB-associated statements and SEI-associated statements. Each subsection discusses the other methodology's associated statements and why they are associated. In discussing the association between statements, the terms "some correlation" and "strong correlation" are used. These terms are intended to give you a feel for the association and its significance. A summary of the correlations is provided in Figures 12.1 and 12.2. A detailed mapping of the correlations is provided in Appendix F and Appendix G.

## ■ 12.1 ISO 9001, 4.1 MANAGEMENT RESPONSIBILITY

### 12.1.1 ISO 9001, Management Responsibility; MB-Associated Statements

*ISO 9001, Quality Policy; MB-Associated Statements*

The requirement for a quality policy has no direct mapping to Malcolm Baldrige; however, two items are related. Under 1.1 Senior Executive Leadership, there is a strong correlation to the requirement for "creating and reinforcing value and expectations throughout the company's leadership system." Under 1.2 Leadership System and Organization, there is a strong correlation to the requirement for "communicating and reinforcing the values, expectations, and directions of the company throughout the entire work force."

**Figure 12.1** ISO 9001 mapping to Malcolm Baldrige.

| ISO 9001 | Malcolm Baldrige | | | | | | | | | | | | | | | | | | | | | | | |
|---|---|---|---|---|---|---|---|---|---|---|---|---|---|---|---|---|---|---|---|---|---|---|---|---|
| | A | B | C | D | E | F | G | H | I | J | K | L | M | N | O | P | Q | R | S | T | U | V | W | X |
| 4.1 Management Responsibility | ● | ● | | | | | | | | | | | | | | | | | | | | | | |
| 4.2 Quality System | | | | | | | ○ | | | | | | | | | | | | | | | | | |
| 4.3 Contract Review | | | | | | | | | | | | | | | | | | | | ○ | ○ | | | |
| 4.4 Design Control | | | | | | | | | | ○ | | | ● | ● | | | | | | | | | | |
| 4.5 Document and Data Control | | | | ● | | | | | | | | | ○ | ● | | | | | | | | | | |
| 4.6 Purchasing | | | | ● | | | | | | | | | | ● | | ● | | | | | ● | | | |
| 4.7 Control of Customer-Supplied Product | | | | | | | | | | | | | | ○ | | ○ | | | | | | | | |
| 4.8 Product Identification and Traceability | | | | | | | | | | | | | | ○ | | ● | | | | | | | | |
| 4.9 Process Control | | | | | | | | | | | | | ● | ● | | | | | | | | | | |
| 4.10 Inspection and Testing | | | | ● | | | | | | | | | ● | ● | | ● | | | | | | | | |
| 4.11 Control of Inspection, Measuring, and Test Equipment | | | | | | | | | | | | | | ● | | | | | | | | | | |
| 4.12 Inspection and Test Status | | | | | | | | | | | | | | ● | | | | | | | | | | |
| 4.13 Control of Nonconforming Product | | | | | | | | | | | | | | ○ | | ○ | | | | | | | | |
| 4.14 Corrective and Preventative Action | | | | | | ● | | | | | | | ● | ● | ● | ● | | | | | ● | | | |
| 4.15 Handling, Storage, Packaging, Preservation, and Delivery | | | | | | | | | | | | | ● | ○ | | | | | | | | | | |
| 4.16 Control of Quality Records | | | | ● | | | | | | | | | | ○ | | | | | | | | | | |
| 4.17 Internal Quality Audits | | | | | | | | | | | | | | ● | | | | | | | | | | |
| 4.18 Training | | | | | | | | | | | ● | | | | | | | | | | | | | |
| 4.19 Servicing | | | | | | | | | | | | | ● | ● | | | | | | | | | ○ | ○ | |
| 4.20 Statistical Techniques | | | | ● | | ● | | | | | | | | ● | | | | | | | | | | |

## ISO 9001, *Responsibility and Authority; MB-Associated Statements*

There are no associated elements in MB.

## ISO 9001, *Resources; MB-Associated Statements*

There are no associated elements in MB.

**ISO 9001 mapping to Malcolm Baldrige key.**

Note:

○ = Some correlation

● = Strong correlation

A  = 1.1 Senior Executive Leadership
B  = 1.2 Leadership System and Organization
C  = 1.3 Public Responsibility and Corporate Citizenship
D  = 2.1 Management of Information and Data
E  = 2.2 Competitive Comparisons and Benchmarking
F  = 2.3 Analysis and Use of Company-Level Data
G  = 3.1 Strategy Development
H  = 3.2 Strategy Deployment
I  = 4.1 Human Resource Planning and Evaluation
J  = 4.2 High Performance Work Systems
K  = 4.3 Employee Education, Training, and Development
L  = 4.4 Employee Well-Being and Satisfaction
M  = 5.1 Design and Introduction of Products and Services
N  = 5.2 Process Management: Product and Service Production and Delivery
O  = 5.3 Process Management: Support Services
P  = 5.4 Management of Supplier Performance
Q  = 6.1 Product and Service Quality Results
R  = 6.2 Company Operational and Financial Results
S  = 6.3 Supplier Performance Results
T  = 7.1 Customer and Market Knowledge
U  = 7.2 Customer Relationship Management
V  = 7.3 Customer Satisfaction Determination
W  = 7.4 Customer Satisfaction Results
X  = 7.5 Customer Satisfaction Comparison

### ISO 9001, *Management Representative; MB-Associated Statements*

There are no associated elements in MB.

### ISO 9001, *Management Review; MB-Associated Statements*

Under 1.1 Senior Executive Leadership, there is a strong correlation to the requirement for "reviewing overall company performance, including customer-related and operational performance(senior executives)." Under 1.2 Leadership System and Organization, there is a strong correlation to the requirement for "reviewing overall company and work unit performance."

**Figure 12.2** ISO 9001 mapping to SEI CMM.

| ISO 9001 | A | B | C | D | E | F | G | H | I | J | K | L | M | N | O | P | Q | R | S | T | U | V | W | X |
|---|---|---|---|---|---|---|---|---|---|---|---|---|---|---|---|---|---|---|---|---|---|---|---|---|
| 4.1 Management Responsibility | ● | ● | ● | ○ |  | ○ | ● | ● | ● | ● | ● | ● | ● |  | ● |  | ● |  | ● |  | ● | ● |  |  |
| 4.2 Quality System |  |  |  | ● |  | ○ |  | ● |  |  |  |  |  |  |  |  |  |  |  |  |  |  |  |  |
| 4.3 Contract Review |  |  |  |  |  |  | ○ | ○ | ○ |  |  |  |  |  |  |  |  |  |  |  |  |  |  |  |
| 4.4 Design Control |  |  |  |  |  |  | ○ | ● | ● |  |  | ● |  |  |  |  | ● | ● | ● |  |  |  |  |  |
| 4.5 Document and Data Control |  |  |  |  |  |  |  |  |  |  |  | ● |  |  |  |  |  |  |  |  |  |  |  |  |
| 4.6 Purchasing |  |  |  |  |  |  |  |  |  | ● |  |  |  |  |  |  |  |  |  |  | ● |  |  |  |
| 4.7 Control of Customer-Supplied Product |  |  |  |  |  |  |  |  |  |  |  |  |  |  |  |  |  |  |  |  |  |  |  |  |
| 4.8 Product Identification and Traceability |  |  |  |  |  |  |  |  |  |  |  | ● |  |  |  |  |  |  |  |  |  |  |  |  |
| 4.9 Process Control |  |  |  | ● |  |  |  | ● |  |  |  |  |  |  |  |  |  |  |  |  |  |  |  |  |
| 4.10 Inspection and Testing |  |  |  |  |  |  |  |  |  | ● |  |  |  |  |  |  | ● |  | ● |  |  |  |  |  |
| 4.11 Control of Inspection, Measuring, and Test Equipment |  |  |  |  |  |  |  |  |  |  |  |  |  |  |  |  |  |  |  |  |  |  |  |  |
| 4.12 Inspection and Test Status |  |  |  |  |  |  |  |  |  |  |  | ● |  |  |  |  |  |  |  |  |  |  |  |  |
| 4.13 Control of Nonconforming Product |  |  |  |  |  |  |  |  |  |  |  | ● |  |  |  |  | ● |  |  |  |  |  |  |  |
| 4.14 Corrective and Preventative Action |  |  |  |  |  |  |  |  | ● |  |  |  |  |  |  |  |  |  |  |  |  |  | ● |  |
| 4.15 Handling, Storage, Packaging, Preservation, and Delivery |  |  |  |  |  |  |  |  |  |  |  |  |  |  |  |  |  |  |  |  |  |  |  |  |
| 4.16 Control of Quality Records |  |  |  | ● |  |  |  |  |  |  |  | ● |  |  |  |  |  |  |  |  |  |  |  |  |
| 4.17 Internal Quality Audits |  |  |  |  |  |  |  |  |  |  | ● |  |  |  |  |  |  |  |  |  |  |  |  |  |
| 4.18 Training |  | ● |  |  |  |  |  |  |  |  |  |  |  |  |  | ● |  |  |  |  |  |  |  |  |
| 4.19 Servicing |  |  |  |  |  |  |  |  |  |  |  |  |  |  |  |  |  |  |  |  |  |  |  |  |
| 4.20 Statistical Techniques |  |  |  | ● |  |  |  |  |  |  |  |  |  |  |  |  |  |  |  |  | ● | ● |  |  |

## 12.1.2 ISO 9001, Management Responsibility; SEI-Associated Statements

### ISO 9001, Quality Policy; SEI-Associated Statements

SEI has no generic quality policy, but it does identify two areas that have a strong correlation to ISO. These practices require organizational policies regarding quality. ISO is looking for management to define quality objectives. SEI does not specifically address

ISO 9001 mapping to SEI CMM Key.[a]

---

**Note:**

○ = Some correlation

● = Strong correlation

A   = Goals (GO)

B   = Commitment to Perform (CO)

C   = Ability to Perform (AB)

D   = Activities Performed (AC)

E   = Measurement and Analysis (ME)

F   = Verifying Implementation (VE)

G   = Requirements Management (RM)

H   = Software Project Planning (PP)

I   = Software Project Tracking and Oversight (PT)

J   = Software Subcontract Management (SM)

K   = Software Quality Assurance (QA)

L   = Software Configuration Management (CM)

M   = Organization Process Focus (PF)

N   = Organization Process Definition (PD)

O   = Training Program (TP)

P   = Integrated Software Management (IM)

Q   = Software Product Engineering (PE)

R   = Intergroup Coordination (IC)

S   = Peer Reviews (PR)

T   = Quantitative Process Management (QP)

U   = Software Quality Management (QM)

V   = Defect Prevention (DP)

W   = Technology Change Management (TM)

X   = Process Change Management (PC)

---

[a]**Note:** In comparisons with the SEI CMM, the reader should make note that the SEI CMM common features are requirement themes that cut across the SEI CMM key process areas. A particular key process area may not show any direct requirement relationships, but may have correlations through the common feature themes. Refer to Chapter 7, "1993 SEI CMM for Software" for a more detailed discussion of SEI's common features and key process areas. Details on key process area requirements included under the common feature themes are provided in Appendix C.

"quality" objectives; however, SEI's Goals (GO), which summarize the key practices for each key process area, can be thought of as quality objectives. ISO is also looking to ensure that the quality policy is implemented and maintained. SEI's Commitment to Perform (CO) common feature is intended to "ensure that the process is established and will endure." Within the Commitment to Perform (CO) common feature, the need for "organizational policy" is identified in the Software Quality Assurance (QA) key process area.

*ISO 9001, Responsibility and Authority; SEI-Associated Statements*

SEI has a number of key practices that have a strong correlation to ISO's Responsibility and Authority requirement. The Intergroup Coordination (IC) process area is especially focused on this requirement. Other process areas with practices which have a strong correlation include Requirements Management (RM), Software Project Planning (PP), Software Project Tracking and Oversight (PT), Software Subcontract Management (SM), Software Quality Assurance (QA), Software Configuration Management (CM), Organization Process Focus (PF), Training Program (TP), Quantitative Process Management (QP), Defect Prevention (DP), and Technology Change Management (TM). Most of these practices involve the establishment of a team or group.

*ISO 9001, Resources; SEI-Associated Statements*

SEI has a strong correlation to ISO's Resources requirement. All 18 of SEI's key process areas have one or more practices devoted to the requirements for "identifying resource requirements" or "providing adequate resources." These practices fall under the Ability to Perform (AB) common feature.

*ISO 9001, Management Representative; SEI-Associated Statements*

There are no associated elements in SEI.

*ISO 9001, Management Review; SEI-Associated Statements*

ISO's Management Review requires "reviewing the quality system at defined intervals sufficient to ensure its continuing suitability and effectiveness." This requirement is focused on the findings of internal audits of the quality management system, as defined by the ISO 9001 standard. This is a very explicit requirement of ISO and is much more specific than SEI. This has some correlation with the SEI practices for senior and project management reviews. These practices follow the Verifying Implementation (VE) common feature and span all 18 SEI key process areas. There are also some Activities Performed (AC) practices, which identify management reviews and reviews by groups such as the software quality assurance group.

## ■ 12.2  ISO 9001, 4.2 QUALITY SYSTEM

### 12.2.1  ISO 9001, Quality System; MB-Associated Statements

*ISO 9001, General; MB-Associated Statements*

There are no associated elements in MB.

### ISO 9001, *Quality-System Procedures; MB-Associated Statements*

There are no associated elements in MB.

### ISO 9001, *Quality Planning; MB-Associated Statements*

Malcolm Baldrige has some correlation with this ISO requirement in its 3.1 Strategy Development examination item. ISO requires "defining and documenting how the requirements for quality will be met." Malcolm Baldrige addresses this requirement with its general requirement for "planning overall performance and competitive leadership for short term and longer term." Malcolm Baldrige is much broader in this area than ISO requires.

## 12.2.2 ISO 9001, Quality System; SEI-Associated Statements

### ISO 9001, *General; SEI-Associated Statements*

There are no associated elements in SEI.

### ISO 9001, *Quality-System Procedures; SEI-Associated Statements*

SEI has a strong correlation with the ISO Quality-System Procedures *a* requirement for "preparing documented procedures" in 15 of its 18 key process areas. These key process areas are Software Project Planning (PP), Software Project Tracking and Oversight (PT), Software Subcontract Management (SM), Software Quality Assurance (QA), Software Configuration Management (CM), Organization Process Definition (PD), Training Program (TP), Integrated Software Management (IM), Intergroup Coordination (IC), Peer Reviews (PR), Quantitative Process Management (QP), Software Quality Management (QM), Defect Prevention (DP), Technology Change Management (TM), and Process Change Management (PC). SEI identifies key practices that require the use of documented procedures. These practices follow the Activities Performed (AC) common feature.

SEI also has some correlation with the ISO Quality-System Procedures *b* requirement for "implementing the quality system and its documented procedures effectively" in all 18 of its key process areas. These practices mostly involve reviews of the activities with the specific key process areas. These practices follow the Verifying Implementation (VE) common feature.

### ISO 9001, *Quality Planning; SEI-Associated Statements*

SEI has a strong correlation with the ISO requirement for Quality Planning. This ISO requirement is looking for a quality plan that identifies how the quality requirements will be achieved for a given project. SEI does not refer to one quality plan specifically. SEI does, however, address the suggested guidelines for a quality plan (as indicated in ISO 9004-1 and ISO 9000-3) via a Software Development Plan as part of Software Project Planning (PP). Additionally, SEI addresses quality planning in many of the Capability Maturity Model key process areas. For more information on ISO and SEI in this area, refer to Appendix J.

# ■ 12.3  ISO 9001, 4.3 CONTRACT REVIEW

## 12.3.1 ISO 9001, Contract Review; MB-Associated Statements

Malcolm Baldrige has some correlation with this ISO requirement in its 7.1 Customer and Market Knowledge examination item. In this clause, ISO is focused on a single contract situation and having a specific "contract" or agreement in place. This clause has some correlation to Malcolm Baldrige. Malcolm Baldrige can apply to the specific contractual situation but, more generally, is aimed at the situation where a product is being created for a "market." In creating products for a market, there is a different set of issues and problems than those encountered in a specific contract situation.

Malcolm Baldrige has some correlation with this ISO requirement in its 7.2 Customer Relationship Management requirement for "providing effective management of the company's responses and follow ups with customers to preserve and build relationships and to increase knowledge about specific customers and about general customer expectations."

## 12.3.2 ISO 9001, Contract Review; SEI-Associated Statements

SEI is a software perspective in the context of a larger system development. In general, Contract Review for SEI is limited in its scope to software requirements and does not address requirements and the customer in the larger context of purchasing the final delivered product. However, SEI does have some correlation to the requirements of ISO Contract Review in the context of the software development portion of a system development. ISO's Contract Review general requirement for "establishing and maintaining documented procedures for contract review and for the coordination of these activities" is addressed by SEI's Requirements Management (RM) and Software Project Planning (PP) key practices. ISO identifies Review requirements to ensure that the "requirements are adequately defined and documented" and "agreed before their acceptance," any differences are resolved, and the supplier has the capability to meet the requirements. ISO's Amendment to Contract requires "identifying how an amendment to a contract is made." SEI addresses this requirement in its Software Project Tracking and Oversight (PT) key process area. ISO also has a requirement for "establishing channels for communication and interfaces with the customer's organization." SEI has no practices that address this requirement.

# ■ 12.4 ISO 9001, 4.4 DESIGN CONTROL

## 12.4.1 ISO 9001, Design Control; MB-Associated Statements

Malcolm Baldrige has an overall strong correlation to ISO's Design Control requirement. ISO's General and Design and Development Planning requirements are addressed by Malcolm Baldrige's 5.1 Design and Introduction of Products and Services. ISO's Organizational and Technical Interfaces requirement has some correlation to Malcolm Baldrige's 4.2 High Performance Work Systems "ensuring effective communications across functions...." ISO's Design Input and Design Output requirements are addressed by Malcolm Baldrige's 5.1.a translating customer requirements into design requirements, translating design requirements into processes, and "addressing all requirements...to ensure integration, coordination, and capability." ISO's Design Review, Design Verification, and Design Validation requirements are addressed by Malcolm Baldrige's 5.1.b "reviewing and/or testing product, service, and production/delivery process designs in detail to ensure trouble-free launch." ISO's verification and validation requirements are also addressed by Malcolm Baldrige's 5.2 Process Management: Product and Service Production and Delivery by requiring "that design requirements are met." ISO's Design Changes requirement is not addressed by Malcolm Baldrige.

## 12.4.2 ISO 9001, Design Control; SEI-Associated Statements

SEI has an overall strong correlation to ISO's Design Control requirement. ISO's General requirement is addressed by SEI's Software Product Engineering (PE), Software Configuration Management (CM), and Software Project Tracking and Oversight (PT) key process areas. SEI calls for "defined software process" as opposed to the "procedures" called for in ISO.

ISO's Design and Development Planning requirement is addressed by SEI's Software Project Planning (PP) and Software Project Tracking and Oversight (PT) key process areas, which have a strong correlation and require a software development plan.

ISO's Organizational and Technical Interfaces requirement is addressed by SEI's Intergroup Coordination (IC) key process area. Intergroup Coordination (IC) has a strong correlation to ISO and is looking for interfaces and interactions between groups to be "planned and managed."

ISO's Design Input requirement is addressed by SEI's Requirements Management (RM) and Software Product Engineering (PE) key process areas. Requirements Management (RM) has some correlation to ISO and is focused on "establishing and maintaining an agreement with the customer on the requirements for the software project." SEI frames this key process area with the notion of system requirements, which are allocated to software, hardware, and other system components. This process area addresses the software-only portion of this allocation. Software Product Engineering (PE) includes practices that address "analyzing the allocated requirements systemically in order to develop, maintain, document, and verify the software requirements."

ISO's Design Output requirement is addressed by SEI's Software Product Engineering (PE) key process areas. Software Product Engineering (PE) addresses this requirement in its subpractices [refer to Software Engineering Institute, *CMU/SEI-93-TR-25, Key Practices of the Capability Maturity Model, Version 1.1* (Carnegie Mellon University, 1993) for detailed information on the CMM subpractices], which identifies specific design output requirements.

ISO's Design Review requirement is addressed by SEI's Software Product Engineering (PE) and Peer Reviews (PR) key process areas. Within Software Product Engineering (PE), specific practices are identified and the entire Peer Reviews (PR) process area is devoted to reviews. Peer Reviews (PR) have a strong correlation to ISO and involve many different kinds of software work products. Some examples provided under the subpractices include

 ✦ operational software and support software,
 ✦ deliverable and nondeliverable software work products,
 ✦ software (e.g., source code) and nonsoftware work products (e.g., documents), and
 ✦ process descriptions.

ISO's Design Verification and Design Validation requirements are addressed by SEI's Software Product Engineering (PE) key process areas.

ISO's Design Changes requirement is addressed principally by SEI's Software Configuration Management (CM) and Software Product Engineering (PE) key process areas, which have a strong correlation to ISO.

Practices under Software Configuration Management (CM), like the practices under Peer Reviews (PR), involve different kinds of software work products. Some examples of SEI software work products provided under the subpractices include

 ✦ process-related documentation (e.g., plans, standards, or procedures),
 ✦ software requirements,
 ✦ software design,
 ✦ software code units,
 ✦ software test procedures,
 ✦ software system build for the software test activity,
 ✦ software system build for delivery to the customer or end users,
 ✦ compilers, and
 ✦ other support tools.

# ■ 12.5 ISO 9001, 4.5 Document and Data Control

## 12.5.1 ISO 9001, Document and Data Control; MB-Associated Statements

Malcolm Baldrige has an overall strong correlation to ISO's Document and Data Control requirement. ISO's General, Document and Data Approval and Issue, and Document and Data Changes requirements are addressed by Malcolm Baldrige's 2.1 Management of Information and Data examination item. ISO requires "establishing and maintaining documented procedures to control all documents and data" that relate to the standard. Malcolm Baldrige has a similar requirement for "selecting and managing information and data." Malcolm Baldrige is not specific about what constitutes "managing" or what "information and data" should be selected and managed. The Malcolm Baldrige requirement for "efficient and effective production/delivery processes, including an appropriate measurement plan" under 5.1 Design and Introduction of Products and Services has some correlation to ISO. Malcolm Baldrige 5.2 Process Management: Product and Service Production and Delivery has a strong correlation to ISO with its requirement for describing "the key processes and their principal requirements." This Malcolm Baldrige item is focused on the maintenance of process performance as well as the on-going evaluation and improvement of processes.

## 12.5.2 ISO 9001, Document and Data Control; SEI-Associated Statements

SEI has a strong correlation to ISO's Document and Data Control requirement. Practices under Software Configuration Management (CM) identify different kinds of software work products. Some examples of SEI software work products are provided on page 96.

# ■ 12.6 ISO 9001, 4.6 Purchasing

## 12.6.1 ISO 9001, Purchasing; MB-Associated Statements

The Malcolm Baldrige 2.1 Management of Information and Data general requirement for "selecting and managing information and data used for planning, management, and evaluation of overall performance by the company" has a strong correlation to this ISO requirement.

Malcolm Baldrige 5.2 Process Management: Product and Service Production and Delivery, with its requirement for describing "the key processes and their principal requirements," has a strong correlation to ISO. This Malcolm Baldrige item is focused on the maintenance of process performance as well as the on-going evaluation and improvement of processes.

Malcolm Baldrige 5.4 Management of Supplier Performance has a strong correlation to ISO's Purchasing requirement. ISO's General requirement has a strong correlation with Malcolm Baldrige's 5.4 Management of Supplier Performance. ISO's Evaluation of Sub-Contractors, Purchasing Data, and Verification of Purchased Product requirements are addressed by Malcolm Baldrige's 5.4.a area to address. Evaluation of Sub-Contractors has some correlation to Malcolm Baldrige 5.4.a, since there is no explicit Baldrige requirement. Purchasing Data has a strong correlation with Malcolm Baldrige 5.4.a "communicating the company's requirements to suppliers." Verification of Purchased Product has a strong correlation with Malcolm Baldrige 5.4.a "determining whether or not the company's requirements are met by suppliers."

Malcolm Baldrige 7.2 Customer Relationship Management requirement for "providing information and easy access to enable customers to seek information and assistance, to comment, and to complain" has a strong correlation to ISO's 4.6.4.2 Customer Verification of Subcontracted Product requirement.

### 12.6.2 ISO 9001, Purchasing; SEI-Associated Statements

SEI has a strong correlation to ISO's Purchasing requirement. ISO's General requirement has a strong correlation with SEI's Software Subcontract Management (SM) and Software Quality Management (QM)'s QM.AC.5 requirement. SEI is focused on selecting software subcontractors. ISO is much broader and is focused on purchased product that becomes part of the company's product and may affect its product quality. This includes services provided, such as calibration or special processes. ISO's Evaluation of Sub-Contractors requirement has a strong correlation with SEI's Software Subcontract Management (SM) requirements. SEI does not address the requirement to keep "records of acceptable subcontractors." ISO's Purchasing Data and Verification of Purchased Product requirements have a strong correlation with SEI's Software Subcontract Management (SM) requirements.

## ■ 12.7 ISO 9001, 4.7 CONTROL OF CUSTOMER-SUPPLIED PRODUCT

### 12.7.1 ISO 9001, Control of Customer-Supplied Product; MB-Associated Statements

Malcolm Baldrige 5.2 Process Management: Product and Service Production and Delivery, with its requirement for describing "the key processes and their principal requirements," has some correlation to ISO. This Malcolm Baldrige item is focused on the maintenance of process performance as well as the on-going evaluation and improvement of processes.

Malcolm Baldrige 5.4 Management of Supplier Performance, with its requirement for "assuring that materials, components, and services furnished by other businesses meet the company's performance requirements," has some correlation to ISO.

### 12.7.2 ISO 9001, Control of Customer-Supplied Product; SEI-Associated Statements

There are no associated elements in SEI.

## ▇ 12.8 ISO 9001, 4.8 PRODUCT IDENTIFICATION AND TRACEABILITY

### 12.8.1 ISO 9001, Product Identification and Traceability; MB-Associated Statements

Malcolm Baldrige 5.2 Process Management: Product and Service Production and Delivery, with its requirement for describing "the key processes and their principal requirements," has some correlation to ISO. This MB item is focused on the maintenance of process performance as well as the on-going evaluation and improvement of processes.

Malcolm Baldrige 5.4 Management of Supplier Performance, with its requirement for "assuring that materials, components, and services furnished by other businesses meet the company's performance requirements," has some correlation to ISO.

### 12.8.2 ISO 9001, Product Identification and Traceability; SEI-Associated Statements

SEI's Software Configuration Management (CM) key practice area has a strong correlation to ISO's Product Identification and Traceability requirement. Software Configuration Management (CM) identifies different kinds of software work products. In general, software has two products, the program itself and the documentation of how the program works.

## ▇ 12.9 ISO 9001, 4.9 PROCESS CONTROL

### 12.9.1 ISO 9001, Process Control; MB-Associated Statements

Malcolm Baldrige has a strong correlation to ISO's Process Control requirement. Malcolm Baldrige's 5.2 Process Management: Product and Service Production and Delivery item 5.2.a and 5.3 Process Management: Support Services item 5.3.b require "maintaining the performance of key...processes to ensure that such processes meet design requirements." ISO requires that processes be "carried out under controlled conditions" and defines what controlled conditions include. Malcolm Baldrige specifies that processes should be maintained "by use of the measurement plan and measurements and/or observations." Malcolm Baldrige makes a distinction between the types of processes addressed in 5.2.a and 5.3.b as "production/delivery" and "support service," respectively. Malcolm Baldrige's 5.2.b and 5.3.c areas to address go beyond ISO's requirements and look for "evaluating and improving processes to achieve better operational performance."

## 12.9.2 ISO 9001, Process Control; SEI-Associated Statements

SEI has an overall strong correlation to ISO's Process Control requirement. SEI's Software Project Planning (PP) key process area has a strong correlation to ISO's requirement for "identifying and planning the production, installation, and servicing processes which directly affect quality." Under Process Control, ISO identifies the requirement for "ensuring that these processes are carried out under controlled conditions." ISO also identifies specific items that are considered part of "controlled conditions" such as "documented procedures defining the manner of production, installation, and servicing, where the absence of such procedures would adversely affect quality." SEI follows this theme of "controlled conditions" throughout 13 of its 18 key process areas, by requiring documented procedures. These key process areas follow the Activities Performed (AC) common feature and the theme of requiring that certain tasks or activities be executed "according to a documented procedure." These key process areas include

- ✧ Software Project Planning (PP)
- ✧ Software Project Tracking and Oversight (PT)
- ✧ Software Subcontract Management (SM)
- ✧ Software Quality Assurance (QA)
- ✧ Software Configuration Management (CM)
- ✧ Organization Process Definition (PD)
- ✧ Integrated Software Management (IM)
- ✧ Software Product Engineering (PE)
- ✧ Intergroup Coordination (IC)
- ✧ Peer Reviews (PR)
- ✧ Quantitative Process Management (QP)

✧  Software Quality Management (QM)
✧  Technology Change Management (TM)

In many cases, the requirements of SEI could be considered to exceed those of ISO. This would have to be considered on an individual basis and by the specific circumstances. One example of this is the Technology Change Management (TM) key process area of SEI. This key process area is part of SEI's highest maturity level, Level 5: Optimizing. The stated objective of this key process area "is to improve software quality, increase productivity, and decrease the cycle time for product development." This requirement seems to fit more with the Malcolm Baldrige/TQM focus on continuous improvement. At first glance, this would appear to be outside the scope of ISO. A closer examination, however, finds that certain parts of Technology Change Management (TM) in fact do fall under the ISO standard. ISO Process Control requires identifying and planning the "production, installation, and servicing processes which directly affect quality" and ensuring that "these processes are carried out under controlled conditions." So, while Technology Change Management (TM) is not a requirement of ISO, it can fall under the requirements of ISO, when an organization establishes Technology Change Management (TM) to introduce new technologies that can adversely affect the product quality. SEI defines technology as the "application of science and/or engineering in accomplishing some particular results." SEI further provides examples of new technologies, such as tools, methods, and processes.

ISO does not have a specific requirement for "continuous improvement," but it does have an implied "continuous improvement" just through the on-going process of Corrective and Preventative Action (ISO 4.14), which can be characterized as more of an incremental type of improvement. ISO's form of "continuous improvement" is not on the same scale or as consistent a theme as SEI and Malcolm Baldrige.

# ■ 12.10 ISO 9001, 4.10 INSPECTION AND TESTING

## 12.10.1 ISO 9001, Inspection and Testing; MB-Associated Statements

The Malcolm Baldrige 2.1 Management of Information and Data general requirement for "selecting and managing information and data used for planning, management, and evaluation of overall performance by the company" has a strong correlation to this ISO requirement.

Malcolm Baldrige's 5.1 Design and Introduction of Products and Services item 5.1.b has a strong correlation to ISO's Inspection and Testing requirement. Like other Malcolm Baldrige items, it addresses the ISO requirement at a much higher level and is far less specific than ISO.

Malcolm Baldrige 5.2 Process Management: Product and Service Production and Delivery, with its requirement for "maintaining process performance by use of the measurement plan and measurements and/or observations," has a strong correlation to ISO.

Malcolm Baldrige 5.4 Management of Supplier Performance, with its requirement for "assuring that materials, components, and services furnished by other businesses meet the company's performance requirements," has a strong correlation to ISO.

### 12.10.2  ISO 9001, Inspection and Testing; SEI-Associated Statements

SEI has a strong correlation to ISO's Inspection and Testing requirement. ISO's General requirement has a strong correlation with two SEI key process areas—Software Product Engineering (PE) and Peer Reviews (PR). ISO's Receiving Inspection and Testing requirement has a strong correlation with key practice SM.AC.12 in the Software Subcontract Management (SM) key process area. ISO's In-Process Inspection and Testing and Final Inspection and Testing requirements are strongly correlated with two key process areas—Software Product Engineering (PE) and Peer Reviews (PR). ISO's Inspection and Test Records requirement has strong correlation with key practices PE.AC.9 and PR.AC.3 in the Software Product Engineering (PE) and Peer Reviews (PR) key process areas.

## ◼ 12.11  ISO 9001, 4.11 CONTROL OF INSPECTION, MEASURING, AND TEST EQUIPMENT

### 12.11.1  ISO 9001, Control of Inspection, Measuring, and Test Equipment; MB-Associated Statements

Malcolm Baldrige 5.2 Process Management: Product and Service Production and Delivery, with its requirement for "maintaining process performance by use of the measurement plan and measurements and/or observations," has a strong correlation to ISO.

### 12.11.2  ISO 9001, Control of Inspection, Measuring, and Test Equipment; SEI-Associated Statements

There are no associated elements in SEI.

# ■ 12.12  ISO 9001, 4.12 INSPECTION AND TEST STATUS

## 12.12.1  ISO 9001, Inspection and Test Status; MB-Associated Statements

Malcolm Baldrige 5.2 Process Management: Product and Service Production and Delivery, with its requirement for "maintaining process performance by use of the measurement plan and measurements and/or observations," has a strong correlation to ISO.

## 12.12.2  ISO 9001, Inspection and Test Status; SEI-Associated Statements

SEI's Software Configuration Management (CM) key process area has a strong correlation to ISO's Inspection and Test Status requirement. Software Configuration Management (CM) is intended to allow identification of the software work products throughout the entire process, as well as "systematically controlling changes to the configuration, and maintaining the integrity and traceability of the configuration throughout the software life cycle."

# ■ 12.13  ISO 9001, 4.13 CONTROL OF NONCONFORMING PRODUCT

## 12.13.1  ISO 9001, Control of Nonconforming Product; MB-Associated Statements

Malcolm Baldrige 5.2 Process Management: Product and Service Production and Delivery, with its requirement for describing "the key processes and their principal requirements," has some correlation to ISO. This Malcolm Baldrige item is focused on the maintenance of process performance as well as the on-going evaluation and improvement of processes.

Malcolm Baldrige 5.4 Management of Supplier Performance, with its requirement for "assuring that materials, components, and services furnished by other businesses meet the company's performance requirements," has some correlation to ISO.

## 12.13.2  ISO 9001, Control of Nonconforming Product; SEI-Associated Statements

SEI's Software Configuration Management (CM) and Software Product Engineering (PE) key process areas have a strong correlation to ISO's Control of Nonconforming Product requirement. Software Configuration Management (CM) is intended to identify and control software work products throughout the entire process by "systematically controlling changes to the configuration, and maintaining the integrity and traceability of the configuration throughout the software life cycle." Software Product Engineering (PE)'s PE.AC.9 key practice addresses the ISO requirement for Review and Disposition of Nonconforming Product.

# ■ 12.14 ISO 9001, 4.14 CORRECTIVE AND PREVENTIVE ACTION

### 12.14.1 ISO 9001, Corrective and Preventative Action; MB-Associated Statements

Malcolm Baldrige has a strong correlation to ISO's Corrective and Preventative Action requirement. ISO's General requirement has no direct correlation to Malcolm Baldrige. ISO's Corrective Action requirement has a strong correlation with Malcolm Baldrige requirements in 7.2 Customer Relationship Management, 7.2.b and 7.2.c. These requirements address interaction with the customer. ISO's Preventative Action requirement has a strong correlation with Malcolm Baldrige requirements in 2.3 Analysis and Use of Company-Level Data; 5.1 Design and Introduction of Products and Services; 5.2 Process Management: Product and Service Production and Delivery; 5.3 Process Management: Support Services; 5.4 Management of Supplier Performance; and 7.2 Customer Relationship Management. The following are the specific Malcolm Baldrige areas to address:

- ❖ 2.3.b,
- ❖ 5.1.c,
- ❖ 5.2.b,
- ❖ 5.3.c,
- ❖ 5.4.b, and
- ❖ 7.2.d.

Malcolm Baldrige 7.2 Customer Relationship Management can be considered proactive in its approach. ISO's Corrective Action and Preventative Action can generally be regarded as reactive to a problem, in that no preventative action is taken until a problem is discovered. As identified in ISO, preventative action is a natural extension to corrective action and very important to operational quality issues. Malcolm Baldrige, however, identifies another level of corrective and preventive action that takes a proactive approach, in that it makes the process an anticipative one. This approach also includes a much broader business view, as opposed to a strictly operational quality view.

### 12.14.2 ISO 9001, Corrective and Preventative Action; SEI-Associated Statements

SEI's Software Project Tracking and Oversight (PT) and Defect Prevention (DP) key process areas have a strong correlation to ISO's Corrective and Preventative Action requirement. ISO's General and Corrective Action requirements are addressed by SEI's Software Project Tracking and Oversight (PT) key practices. ISO's Preventative Action requirement is addressed by SEI's Defect Prevention (DP) key process area. Defect Prevention (DP) provides practices that institutionalize preventative action.

## ■ 12.15  ISO 9001, 4.15 HANDLING, STORAGE, PACKAGING, PRESERVATION, AND DELIVERY

### 12.15.1 ISO 9001, Handling, Storage, Packaging, Preservation, and Delivery; MB-Associated Statements

Malcolm Baldrige 5.1 Design and Introduction of Products and Services, with its requirement for "translating customer requirements into efficient and effective production/delivery..." processes, has a strong correlation to ISO. Malcolm Baldrige is at higher level and is less specific than ISO.

Malcolm Baldrige 5.2 Process Management: Product and Service Production and Delivery, with its requirement for describing "the key processes and their principal requirements," has some correlation to ISO. This Malcolm Baldrige item is focused on the maintenance of process performance as well as the on-going evaluation and improvement of processes.

### 12.15.2 ISO 9001, Handling, Storage, Packaging, Preservation, and Delivery; SEI-Associated Statements

There are no associated elements in SEI.

## ■ 12.16  ISO 9001, 4.16 CONTROL OF QUALITY RECORDS

### 12.16.1 ISO 9001, Control of Quality Records; MB-Associated Statements

The Malcolm Baldrige 2.1 Management of Information and Data general requirement for "selecting and managing information and data used for planning, management, and evaluation of overall performance by the company" has a strong correlation to this ISO requirement. ISO covers very specific ways that documents, data, and records must be controlled and managed. This includes the requirement for documented procedures.

Malcolm Baldrige 5.2 Process Management: Product and Service Production and Delivery, with its requirement for describing "the key processes and their principal requirements," has some correlation to ISO. This Malcolm Baldrige item is focused on the maintenance of process performance as well as the on-going evaluation and improvement of processes.

## 12.16.2 ISO 9001, Control of Quality Records; SEI-Associated Statements

SEI's Software Configuration Management (CM) key process area has a strong correlation to ISO's Control of Quality Records requirement. Software Configuration Management (CM) is intended to identify and control software work products throughout the entire process by "systematically controlling changes to the configuration, and maintaining the integrity and traceability of the configuration throughout the software life cycle." SEI has no specific procedures identified for control of quality records in general. Many practices require the recording of data [refer to Software Project Tracking and Oversight (PT)]. Software Configuration Management (CM) is scoped to

1. externally deliverable software products,
2. designated internal software work products,
3. designated support tools used inside a project (e.g., compilers).

Item #2 specifically addresses the ISO requirement. Control of specific documents is identified throughout the key practices. SEI requires documented procedures, which in turn identify the need for documenting specific items, which can be considered quality records. Many of these items are identified as part of the subpractices (refer to Software Engineering Institute, *CMU/SEI-93-TR-25*, *Key Practices of the Capability Maturity Model, Version 1.1* [Carnegie Mellon University, 1993] for detailed information on the CMM subpractices) within the Activities Performed (AC) common feature and have a strong correlation to ISO. These subpractices often require these items be "managed and controlled." Some examples of these items include

- ✧ allocated requirements,
- ✧ software development plan,
- ✧ software replanning data,
- ✧ subcontract statement of work,
- ✧ software quality assurance plan, and
- ✧ organization's training plan

# ■ 12.17 ISO 9001, 4.17 INTERNAL QUALITY AUDITS

### 12.17.1 ISO 9001, Internal Quality Audits; MB-Associated Statements

Malcolm Baldrige 5.2 Process Management: Product and Service Production and Delivery, with its requirement for "maintaining process performance by use of the measurement plan and measurements and/or observations," has a strong correlation to ISO.

### 12.17.2 ISO 9001, Internal Quality Audits; SEI-Associated Statements

SEI's Software Quality Assurance (QA) key process area has a strong correlation to ISO's Internal Quality Audits requirement. Software Quality Assurance (QA) directly addresses the ISO requirement for internal quality audits. Software Quality Assurance (QA) goes beyond the requirements of ISO and provides for a software quality assurance group that is involved early in the product cycle with the various product groups. This role is one of assisting in the establishment of plans, standards, and procedures, ensuring that they are sufficient. Software Quality Assurance (QA) also addresses, in a subpractice, the ISO requirement for auditing to be done by "personnel independent of those having direct responsibility for the activity being audited." SEI is more specific in that it requires that the Software Quality Assurance (QA) group "has a reporting channel to senior management that is independent" of product management.

# ■ 12.18 ISO 9001, 4.18 TRAINING

### 12.18.1 ISO 9001, Training; MB-Associated Statements

Malcolm Baldrige's 4.3 Employee Education, Training, and Development has a strong correlation to ISO's Training requirement. Malcolm Baldrige goes beyond the requirements of ISO by addressing items such as "employee motivation, progression, and development."

### 12.18.2 ISO 9001, Training; SEI-Associated Statements

SEI has a strong correlation to ISO's Training requirement. SEI addresses this requirement through the Training Program (TP) key process area, and as an Ability to Perform (AB) common feature across all 18 key process areas. The Training Program (TP) identifies the practices for the group that provides the training function. Specific training requirements are identified within the individual key process areas.

# ■ 12.19  ISO 9001, 4.19 SERVICING

### 12.19.1  ISO 9001, Servicing; MB-Associated Statements

Malcolm Baldrige has a strong correlation to ISO's Servicing requirement. Malcolm Baldrige addresses this requirement in its 5.1 Design and Introduction of Products and Services; 5.2 Process Management: Product and Service Production and Delivery; 7.3 Customer Satisfaction Determination; and 7.4 Customer Satisfaction Results examination items. Malcolm Baldrige 7.3 Customer Satisfaction Determination and 7.4 Customer Satisfaction Results have some correlation to ISO's Servicing requirement. Baldrige is very focused on customer satisfaction in its clauses. ISO requires "meeting requirements," which doesn't necessarily mean that the customer will be satisfied.

Malcolm Baldrige 5.2 Process Management: Product and Service Production and Delivery, with its requirement for describing "the key processes and their principal requirements," has a strong correlation to ISO. This Malcolm Baldrige item is focused on the maintenance of process performance as well as the on-going evaluation and improvement of processes.

### 12.19.2  ISO 9001, Servicing; SEI-Associated Statements

There are no associated elements in SEI.

# ■ 12.20  ISO 9001, 4.20 STATISTICAL TECHNIQUES

### 12.20.1  ISO 9001, Statistical Techniques; MB-Associated Statements

Malcolm Baldrige 2.1 Management of Information and Data, 2.3 Analysis and Use of Company-Level Data, and 5.2 Process Management: Product and Service Production and Delivery have a strong correlation to ISO's Statistical Techniques requirement. ISO's Identification of Need requirement is addressed by Malcolm Baldrige 2.1 Management of Information and Data, which identifies "selecting and managing information and data." ISO's Procedures requirement is addressed by Malcolm Baldrige 2.3 Analysis and Use of Company-Level Data in the requirement for "analyzing data related to quality, customers, and operational performance...to support company-level review, action, and planning." Malcolm Baldrige 5.2 Process Management: Product and Service Production and Delivery, with its requirement for describing "the key processes and their principal requirements," has a strong correlation to ISO. This Malcolm Baldrige item is focused on the maintenance of process performance as well as the on-going evaluation and improvement of processes.

## 12.20.2 ISO 9001, Statistical Techniques; SEI-Associated Statements

SEI has a strong correlation to ISO's Statistical Techniques requirement. SEI addresses these requirements through its Quantitative Process Management (QP) and Software Quality Management (QM) key process areas. Quantitative Process Management (QP) is focused on processes and Software Quality Management (QM) is focused on products. SEI also addresses these requirements through its Measurement and Analysis (ME) common feature across all 18 key process areas. Quantitative Process Management (QP) defines *quantitative control* as "any quantitative or statistically based technique appropriate to analyze a software process, identify special causes of variations in the performance of the software process, and bring the performance of the software process within well-defined limits." Software Quality Management (QM) is also looking to "develop a quantitative understanding of the quality of the project's software products."

# 13

# Comparison from an SEI CMM Perspective

This chapter covers the goals, 5 common features, and the 18 key process areas of the Software Engineering Institute's Capability Maturity Model. Each of these SEI CMM components is addressed in two subsections—MB-associated statements and ISO-associated statements. Each subsection discusses the other methodology's associated statements and why they are associated. In discussing the association between statements, the terms "some correlation" and "strong correlation" are used. These terms are intended to give you a feel for the association and its significance. A summary of the correlations is provided in Figures 13.1 and 13.2. A detailed mapping of the correlations is provided in Appendix H and Appendix I.

## ■ 13.1 SEI CMM, GOALS

"Summarizes the key practices of a key process area and can be used to determine whether an organization or project has effectively implemented the key process area. The Goals signify the scope, boundaries, and intent of each key process area."[1]

---

1. Software Engineering Institute, CMU/SEI-93-TR-25, *Key Practices of the Capability Maturity Model, Version 1.1* (Carnegie Mellon University, 1993), p. O-11.

**Figure 13.1** SEI CMM mapping to Malcolm Baldrige.

| SEI CMM | Malcolm Baldrige | | | | | | | | | | | | | | | | | | | | | | | |
|---|---|---|---|---|---|---|---|---|---|---|---|---|---|---|---|---|---|---|---|---|---|---|---|---|
| | A | B | C | D | E | F | G | H | I | J | K | L | M | N | O | P | Q | R | S | T | U | V | W | X |
| Goals (GO) | ○ | | | ○ | | | | | | | | | | ● | | | | | | | | | | |
| Commitment to Perform (CO) | ● | | | | | | | | | | | | | | | | | | | | | | | |
| Ability to Perform (AB) | ● | | | ○ | | | | | | | ● | | | | | | | | | | | | | |
| Activities Performed (AC) | | | | ○ | | | | | | | | | | | | | | | | | | | | |
| Measurement and Analysis (ME) | | | | ○ | | ● | | | | | | | | ● | | | | | | | | | | |
| Verifying Implementation (VE) | ● | ● | | | | | | | | | | | | ● | | | | | | | | | | |
| Requirements Management (RM) | | | | | | ○ | | | | | | | ● | | | | | | | ○ | | | | |
| Software Project Planning (PP) | | | | | | | | | | | | | | | | | | | | | | | | |
| Software Project Tracking and Oversight (PT) | | | | | | | | | | | | | | | | | | | | | | | | |
| Software Subcontract Management (SM) | | | | | | | | | | | | | | | | ● | | | | | | | | |
| Software Quality Assurance (QA) | | | | | | | | | | | | | | | | | | | | | ○ | | | |
| Software Configuration Management (CM) | | | | | | | | | | | | | | | | | | | | | | | | |
| Organization Process Focus (PF) | | | | ○ | | | | | | | | | | ● | | | | | | | | | | |
| Organization Process Definition (PD) | | | | ○ | | | | | | | | | | ● | | | | | | | | | | |
| Training Program (TP) | | | | | | | | | | | ● | | | | | | | | | | | | | |
| Integrated Software Management (IM) | | | | | | | | | | | | | | | | | | | | | ○ | | | |
| Software Product Engineering (PE) | | | | | | ○ | | | | | | | ● | | | | | | | | | | | |
| Intergroup Coordination (IC) | | | | | | | | | | ● | | | ● | | | | | | | | ○ | | | |
| Peer Reviews (PR) | | | | | | | | | | | | | ● | | | | | | | | | | | |
| Quantitative Process Management (QP) | | | | | | ● | | | | | | | | | | | | | | | | | | |
| Software Quality Management (QM) | | | | | | ● | | | | | | | ● | | | | | | | | | | | |
| Defect Prevention (DP) | | | | | | ○ | | | | | | | | | | | | | | | | | | |
| Technology Change Management (TM) | | | | ○ | | | | | | | | | | ● | | | | | | | | | | |
| Process Change Management (PC) | | | | ○ | | | | | | | | | | ● | | | | | | | | | | |

SEI CMM mapping to Malcolm Baldrige key.[a]

---

**Note:**

○ = Some correlation

● = Strong correlation

A = 1.1 Senior Executive Leadership

B = 1.2 Leadership System and Organization

C = 1.3 Public Responsibility and Corporate Citizenship

D = 2.1 Management of Information and Data

E = 2.2 Competitive Comparisons and Benchmarking

F = 2.3 Analysis and Use of Company-Level Data

G = 3.1 Strategy Development

H = 3.2 Strategy Deployment

I = 4.1 Human Resource Planning and Evaluation

J = 4.2 High Performance Work Systems

K = 4.3 Employee Education, Training, and Development

L = 4.4 Employee Well-Being and Satisfaction

M = 5.1 Design and Introduction of Products and Services

N = 5.2 Process Management: Product and Service Production and Delivery

O = 5.3 Process Management: Support Services

P = 5.4 Management of Supplier Performance

Q = 6.1 Product and Service Quality Results

R = 6.2 Company Operational and Financial Results

S = 6.3 Supplier Performance Results

T = 7.1 Customer and Market Knowledge

U = 7.2 Customer Relationship Management

V = 7.3 Customer Satisfaction Determination

W = 7.4 Customer Satisfaction Results

X = 7.5 Customer Satisfaction Comparison

---

[a]**Note:** In comparisons with the SEI CMM, note that the SEI CMM common features are requirement themes that cut across the SEI CMM key process areas. A particular key process area may not show any direct requirement relationships, but may have correlations through the common feature themes. Refer to Chapter 7, "1993 SEI CMM for Software" for a more detailed discussion of SEI's common features and key process areas. Details on key process area requirements included under the common feature themes are provided in Appendix C.

## 13.1.1  SEI CMM, Goals; MB-Associated Statements

Malcolm Baldrige 1.1 Senior Executive Leadership has some correlation to one key practice, QA.GO.4, which falls under the Goals and Software Quality Assurance key process area. Malcolm Baldrige has a requirement for "setting directions through leadership and personal involvement." QA.GO.4 requires senior management to act as an escalation point for unresolvable issues.

**Figure 13.2** SEI CMM mapping to ISO 9001.

| SEI CMM | ISO 9001 | | | | | | | | | | | | | | | | | | | |
|---|---|---|---|---|---|---|---|---|---|---|---|---|---|---|---|---|---|---|---|---|
| | A | B | C | D | E | F | G | H | I | J | K | L | M | N | O | P | Q | R | S | T |
| Goals (GO) | ● | | | | | | | | | | | | | | | | | | | |
| Commitment to Perform (CO) | ● | | | | | | | | | | | | | | | | | | | |
| Ability to Perform (AB) | ● | | | | | | | | | | | | | | | | | ● | | |
| Activities Performed (AC) | ○ | ● | | | | | | | ● | | | | | | ● | | | | | |
| Measurement and Analysis (ME) | | | | | | | | | | | | | | | | | | | | ● |
| Verifying Implementation (VE) | ○ | ○ | | | | | | | | | | | | | | | | | | |
| Requirements Management (RM) | ● | | ○ | ○ | | | | | | | | | | | | | | | | |
| Software Project Planning (PP) | ● | ● | ○ | ● | | | | | ● | | | | | | | | | | | |
| Software Project Tracking and Oversight (PT) | ● | | ○ | ● | | | | | | | | | | ● | | | | | | |
| Software Subcontract Management (SM) | ● | | | | | ● | | | | ● | | | | | | | | | | |
| Software Quality Assurance (QA) | ● | | | | | | | | | | | | | | | | ● | | | |
| Software Configuration Management (CM) | ● | | | ● | ● | | | ● | | | | ● | ● | | | ● | | | | |
| Organization Process Focus (PF) | ● | | | | | | | | | | | | | | | | | | | |
| Organization Process Definition (PD) | | | | | | | | | | | | | | | | | | | | |
| Training Program (TP) | ● | | | | | | | | | | | | | | | | | ● | | |
| Integrated Software Management (IM) | | | | | | | | | | | | | | | | | | | | |
| Software Product Engineering (PE) | | | | ● | | | | | | ● | | | ● | | | | | | | |
| Intergroup Coordination (IC) | ● | | | ● | | | | | | | | | | | | | | | | |
| Peer Reviews (PR) | | | | ● | | | | | | ● | | | | | | | | | | |
| Quantitative Process Management (QP) | ● | | | | | | | | | | | | | | | | | | | ● |
| Software Quality Management (QM) | | | | | | ● | | | | | | | | | | | | | | ● |
| Defect Prevention (DP) | ● | | | | | | | | | | | | ● | | | | | | | |
| Technology Change Management (TM) | ● | | | | | | | | | | | | | | | | | | | |
| Process Change Management (PC) | | | | | | | | | | | | | | | | | | | | |

Malcolm Baldrige 2.1 Management of Information and Data has some correlation to one key practice, PD.GO.2, which falls under the Goals and Organization Process Definition key process area. Malcolm Baldrige has a requirement for "selecting and managing information and data used for planning, management, and evaluation...." PD.GO.2 requires "collecting, reviewing, and making available information."

Malcolm Baldrige 5.2 Process Management: Product and Service Production and Delivery has a strong correlation to the Goals requirements within the process areas of

SEI CMM mapping to ISO 9001 key.[a]

**Note:**

○ = Some correlation

● = Strong correlation

A  = 4.1 Management Responsibility

B  = 4.2 Quality System

C  = 4.3 Contract Review

D  = 4.4 Design Control

E  = 4.5 Document and Data Control

F  = 4.6 Purchasing

G  = 4.7 Control of Customer-Supplied Product

H  = 4.8 Product Identification and Traceability

I  = 4.9 Process Control

J  = 4.10 Inspection and Testing

K  = 4.11 Control of Inspection, Measuring, and Test Equipment

L  = 4.12 Inspection and Test Status

M = 4.13 Control of Nonconforming Product

N  = 4.14 Corrective and Preventative Action

O  = 4.15 Handling, Storage, Packaging, Preservation, and Delivery

P  = 4.16 Control of Quality Records

Q  = 4.17 Internal Quality Audits

R  = 4.18 Training

S  = 4.19 Servicing

T  = 4.20 Statistical Techniques

[a]**Note:** In comparisons with the SEI CMM, note that the SEI CMM common features are requirement themes that cut across the SEI CMM key process areas. A particular key process area may not show any direct requirement relationships, but may have correlations through the common feature themes. Refer to Chapter 7, "1993 SEI CMM for Software" for a more detailed discussion of SEI's common features and key process areas. Details on key process area requirements included under the common feature themes are provided in Appendix C.

Software Project Tracking and Oversight (PT), Software Quality Assurance (QA), Software Configuration Management (CM), and Integrated Software Management (IM). Malcolm Baldrige, with its requirement for "maintaining process performance by the use of the measurement plan and measurements and/or observations," addresses the SEI CMM requirements for "managing."

## 13.1.2  SEI CMM, Goals; ISO-Associated Statements

ISO 9001 4.1.1 Quality Policy has a strong correlation to SEI's Goals. ISO is looking for management to define quality objectives. SEI does not specifically address "quality" objectives; however, SEI's Goals, which summarize the key practices for each key process area, can be thought of as quality objectives. The Goals "can be used to determine whether an organization or project has effectively implemented the Key Process Area." Many of SEI's Goals go beyond the requirements of ISO 9001. It is important to note, however, that ISO, being a tell-me-then-show-me type of quality management system assessment, will not only check that you are adhering to the requirements of the standard but also that you are adhering to any additional requirements that your QMS requires. If your QMS goes beyond the requirements of ISO, you can be audited to those requirements as well, unless they are defined as outside the scope of the audit and do not directly affect the product quality.

## ■ 13.2  SEI CMM, COMMON FEATURES

"The key practices in each key process area are organized by a set of common features. The common features are attributes that indicate whether the implementation and institutionalization of a key process area is effective, repeatable, and lasting."[2]

## ■ 13.3  SEI CMM, COMMITMENT TO PERFORM

"Describes the actions the organization must take to ensure that the process is established and will endure. Commitment to Perform typically involves establishing organizational policies and senior management sponsorship."[3]

### 13.3.1  SEI CMM, Commitment to Perform; MB-Associated Statements

Malcolm Baldrige 1.1 Senior Executive Leadership has a strong correlation to key practices that fall under the Commitment to Perform common feature. The Malcolm Baldrige requirement for "providing effective leadership and direction in building and improving company competitiveness, performance, and capabilities" and "creating and reinforcing values and expectations throughout the company's leadership system" addresses the SEI key practices, which are looking for senior management to "sponsor" and "oversee."

---

2. Software Engineering Institute, *CMU/SEI-93-TR-24, Capability Maturity Model for Software, Version 1.1* (Carnegie Mellon University, 1993), p. 37.

3. Software Engineering Institute, *CMU/SEI-93-TR-25, Key Practices of the Capability Maturity Model, Version 1.1* (Carnegie Mellon University, 1993), pp. O-27–O-28.

### 13.3.2  SEI CMM, Commitment to Perform; ISO-Associated Statements

ISO 9001 4.1.1 Quality Policy has a strong correlation to the Commitment to Perform common feature. Commitment to Perform is intended to "ensure that the process is established and will endure" and "typically involves establishing organizational policies and senior management sponsorship." ISO is looking to ensure that the 4.1.1 Quality Policy is "understood, implemented, and maintained."

# ■ 13.4  SEI CMM, ABILITY TO PERFORM

"Describes the preconditions that must exist in the project or organization to implement the software process competently. Ability to Perform typically involves resources, organizational structures, and training."[4]

### 13.4.1  SEI CMM, Ability to Perform; MB-Associated Statements

Malcolm Baldrige 1.1 Senior Executive Leadership has a strong correlation to Process Change Management key practice PC.AB.4, which falls under the Ability to Perform common feature. The Malcolm Baldrige requirement for "developing and maintaining a leadership system for performance excellence" addresses this key practice, which looks for senior management to receive training in software process improvement.

Malcolm Baldrige 2.1 Management of Information and Data has some correlation to one key practice, QP.AB.2, which falls under the Ability to Perform common feature and Quantitative Process Management key process area. Malcolm Baldrige has a requirement for "selecting and managing information and data used for planning, management, and evaluation...." QP.AB.2 requires "establishing support for collecting, recording, and analyzing data for selected process and product measures."

Malcolm Baldrige 4.3 Employee Education, Training, and Development has a strong correlation to the Ability to Perform "training" thread found throughout most of the SEI CMM's 18 key process areas. SEI CMM also devotes the entire Training Program key process area to this area as well. The practices under Ability to Perform are specific to the process area and identify the particular needs of that key process area.

---

4. Ibid.

### 13.4.2 SEI CMM, Ability to Perform; ISO-Associated Statements

ISO's 4.1.2.2 Resources requirement has a strong correlation to SEI's Ability to Perform, which "typically involves resources, organizational structures, and training." ISO requires "identifying resource requirements" and "providing adequate resources."

ISO 9001 4.18 Training has a strong correlation to the Ability to Perform common feature. Ability to Perform has a thread of "training" and "orienting" key practices. Specific training requirements are identified within the individual key process areas. ISO requires "procedures for identifying training needs" and for providing "for the training of all personnel performing activities affecting quality."

## ■ 13.5  SEI CMM, ACTIVITIES PERFORMED

"Describes the roles and procedures necessary to implement a key process area. Activities Performed typically involve establishing plans and procedures, performing the work, tracking it, and taking corrective actions as necessary."[5]

### 13.5.1 SEI CMM, Activities Performed; MB-Associated Statements

Malcolm Baldrige 2.1 Management of Information and Data has some correlation with SEI elements in most of the 18 key process areas. Malcolm Baldrige is not specific about what information and data should be "selected and managed." Baldrige instead leaves it up to the applicant to decide what information and data are needed for "planning, management, and evaluation" and "to drive improvement" in overall company performance.

### 13.5.2 SEI CMM, Activities Performed; ISO-Associated Statements

ISO's 4.1.3 Management Review requirement has some correlation to SEI Activities Performed. Activities Performed has a "thread" or "theme" that involves key practices for reviews. These practices identify management reviews and reviews by groups such as the software quality assurance group. ISO requires reviews of the "quality system at defined intervals sufficient to ensure its continuing suitability and effectiveness."

ISO 4.2.2 Quality-System Procedures *a* requirement for "preparing documented procedures" has a strong correlation with SEI in 15 of its 18 key process areas. These key process areas are

---

5. Ibid.

- ✧  Software Project Planning (PP)
- ✧  Software Project Tracking and Oversight (PT)
- ✧  Software Subcontract Management (SM)
- ✧  Software Quality Assurance (QA)
- ✧  Software Configuration Management (CM)
- ✧  Organization Process Definition (PD)
- ✧  Training Program (TP)
- ✧  Integrated Software Management (IM)
- ✧  Intergroup Coordination (IC)
- ✧  Peer Reviews (PR)
- ✧  Quantitative Process Management (QP)
- ✧  Software Quality Management (QM)
- ✧  Defect Prevention (DP)
- ✧  Technology Change Management (TM)
- ✧  Process Change Management (PC)

SEI identifies key practices that require the use of documented procedures.

Activities Performed has another theme that involves key practices for following documented procedures to accomplish a task. ISO has a strong correlation with this theme through its 4.2.2 Quality-System Procedures requirement. ISO requires "preparing documented procedures" and "implementing...documented procedures effectively."

ISO's 4.9 Process Control has an overall strong correlation to the SEI Activities Performed theme of requiring that certain tasks or activities be executed "according to a documented procedure." Under 4.9 Process Control, ISO identifies the requirement for "ensuring that these processes are carried out under controlled conditions." ISO also identifies specific items that are considered part of "controlled conditions," such as "documented procedures defining the manner of production, installation, and servicing, where the absence of such procedures would adversely affect quality." Refer to the section entitled "ISO 9001, Process Control; SEI-Associated Statements" in Chapter 12 for additional discussion.

ISO 9001 4.16 Control of Quality Records has a strong correlation to Activities Performed. ISO has a strong correlation with the Activities Performed theme of "placed under configuration management versus managed and controlled." ISO requires "documented procedures for identification, collection, indexing, access, filing, storage, maintenance, and disposition of quality records." Refer to the section entitled "ISO 9001, Control of Quality Records; SEI-Associated Statements" in Chapter 12 for additional discussion.

# ■ 13.6 SEI CMM, MEASUREMENT AND ANALYSIS

"Describes the need to measure the process and analyze the measurement. Measurement and Analysis typically includes examples of the measurements that could be taken to determine the status and effectiveness of the Activities Performed."[6]

## 13.6.1 SEI CMM, Measurement and Analysis; MB-Associated Statements

Malcolm Baldrige 2.1 Management of Information and Data has some correlation with SEI elements in most of the 18 key process areas. Malcolm Baldrige is not specific about what information and data should be "selected and managed." Baldrige instead leaves it up to the applicant to decide what information and data are needed for "planning, management, and evaluation" and "to drive improvement" in overall company performance. The key practices that follow this thread are specific to the process area they address and involve the recording of data and the measurement of activities.

Malcolm Baldrige 2.3 Analysis and Use of Company-Level Data has a strong correlation with SEI elements in most of the 18 key process areas. Malcolm Baldrige requires "using analysis to gain an understanding of operational performance and company capabilities."

Malcolm Baldrige 5.2 Process Management: Product and Service Production and Delivery has a strong correlation with this SEI common feature. Malcolm Baldrige is looking for "maintaining process performance by use of the measurement plan and measurements and/or observations." Malcolm Baldrige requires that the measurement plan identify "what is to be measured, how and when measurements are to be made, and performance levels or standards to ensure that the results of measurements provide information to guide, monitor, control, or improve the process."

## 13.6.2 SEI CMM, Measurement and Analysis; ISO-Associated Statements

ISO 9001 4.20 Statistical Techniques has a strong correlation to the Measurement and Analysis common feature. Measurement and Analysis describes "basic measurement practices that are necessary to determine status related to the Activities Performed Common Feature of Key Practices." ISO 4.20.2 Procedures addresses this feature by requiring "documented procedures to implement and control the application of statistical techniques."

---

6. Ibid.

# ■ 13.7 SEI CMM, VERIFYING IMPLEMENTATION

"Describes the steps to ensure that the activities are performed in compliance with the process that has been established. Verification typically encompasses reviews and audits by management and software quality assurance."[7]

## 13.7.1 SEI CMM, Verifying Implementation; MB-Associated Statements

Malcolm Baldrige 1.1 Senior Executive Leadership has a strong correlation with this SEI common feature. Malcolm Baldrige follows the SEI thread of senior management oversight. Malcolm Baldrige defines *senior executives* as "the applicant's highest official and those reporting directly to that official." SEI defines *senior manager* as "a management role at a high enough level in an organization that the primary focus is the long-term vitality of the organization, rather than short-term project and contractual concerns and pressures. In general, a senior manager for engineering would have responsibility for multiple projects." Many of SEI's key practices require reviews "with senior management."

Malcolm Baldrige 1.2 Leadership System and Organization has a strong correlation with this SEI common feature. Malcolm Baldrige addresses the SEI thread of senior management oversight through its requirement for "focusing the company's leadership system, management, and organization on customers and high performance objectives."

Malcolm Baldrige 5.2 Process Management: Product and Service Production and Delivery has a strong correlation with this SEI common feature. Malcolm Baldrige addresses the SEI thread of management reviews through its requirement for "managing the company's key product and service production/delivery processes...." Malcolm Baldrige also addresses the SEI thread of software quality assurance activities through its requirement for "maintaining process performance by...measurements and/or observations."

## 13.7.2 SEI CMM, Verifying Implementation; ISO-Associated Statements

ISO's 4.1.3 Management Review requirement has some correlation to SEI Verifying Implementation. Verifying Implementation has a thread or theme that involves key practices for reviews. These practices identify management reviews and reviews by groups such as the software quality assurance group. ISO requires reviews of the "quality system at defined intervals sufficient to ensure its continuing suitability and effectiveness."

---

7. Ibid.

ISO 4.2.2 Quality-System Procedures has some correlation with the requirements of Verifying Implementation with its *b* requirement for "implementing the quality system and its documented procedures effectively." Verifying Implementation practices mostly involve reviews of the activities within the specific key process areas.

# ■ 13.8  SEI CMM, KEY PROCESS AREAS

"Each key process area identifies a cluster of related activities that, when performed collectively, achieve a set of goals considered important for enhancing process capability. The key process areas have been defined to reside at a single maturity level. The key process areas are building blocks that indicate the areas an organization should focus on to improve its software process. Key process areas identify the issues that must be addressed to achieve a maturity level."[8]

# ■ 13.9  SEI CMM, LEVEL 1—INITIAL

"The software process is characterized as ad hoc, and occasionally even chaotic. Few processes are defined, and success depends on individual effort."[9]

# ■ 13.10  SEI CMM, LEVEL 2—REPEATABLE

"Basic project management processes are established to track cost, schedule, and functionality. The necessary process discipline is in place to repeat earlier successes on projects with similar applications."[10]

# ■ 13.11  SEI CMM, LEVEL 2 REQUIREMENTS MANAGEMENT

## 13.11.1  SEI CMM, Requirements Management; MB-Associated Statements

Malcolm Baldrige's 2.3 Analysis and Use of Company-Level Data requirement for "using analysis to gain an understanding of customers..." has some correlation with the Require-

---

8. Ibid, p. O-18.

9. Software Engineering Institute, CMU/SEI-93-TR-24, *Capability Maturity Model for Software, Version 1.1* (Carnegie Mellon University, 1993), p. xi.

10. Ibid,

ments Management practice (RM.AB.1) for establishing "responsibility for analyzing system requirements and allocating them to hardware, software, and other system components."

Malcolm Baldrige 5.1 Design and Introduction of Products and Services has a strong correlation to SEI through the common features of Measurement and Analysis and Verifying Implementation. The Measurement and Analysis common feature practices are used to determine the status of specific activities. The Verifying Implementation common feature practices identify management reviews. In addition, Verifying Implementation practices also identify audit practices, which are conducted by an independent group (e.g., the software quality assurance group). Malcolm Baldrige addresses these practices through its requirement for "maintaining process performance by use of the measurement plan and measurements and/or observations." Malcolm Baldrige requires that the measurement plan identify "what is to be measured, how and when measurements are to be made, and performance levels or standards to ensure that the results of measurements provide information to guide, monitor, control, or improve the process."

Like ISO, SEI is focused on a single contract situation and having a specific contract or agreement in place. Malcolm Baldrige 7.1 Customer and Market Knowledge has some correlation to this requirement. Malcolm Baldrige can apply to specific contractual situations but, more generally, is aimed at the situation where a product is being created for a market. In creating products for a market there is a different set of issues and problems than those encountered in a specific contract situation. These problems are related to understanding the markets that the products are intended for and providing a product for a potentially wide range of customer wants and needs.

## 13.11.2  SEI CMM, Requirements Management; ISO-Associated Statements

ISO 4.1.2.1 Responsibility and Authority has a strong correlation to the SEI practice(s) for assigning responsibility. ISO requires defining and documenting the "responsibility, authority, and the interrelation of personnel." SEI requires establishing "responsibility for analyzing the system requirements and allocating them...."

ISO 9001 4.3 Contract Review has some correlation with SEI in its 4.3.1 General requirement for "establishing and maintaining documented procedures for contract review and for the coordination of these activities." SEI is a software perspective in the context of a larger system development. SEI in general is limited in its scope to software requirements and does not address requirements and the customer in the larger context of purchasing the final delivered product. However, SEI does have some correlation to the requirements of ISO 4.3 Contract Review in the context of the software development portion of a system development.

ISO 9001 4.4 Design Control has some correlation to Requirements Management through its 4.4.4 Design Input requirement. Requirements Management requires "establishing and maintaining an agreement with the customer on the requirements for the software project." SEI frames this key process area with the notion of system requirements, which are allocated to software, hardware, and other system components. This process area addresses the software-only portion of this allocation. ISO 4.4.4 Design Input ties itself to 4.3 Contract Review by requiring "taking into consideration the results of any contract-review."

Refer to Section 13.1, "SEI CMM, Goals," and Section 13.2, "SEI CMM, Common Features," for additional associated statements.

# ■ 13.12  SEI CMM, LEVEL 2 SOFTWARE PROJECT PLANNING

## 13.12.1  SEI CMM, Software Project Planning; MB-Associated Statements

Associated statements are addressed in Section 13.1, "SEI CMM, Goals," and Section 13.2, "SEI CMM, Common Features."

## 13.12.2  SEI CMM, Software Project Planning; ISO-Associated Statements

ISO 4.1.2.1 Responsibility and Authority has a strong correlation to the SEI practice(s) for assigning responsibility. ISO requires defining and documenting the "responsibility, authority, and the interrelation of personnel."

ISO 9001 4.2.3 Quality Planning has a strong correlation with SEI. This ISO requirement is looking for a quality plan that identifies how the quality requirements will be achieved for a given project. SEI does not refer to one quality plan specifically. SEI does, however, address the suggested guidelines for a quality plan (as indicated in ISO 9004-1 and ISO 9000-3) via a Software Development Plan as part of Software Project Planning. Additionally, SEI addresses quality planning in many of the Capability Maturity Model key process areas. For more information on ISO and SEI in this area, refer to Appendix J.

ISO 9001 4.3 Contract Review has some correlation with SEI. Refer to the preceding section entitled "SEI CMM, Requirements Management; ISO Associated Statements," for a complete discussion.

ISO 9001 4.4 Design Control has a strong correlation to Software Project Planning through its 4.4.2 Design and Development Planning requirement. Software Project

Planning requires "developing the project's software development plan." ISO 4.4.2 Design and Development Planning requires "preparing plans for each design and development activity."

ISO 9001 4.9 Process Control has a strong correlation to Software Project Planning through its requirement for "identifying and planning the production, installation, and servicing processes which directly affect quality."

Refer to Section 13.1, "SEI CMM, Goals," and Section 13.2, "SEI CMM, Common Features," for additional associated statements.

# ■ 13.13  SEI CMM, LEVEL 2 SOFTWARE PROJECT TRACKING AND OVERSIGHT

## 13.13.1  SEI CMM, Software Project Tracking and Oversight; MB-Associated Statements

Associated statements are addressed from Section 13.1, "SEI CMM, Goals," and Section 13.2, "SEI CMM, Common Features."

## 13.13.2  SEI CMM, Software Project Tracking and Oversight; ISO-Associated Statements

ISO 4.1.2.1 Responsibility and Authority has a strong correlation to the SEI practice(s) for assigning responsibility. ISO requires defining and documenting the "responsibility, authority, and the interrelation of personnel."

ISO 9001 4.3 Contract Review has some correlation with SEI. Refer to a preceding section entitled "SEI CMM, Requirements Management; ISO-Associated Statements" for a complete discussion.

ISO 4.4 Design Control has a strong correlation to SEI in its 4.4.1 General requirement. ISO requires "procedures to control and verify the design of the product." SEI calls for "defined software process" as opposed to the "procedures" called for in ISO.

ISO 4.14 Corrective and Preventative Action has a strong correlation to SEI. SEI requires "taking corrective actions" throughout its key practices. ISO's 4.14.1 General and 4.14.2 Corrective Action address this requirement through "taking corrective or preventive action" and "determining the corrective action needed."

Refer to Section 13.1, "SEI CMM, Goals," and Section 13.2, "SEI CMM, Common Features," for additional associated statements.

# ■ 13.14 SEI CMM, LEVEL 2 SOFTWARE SUBCONTRACT MANAGEMENT

## 13.14.1 SEI CMM, Software Subcontract Management; MB-Associated Statements

SEI provides a comprehensive set of practices for "selecting qualified software subcontractors and managing them effectively." Malcolm Baldrige 5.4 Management of Supplier Performance has a strong correlation to these SEI requirements. Malcolm Baldrige requires "assuring that materials, components, and services furnished by other businesses meet the company's performance requirements" and "communicating the company's requirements to suppliers."

## 13.14.2 SEI CMM, Software Subcontract Management; ISO-Associated Statements

ISO 4.1.2.1 Responsibility and Authority has a strong correlation to the SEI practices for assigning responsibility. ISO requires defining and documenting the "responsibility, authority, and the interrelation of personnel."

ISO 4.6 Purchasing has a strong correlation to SEI. SEI is focused on selecting software subcontractors. ISO is broader and addresses purchased product that becomes part of the company's product and may affect its product quality. This includes services provided, such as calibration or special processes. ISO also requires keeping "records of acceptable subcontractors."

ISO's 4.10.2 Receiving Inspection and Testing requirement has a strong correlation with key practice SM.AC.12, which requires acceptance testing as part of delivery.

# ■ 13.15 SEI CMM, LEVEL 2 SOFTWARE QUALITY ASSURANCE

## 13.15.1 SEI CMM, Software Quality Assurance; MB-Associated Statements

SEI calls for periodic customer reviews, and this requirement has some correlation with Malcolm Baldrige 7.2 Customer Relationship Management. Malcolm Baldrige requires "providing effective management of the company's responses and follow ups with customers to preserve and build relationships and to increase knowledge about specific customers and about general customer expectations." Malcolm Baldrige is much broader and is focused on organizations that are marketing to more than just a single customer.

### 13.15.2  SEI CMM, Software Quality Assurance; ISO-Associated Statements

ISO 4.1.2.1 Responsibility and Authority has a strong correlation to the SEI practice(s) for assigning responsibility. ISO requires defining and documenting the "responsibility, authority, and the interrelation of personnel."

ISO 4.17 Internal Quality Audits has a strong correlation to SEI. ISO's requirement for internal quality audits directly addresses SEI's requirement for auditing. SEI goes beyond the requirements of ISO and provides for a software quality assurance group that is involved early in the product cycle with the various product groups. This role is one of assisting in the establishment of plans, standards, and procedures, ensuring that they are sufficient. Software Quality Assurance also addresses, in a subpractice, the ISO requirement for auditing to be done by "personnel independent of those having direct responsibility for the activity being audited." SEI is more specific in that it requires that the Software Quality Assurance group "has a reporting channel to senior management that is independent" of product management.

Refer to Section 13.1, "SEI CMM, Goals," and Section 13.2, "SEI CMM, Common Features," for additional associated statements.

## ■ 13.16  SEI CMM, Level 2 Software Configuration Management

### 13.16.1  SEI CMM, Software Configuration Management; MB-Associated Statements

Associated statements are addressed in Section 13.1, "SEI CMM, Goals," and Section 13.2, "SEI CMM, Common Features."

### 13.16.2  SEI CMM, Software Configuration Management; ISO-Associated Statements

ISO 4.1.2.1 Responsibility and Authority has a strong correlation to the SEI practice(s) for assigning responsibility. ISO requires defining and documenting the "responsibility, authority, and the interrelation of personnel."

ISO 4.4 Design Control has a strong correlation to SEI in its 4.4.1 General requirement. ISO requires "procedures to control and verify the design of the product." SEI calls for "defined software process" as opposed to the "procedures" called for in ISO.

SEI requires "initiating, recording, reviewing, approving, and tracking change requests and problems reports for all configuration items/units according to a documented procedure." ISO 4.4.9 Design Changes addresses this requirement through "identifying, documenting, reviewing, and approving by authorized personnel, all design changes and modifications, before their implementation." Practices under Software Configuration Management involve different kinds of software work products. Some examples provided under the subpractices include

✧ process-related documentation (e.g., plans, standards, or procedures),

✧ software requirements,

✧ software design,

✧ software code units,

✧ software test procedures,

✧ software system build for the software test activity,

✧ software system build for delivery to the customer or end users,

✧ compilers, and

✧ other support tools.

Software Configuration Management's purpose is to "establish and maintain the integrity of the products of the software project throughout the project's life cycle." ISO 4.5 Document and Data Control has a strong correlation with SEI through its requirement for "procedures to control all documents and data that relate to the requirements" of the standard. Practices under Software Configuration Management identify different kinds of software work products. Refer to previous examples of software work products.

ISO 4.8 Product Identification and Traceability has a strong correlation to SEI. ISO requires "procedures for identifying the product by suitable means from receipt and during all stages of production, delivery, and installation."

ISO 4.12 Inspection and Test Status and 4.13 Control of Nonconforming Product have a strong correlation to SEI. Software Configuration Management is intended to allow identification of the software work products throughout the entire process as well as "systematically controlling changes to the configuration, and maintaining the integrity and traceability of the configuration throughout the software life cycle." ISO addresses this requirement in 4.12 Inspection and Test Status by requiring "maintaining the identification of inspection and test status...throughout production, installation, and servicing of the product." ISO addresses this requirement in 4.13 Control of Nonconforming Product by requiring "providing for identification, documentation, evaluation, segregation (when practical), disposition of nonconforming product...."

ISO 4.16 Control of Quality Records has a strong correlation to SEI. Refer to the section entitled "ISO 9001, Control of Quality Records; SEI-Associated Statements" for additional discussion.

Refer to Section 13.1, "SEI CMM, Goals," and Section 13.2, "SEI CMM, Common Features," for additional associated statements.

# ■ 13.17 SEI CMM, Level 3—Defined

"The software process for both management and engineering activities is documented, standardized, and integrated into a standard software process for the organization. All projects use an approved, tailored version of the organization's standard software process for developing and maintaining software."[11]

# ■ 13.18 SEI CMM, Level 3 Organization Process Focus

## 13.18.1 SEI CMM, Organization Process Focus; MB-Associated Statements

SEI puts a strong emphasis on "establishing organizational responsibility for software process activities." This requirement has some correlation to Malcolm Baldrige 2.2 Competitive Comparisons and Benchmarking for "supporting the company's improvement of overall performance by the use of its processes."

Malcolm Baldrige 5.2 Process Management: Product and Service Production and Delivery has strong correlation with the SEI focus on improvement of processes. Malcolm Baldrige addresses this through its requirement for "evaluating and improving processes to achieve better operational performance, including cycle time; using process analysis, using benchmarking, using alternative technology, considering information from customers of the processes—within and outside the company."

## 13.18.2 SEI CMM, Organization Process Focus; ISO-Associated Statements

ISO 4.1.2.1 Responsibility and Authority has a strong correlation to the SEI practice(s) for assigning responsibility. ISO requires defining and documenting the "responsibility, authority, and the interrelation of personnel."

---

11. Ibid.

Refer to Section 13.1, "SEI CMM, Goals," and Section 13.2, "SEI CMM, Common Features," for additional associated statements.

# ■ 13.19 SEI CMM, LEVEL 3 ORGANIZATION PROCESS DEFINITION

### 13.19.1 SEI CMM, Organization Process Definition; MB-Associated Statements

SEI puts a strong emphasis on improvement throughout its key practices, and particularly within the Organization Process Focus key process area. This requirement provides a means of internal benchmarking across the various projects that comprise the organization and supports the incremental improvement philosophy. It has some correlation to Malcolm Baldrige 2.2 Competitive Comparisons and Benchmarking and its requirements. SEI makes no direct reference to conducting external benchmarks.

Malcolm Baldrige 5.2 Process Management: Product and Service Production and Delivery has strong correlation with SEI. Refer to "SEI CMM, Organization Process Focus; MB-Associated Statements" for a complete discussion.

### 13.19.2 SEI CMM, Organization Process Definition; ISO-Associated Statements

Refer to Section 13.1, "SEI CMM, Goals," and Section 13.2, "SEI CMM, Common Features," for additional associated statements.

# ■ 13.20 SEI CMM, LEVEL 3 TRAINING PROGRAM

### 13.20.1 SEI CMM, Training Program; MB-Associated Statements

SEI's Training Program key practices have a strong correlation with Malcolm Baldrige 4.3 Employee Education, Training, and Development. SEI devotes one of its 18 key process areas solely to training. In addition, it devotes many practices specifically to training. The Training Program process area is focused on the group that will perform the training function for the organization. Malcolm Baldrige addresses training as well as employee motivation, progression, and development.

### 13.20.2 SEI CMM, Training Program; ISO-Associated Statements

ISO 4.1.2.1 Responsibility and Authority has a strong correlation to the SEI practice(s) for assigning responsibility. ISO requires defining and documenting the "responsibility, authority, and the interrelation of personnel."

ISO 9001 4.18 Training has a strong correlation to the SEI CMM Training Program. The Training Program identifies the practices for the group that provides the training function. ISO requires "procedures for identifying training needs" and providing "for the training of all personnel performing activities affecting quality." Refer to the Ability to Perform common feature for additional information on specific training requirements identified within the individual key process areas.

Refer to Section 13.1, "SEI CMM, Goals," and Section 13.2, "SEI CMM, Common Features," for additional associated statements.

# ■ 13.21 SEI CMM, Level 3 Integrated Software Management

## 13.21.1 SEI CMM, Integrated Software Management; MB-Associated Statements

SEI Integrated Software Management has a requirement (IM.AC.11) for reviews to ensure that the "project's performance and results" are "in line with the current and projected needs of the business, customer, and end users." This requirement has some correlation with Malcolm Baldrige 7.2 Customer Relationship Management. Malcolm Baldrige requires "providing effective management of the company's responses and follow ups with customers to preserve and build relationships and to increase knowledge about specific customers and about general customer expectations." Malcolm Baldrige's focus is much broader and is generally aimed at organizations that are marketing to more than just a single customer.

## 13.21.2 SEI CMM, Integrated Software Management; ISO-Associated Statements

Refer to Section 13.1, "SEI CMM, Goals," and Section 13.2, "SEI CMM, Common Features," for additional associated statements.

# ■ 13.22 SEI CMM, Level 3 Software Product Engineering

## 13.22.1 SEI CMM, Software Product Engineering; MB-Associated Statements

The Software Product Engineering practice (PE.AC.2) for analyzing "allocated requirements systematically in order to develop, maintain, document, and verify the software requirements" has some correlation with the Malcolm Baldrige 2.3 Analysis and Use of Company-Level Data requirement for "using analysis to gain an understanding of customers...."

Software Product Engineering has a strong correlation to the Malcolm Baldrige 5.1 Design and Introduction of Products and Services requirement for "translating product and service design requirements into efficient and effective production/delivery processes, including an appropriate measurement plan."

## 13.22.2 SEI CMM, Software Product Engineering; ISO-Associated Statements

SEI has an overall strong correlation to ISO's 4.4 Design Control requirement. ISO 4.4.1 General requires "procedures to control and verify the design of the product." SEI calls for "defined software process" as opposed to the "procedures" called for in ISO.

ISO 4.4.4 Design Input requires "resolving incomplete, ambiguous, or conflicting requirements." SEI CMM defines the notion of system requirements, which are allocated to software, hardware, and other system components. This process area addresses the software-only portion of this allocation. Software Product Engineering includes practices that address "analyzing the allocated requirements systemically in order to develop, maintain, document, and verify the software requirements."

ISO's 4.4.5 Design Output requires "documenting and expressing the design output in terms that can be verified against design-input requirements." SEI requires "developing, maintaining, documenting, and verifying the software design." Software Product Engineering identifies specific design output requirements in its subpractices (refer to Software Engineering Institute, CMU/SEI-93-TR-25, *Key Practices of the Capability Maturity Model, Version 1.1* [Carnegie Mellon University, 1993]).

ISO's 4.4.6 Design Review requires "planning and conducting formal documented design reviews of the design results." Within Software Product Engineering, certain practices require verification and specific subpractices are devoted to reviews.

ISO's 4.4.7 Design Verification and 4.4.8 Design Validation require ensuring that "design-stage output meets the design-stage input requirements" and "that product conforms to defined users needs," respectively. SEI requires "planning and performing system and acceptance testing of the software to demonstrate that the software satisfies its requirements."

ISO's 4.10 Inspection and Testing requirement has a strong correlation with SEI. Many of SEI's key practices are focused on inspection and testing as part of the software development process.

ISO's 4.13 Control of Nonconforming Product requirement has a strong correlation with SEI. Many key practices require the review of defect data and measurement of the product produced.

Refer to Section 13.1, "SEI CMM, Goals," and Section 13.2, "SEI CMM, Common Features," for additional associated statements.

# ■ 13.23  SEI CMM, LEVEL 3 INTERGROUP COORDINATION

## 13.23.1  SEI CMM, Intergroup Coordination; MB-Associated Statements

Malcolm Baldrige 4.2 High Performance Work Systems, through its requirement for "ensuring effective communications across functions...," has a strong correlation to Intergroup Coordination.

Malcolm Baldrige 5.1 Design and Introduction of Products and Services, through its requirement for "addressing all requirements associated with products, services, and production/delivery processes early in design by appropriate company units, suppliers, and partners to ensure integration, coordination, and capability," has a strong correlation to Intergroup Coordination.

Malcolm Baldrige 7.2 Customer Relationship Management, through its requirement for "providing effective management of the company's responses and follow ups with customers to preserve and build relationships and to increase knowledge about specific customers and about general customer expectations," has some correlation with SEI Intergroup Coordination. Malcolm Baldrige's focus is much broader and is focused on organizations that are marketing to more than just a single customer.

## 13.23.2  SEI CMM, Intergroup Coordination; ISO-Associated Statements

ISO 4.1.2.1 Responsibility and Authority has a strong correlation to the SEI practice(s) for assigning responsibility. ISO requires defining and documenting the "responsibility, authority, and the interrelation of personnel."

ISO's 4.4.3 Organizational and Technical Interfaces has a strong correlation to SEI. Intergroup Coordination is looking for interfaces and interactions among groups to be "planned and managed." ISO addresses this requirement by requiring "defining organizational and technical interface between different groups."

Refer to Section 13.1, "SEI CMM, Goals," and Section 13.2, "SEI CMM, Common Features," for additional associated statements.

## ◼ 13.24 SEI CMM, LEVEL 3 PEER REVIEWS

### 13.24.1 SEI CMM, Peer Reviews; MB-Associated Statements

Malcolm Baldrige 5.1 Design and Introduction of Products and Services, through its requirement for "reviewing and/or testing product, service, and production/delivery process designs in detail to ensure trouble-free launch," has a strong correlation with SEI Peer Reviews.

### 13.24.2 SEI CMM, Peer Reviews; ISO-Associated Statements

ISO 4.4.6 Design Review has a strong correlation to SEI. The Peer Reviews key process area is devoted to reviews. Peer Reviews involve many different kinds of software work products. Some examples of subpractice work products can be found on page 128.

ISO 4.10.1 General has a strong correlation to SEI. ISO requires "procedures for inspection...activities," which address SEI's "performing peer reviews according to documented procedures." ISO's 4.10.3 In-Process Inspection and Testing and 4.10.4 Final Inspection and Testing requirements address Peer Reviews as a primary inspection method. ISO's 4.10.5 Inspection and Test Records directly addresses SEI's "recording data on the conduct and results of the peer reviews."

Refer to Section 13.1, "SEI CMM, Goals," and Section 13.2, "SEI CMM, Common Features," for additional associated statements.

## ◼ 13.25 SEI CMM, LEVEL 4—MANAGED

"Detailed measures of the software process and product quality are collected. Both the software process and products are quantitatively understood and controlled."[12]

## ◼ 13.26 SEI CMM, LEVEL 4 QUANTITATIVE PROCESS MANAGEMENT

### 13.26.1 SEI CMM, Quantitative Process Management; MB-Associated Statements

Quantitative Process Management is focused on controlling process performance quantitatively. Malcolm Baldrige 2.3 Analysis and Use of Company-Level Data, through its requirement for "integrating and analyzing information and data from all parts of the

---

12. Ibid.

company to support reviews, business decisions, and planning," has a strong correlation with SEI.

### 13.26.2 SEI CMM, Quantitative Process Management; ISO-Associated Statements

ISO 4.1.2.1 Responsibility and Authority has a strong correlation to the SEI practice(s) for assigning responsibility. ISO requires defining and documenting the "responsibility, authority, and the interrelation of personnel."

ISO 4.20 Statistical Techniques has a strong correlation to SEI. Quantitative Process Management is focused on processes and defines *quantitative control* as "any quantitative or statistically-based technique appropriate to analyze a software process, identify special causes of variations in the performance of the software process, and bring the performance of the software process within well-defined limits." ISO requires "procedures to implement and control the application of...statistical techniques."

Refer to Section 13.1, "SEI CMM, Goals," and Section 13.2, "SEI CMM, Common Features," for additional associated statements.

## ■ 13.27 SEI CMM, LEVEL 4 SOFTWARE QUALITY MANAGEMENT

### 13.27.1 SEI CMM, Software Quality Management; MB-Associated Statements

Software Quality Management is focused on developing "a quantitative understanding of the quality" of the product. Malcolm Baldrige 2.3 Analysis and Use of Company-Level Data, through its "integrating and analyzing information and data from all parts of the company to support reviews, business decisions, and planning" requirement, has a strong correlation with SEI.

Malcolm Baldrige 5.1 Design and Introduction of Products and Services, through its requirement for "designing key production/delivery processes to meet both key product and service quality requirements and company operational performance requirements," has a strong correlation to Software Quality Management.

### 13.27.2 SEI CMM, Software Quality Management; ISO-Associated Statements

ISO 4.6 Purchasing has a strong correlation to SEI. ISO's requirement for "procedures to ensure that purchased product conforms to specified requirements," addresses SEI's requirement for "allocating...quality goals...to the subcontractor's."

ISO's 4.20 Statistical Techniques has a strong correlation to SEI. Software Quality Management is focused on products and is looking to "develop a quantitative understanding of the quality of the project's software products."

Refer to Section 13.1, "SEI CMM, Goals," and Section 13.2, "SEI CMM, Common Features," for additional associated statements.

## ■ 13.28  SEI CMM, LEVEL 5—OPTIMIZING

"Continuous process improvement is enabled by quantitative feedback from the process and from piloting innovative ideas and technologies."[13]

## ■ 13.29  SEI CMM, LEVEL 5 DEFECT PREVENTION

### 13.29.1  SEI CMM, Defect Prevention; MB-Associated Statements

The purpose of Defect Prevention is to "identify the cause of defects and prevent them from recurring." Malcolm Baldrige 2.3 Analysis and Use of Company-Level Data has some correlation with this requirement through its requirement for "using analysis to gain an understanding of operational performance and company capabilities."

### 13.29.2  SEI CMM, Defect Prevention; ISO-Associated Statements

ISO 4.1.2.1 Responsibility and Authority has a strong correlation to the SEI practice(s) for assigning responsibility. ISO requires defining and documenting the "responsibility, authority, and the interrelation of personnel."

ISO 4.14 Corrective and Preventative Action has a strong correlation to SEI. SEI has a requirement to "identify the cause of defects and prevent them from recurring." ISO's 4.14.1 General and 4.14.2 Corrective Action address this requirement through "taking corrective or preventive action" and "determining the corrective action needed." SEI can be considered proactive in its approach. ISO's 4.14.2 Corrective Action and 4.14.3 Preventative Action can generally be regarded as reactive to a problem. In one sense, 4.14.3 Preventative Action can be viewed as proactive; however, as defined in ISO, it is generally a reactive process. As identified in ISO, preventative action is a natural extension to corrective action and is very important to operational quality issues. Defect Prevention, however, identifies another level of preventive action that takes a proactive approach in that it makes the process an anticipative one.

---

13. Ibid.

Refer to Section 13.1, "SEI CMM, Goals," and Section 13.2, "SEI CMM, Common Features," for additional associated statements.

# 13.30 SEI CMM, LEVEL 5 TECHNOLOGY CHANGE MANAGEMENT

## 13.30.1 SEI CMM, Technology Change Management; MB-Associated Statements

SEI puts a large emphasis on improvement in general. Some of its key practices provide for internal benchmarking across the various projects that comprise the organization. This supports the incremental improvement philosophy. SEI makes no direct reference to conducting external benchmarks; however, Technology Change Management does put strong emphasis on identifying new technologies. Malcolm Baldrige 2.2 Competitive Comparisons and Benchmarking does have some correlation with this key process area. SEI defines technologies as tools, methods, and processes.

Malcolm Baldrige 5.2 Process Management: Product and Service Production and Delivery, through its requirement for "evaluating and improving process...using alternative technology," has a strong correlation with SEI. SEI provides a great deal of depth in its requirements for managing and deploying new technologies within an organization.

## 13.30.2 SEI CMM, Technology Change Management; ISO-Associated Statements

ISO 4.1.2.1 Responsibility and Authority has a strong correlation to the SEI practice(s) for assigning responsibility. ISO requires defining and documenting the "responsibility, authority, and the interrelation of personnel."

Refer to Section 13.1, "SEI CMM, Goals," and Section 13.2, "SEI CMM, Common Features," for additional associated statements.

# 13.31 SEI CMM, LEVEL 5 PROCESS CHANGE MANAGEMENT

## 13.31.1 SEI CMM, Process Change Management; MB-Associated Statements

SEI puts a large emphasis on improvement in general. Process Change Management provides for improvement at the organization level, which enables internal benchmarking across the various projects that comprise the organization. This supports the incremental improvement philosophy. Malcolm Baldrige 2.2 Competitive Comparisons and Benchmarking does have some correlation with this key process area.

Malcolm Baldrige 5.2 Process Management: Product and Service Production and Delivery, through its requirement for "evaluating and improving process to achieve better operational performance," has a strong correlation with SEI. SEI provides an excellent infrastructure of practices for continually improving an organization.

## 13.31.2 SEI CMM, Process Change Management; ISO-Associated Statements

Refer to Section 13.1, "SEI CMM, Goals," and Section 13.2, "SEI CMM, Common Features," for additional associated statements.

# IV

# Framework for Comparing QMS Assessment Methodologies

*This section describes the framework used to compare these assessment methodologies. Chapter 14, "Approach," details the steps used for conducting the comparison. Chapter 15, "System Assumptions," outlines some important procedural assumptions and rules used in conducting the study. Then Chapter 16, "Framework High-Level Comparison," compares each of the base QMS elements and base QMS activities for the three assessment methodologies. Finally, Chapter 17, "Framework Comparison Summary," completes the framework discussion.*

*This "framework comparison" provides a different level of comparison for you than that provided in Part III, "Comparing QMS Assessment Methodologies." The framework provides you with a more neutral view of the methodologies using TQM concepts as the basis for comparison. This is in contrast to Part III, which provides a comparison based on each methodology's perspective.*

# Approach

In order to compare and contrast the various QMS assessment methodologies, it was necessary to formulate a framework or common point of reference with which to conduct the comparison. The approach described will explain the framework and the process used in conducting the comparison.

The framework consists of a two-dimensional matrix referred to as the QMS properties matrix. A two-dimensional matrix was chosen to minimize the complexity of comparing the systems. The two dimensions are

✧ QMS elements
✧ QMS activities

## ■ 14.1 QMS ELEMENTS

The first dimension, QMS elements, provides a total quality management context for evaluation of the methodologies. From the *Malcolm Baldrige National Quality Award* application, the elements are based on a set of core values and concepts. The core values and concepts found in Baldrige are the foundation for "integrating the overall customer and company operational performance requirements." The details on each of the core values and concepts can be found in Chapter 3 in the section entitled "Malcolm Baldrige Core Values and Concepts." These core values and concepts are

✧ Customer-Driven Quality
✧ Leadership

✧ Continuous Improvement and Learning
✧ Employee Participation and Development
✧ Fast Response
✧ Design Quality and Prevention
✧ Long-Range View of the Future
✧ Management by Fact
✧ Partnership Development
✧ Corporate Responsibility and Citizenship
✧ Results Orientation

The QMS elements used are the seven categories of the Malcolm Baldrige National Quality Award.[1]

1. Leadership. "The Leadership Category examines senior executives' personal leadership and involvement in creating and sustaining a customer focus, clear values and expectations, and a leadership system that promotes performance excellence. Also examined is how the values and expectations are integrated into the company's management system, including how the company addresses its public responsibilities and corporate citizenship."

2. Information and Analysis. "The Information and Analysis Category examines the management and effectiveness of the use of data and information to support customer-driven performance excellence and marketplace success."

3. Strategic Planning. "The Strategic Planning Category examines how the company sets strategic directions, and how it determines key plan requirements. Also examined is how the plan requirements are translated into an effective performance management system."

4. Human Resource Development and Management. "The Human Resource Development and Management Category examines how the work force is enabled to develop and utilize its full potential, aligned with the company's performance objectives. Also examined are the company's efforts to build and maintain an environment conducive to performance excellence, full participation, and personal and organizational growth."

5. Process Management. "The Process Management Category examines the key aspects of process management, including customer-focused design, product and service delivery processes, support services and supply management involving all work units, including research and development. The Category examines how key pro-

---

1. U.S. Department of Commerce, *The Malcolm Baldrige National Quality Award* (National Institute of Standards and Technology, 1995), pp. 21–36.

cesses are designed, effectively managed, and improved to achieve higher performance."

6. Business Results. "The Business Results Category examines the company's performance and improvement in key business areas—product and service quality, productivity and operational effectiveness, supply quality, and financial performance indicators linked to these areas. Also examined are performance levels relative to those of competitors."

7. Customer Focus and Satisfaction. "The Customer Focus and Satisfaction Category examines the company's systems for customer learning and for building and maintaining customer relationships. Also examined are levels and trends in key measures of business success—customer satisfaction and retention, market share, and satisfaction relative to competitors."

Malcolm Baldrige was selected as the most comprehensive criteria for total quality management.

## ■ 14.2 QMS ACTIVITIES

The second dimension, QMS activities, provides an action context for evaluation. The action context addresses the need to understand what the people in the system are doing. Because people are the key element in the implementation of a quality management system, there arises the need to understand "what should the people be doing?" or "what are the actions that our people should be taking?" in order to implement the various quality system requirements. The QMS activities chosen represent the broadest range of activities found in the three QMS assessment methodologies. These activities evolved during the first step of the process used to conduct this investigation (refer to Section 14.3, "Translating QMS Requirements into Statements of Activity"). During this step, over 65 different action verbs, which represented a broad range of activities, were discovered. The ones chosen represent the most prevalent activities, as well as the most representative activities based on quality principles and concepts. These activities are described below and illustrated in the activity loop in Figure 14.1. The activity loop can be thought of as an expanded Plan-Do-Check-Act cycle. The Plan-Do-Check-Act cycle was popularized by W. Edwards Deming and is more commonly known as the Deming cycle. This cycle is used as a basic model for continuous improvement. Deming called this the Shewhart cycle based on the original concept which came from Walter A. Shewhart, one of the pioneers of modern statistical quality control.[2] The activity loop is best described as

---

2. W. Edwards Deming, *Out of the Crisis* (Massachusetts Institute of Technology, 1982, 1986), p. 88.

✧ Plan/Prepare (planning)
✧ Do/Implement (implementing)
✧ Check/Manage (managing)
✧ Act/Enable (improving, communicating, training, motivating)

The biggest difference between Plan-Do-Check-Act and the activity loop is in the Act/Enable phase. The Act step involves "improving" activities and the Enable step involves the three activity areas of communicating, training, and motivating. The four outer activity areas (planning/implementing/managing/improving) can be thought of as the spokes of the quality wheel. The three activities that make up Enable (communicating/training/motivating) represent the core or hub of the quality wheel. These three hub activities are focused on the most important part of any QMS, the people. These activities, like the hub of a wheel, are the key foundation to the success of the other parts of the system.

1. *Planning* is the beginning of the activity loop, which lays the foundation for all subsequent activity groups. This involves the types of activities that are done in order to establish the correct course of action or goals for quality. This activity establishes the baseline from which to compare the results of later activities, including setting objectives for quality. It represents the Plan/Prepare phase.

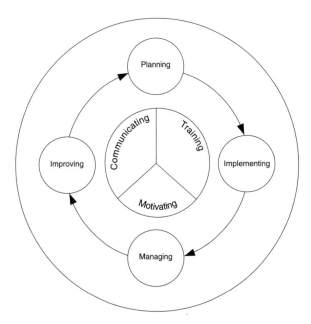

**Fig. 14.1** Activity loop.

2. *Implementing* focuses on the activities necessary to deploy the activities identified in planning. These activities implement the plans and objectives the organization has set for itself. They include the actual performance of the plans and objectives. This represents the Do/Implement phase.

3. *Managing* focuses on the activities necessary to sustain the implemented activities and involves the day-to-day running of the business. These activities are required to ensure that the activities are integrated and run smoothly. This represents the Check/Manage phase.

4. *Improving* focuses on those activities needed to improve the on-going operations and to fine tune them. This group of activities embodies the notion of continuous improvement by incremental means or redesign/reengineering. It is distinct from managing in that it involves activities that would not be considered part of the "normal" operation of the business. This is part of the Act/Enable phase.

5. *Communicating* among the various groups is an important aspect of a well-functioning quality management system. It is especially critical in large organizations where there is a high degree of functional fragmentation. It starts with the senior executive communication of vision, mission, goals, business objectives, and the like. This continues with successive levels of management developing similar business imperatives that can be directly traced to the previous level of management. Also included are intergroup communications among groups, such as marketing and development. This category is intended for what would be termed direct communications as opposed to indirect communications such as documenting and reviewing. This is part of the Act/Enable phase.

6. *Training* focuses on those activities necessary to enable the workforce to perform the activities required in the preceding groups. This is part of the Act/Enable phase.

7. *Motivating* focuses on those activities important to maximizing the performance of the workforce through incentives, recognition, etc. It addresses the human element and drives the goals, plans, and objectives forward. This is part of the Act/Enable phase.

The activities chosen also represent categories or groupings of activities. Grouping activities was necessary because of the large number of activities identified within the assessment methodologies. All statements of activity are verbs and end in *ing* (e.g., planning).

The process for conducting the comparison of QMS assessment methodologies involves four steps:

1. Translating QMS requirements into statements of activity
2. Mapping statements of activity into QMS properties matrix

3. Comparing/contrasting mappings

4. Evaluating mappings

# ■ 14.3 TRANSLATING QMS REQUIREMENTS INTO STATEMENTS OF ACTIVITY

The translation of the QMS requirements into statements of activity involves two steps. First, each sentence in the methodology is examined for action verbs. The action verbs are reviewed, and, based on their context and the author's judgment, the most significant ones are chosen. Second, each sentence is then reworded, using the original phrasing, except that the sentence begins with the action verb (which has also had an *ing* ending added). A detailed example follows.

## 14.3.1 Example Translation Process

1. Original QMS requirement. The ANSI/ASQC Standard Q9001-1994 (ISO 9001) quality requirement is stated as follows:

   **4.5 Document and Data Control**
   **4.5.1 General**
   The supplier shall establish and maintain documented procedures to control all documents and data that relate to the requirements of this American National Standard including, to the extent applicable, documents of external origin such as standards and customer drawings.

2. Selection of significant verbs. Choose *establish* and *maintain*.

3. Translation of original QMS requirement. Establishing and maintaining documented procedures to control all documents and data that relate to the requirements of this American National Standard including, to the extent applicable, documents of external origin such as standards and customer drawings (the supplier).

# ■ 14.4 MAPPING STATEMENTS OF ACTIVITY INTO QMS PROPERTIES MATRIX

The statements of activity are mapped into the QMS properties matrix in two steps. First, the statement is mapped into the most appropriate QMS elements and QMS activities. Second, the statement is mapped into the most appropriate activities/elements based on the context of the activity. Both mappings are based on the author's judgment. It is possible, because of the original wording of the requirement, that a statement could be mapped into more than one cell in the matrix. [Refer to Tables K.1, L.1, and M.1.]

## ■ 14.5 COMPARING/CONTRASTING MAPPINGS

This stage involves reducing data from the original mappings and provides the basis for a high-level view. It is done by summing the various matrix cell counts both for the QMS elements and the QMS activities. Totals for each column and row in the matrix are provided. A percentage of the total number of statements is calculated for each row and column. These summaries are provided in Tables K.2, L.2, and M.2. Table N.1 summarizes the other three tables. This table shows only the percentage of total statements for each row and column.

This step provides the basis for a more comprehensive and detailed mapping from an individual methodology's perspective view.

## ■ 14.6 EVALUATING MAPPINGS

Two evaluations are made based on the preceding step. The first is a high-level evaluation, which reviews the percentage of total statements for each QMS element and QMS activity. In addition, other factors such as investigative assumptions, the context in which the methodology is used, and other system observations are considered in the high-level evaluation. The first evaluation is presented in Chapter 15, "System Assumptions"; Chapter 16, "Framework High-Level Comparison"; and Chapter 17, "Framework Comparison Summary." The second evaluation is provided in Chapter 9, "Comparing QMS Assessment Methodologies." This is a perspective-level evaluation, which involves a detailed view from the perspective of each individual methodology's point of view. This evaluation considers the context of the requirements in its examination, which represents a subset of the original mappings. This evaluation is provided in Chapter 9, "Comparison Overview"; Chapter 10, "High Level Comparison"; Chapter 11, "Comparison from a Malcolm Baldrige Perspective"; Chapter 12, "Comparison from an ISO 9001 Perspective"; and Chapter 13, "Comparison from an SEI CMM Perspective."

# System Assumptions

This investigation, as with any systems investigation, required some simplifying assumptions about the systems under investigation. The process of studying these systems revealed many interesting comparisons, contrasts, and apparent dichotomies. The systems under study are the "systems" that are intended to measure the actual systems themselves. The measurement of any system will, by the act of measuring, cause a loss of information about that system. Information is lost in several ways.

First, information is lost by translation of the original QMS requirements into statements of activity. Variance is introduced during translation based on individual interpretation. One person may interpret or emphasize one part of a given QMS requirement over another. This was minimized by retaining as much of the original phrasing as possible.

Second, information is lost by mapping the statements of activity to the Malcolm Baldrige seven categories. This obviously skews the mapping and makes Baldrige appear to be more balanced than the other two. This trade-off was necessary in order to provide a context that would be the most meaningful to the largest audience.

Third, information is lost by the selection of the seven QMS activities. This information loss is influenced by three factors: activity selection, total number of statements, and the grouping of activities. Activity selection was based on the most prevalent QMS activities found in the methodologies and those judged most representative of quality principles and concepts. Activity selection based on prevalence skews the selection to ISO and SEI since their language was more specific. SEI was more specific in its language than ISO. The total number of statements in each methodology also caused a skew since the methodologies did not have an equal number of statements. SEI had 744 statements, ISO 146, and Malcolm Baldrige 136. This skewing was minimized by normalizing the elements and activities to the total number of statements in their respective methodologies. Note that one QMS requirement could have more than one statement of activity. Many requirements incorporated multiple activities. The grouping of activities introduced a loss of information since the number of action verbs was condensed from over 65 to 7 base QMS activities. This was subjective and, like translation, based on individual views and experiences.

The loss of information is compounded, in the case of quality management systems, by the fact that these systems are not defined based on a common model. Because a common model must be chosen, it results in limiting assumptions in order to make a comparison feasible. As seen earlier, by the various definitions of total quality management, there are many different views of a quality system. There are equally as many views on ways to implement them and on how to measure their effectiveness.

One assumption of this study was that each of the statements of activity was equal in its importance. That is to say, no weighting was given to certain statements over others. It is clear, however, that some statements are written at a much higher level than other statements. In the case of the Malcolm Baldrige assessment, the statements are at a much higher level than either the ISO or SEI statements. Since Malcolm Baldrige is the only assessment of the three that uses a point scoring system, weighting based on points was also not used. The Malcolm Baldrige assessment is scored on a possible 1000 points. The points, however, are not evenly distributed as seen in Table 5.1, "Malcolm Baldrige Examination Items and Point Values." An example of this is category 6 of the Malcolm Baldrige National Quality Award, Business Results, which is worth 250 points or 25.0% of the total available. Yet this category represents less than 5% of the total number of activity statements in MB. This is one of Baldrige's two largest point value categories and is much higher than the other categories. The point scoring is obviously important to those applying for the Malcolm Baldrige National Quality Award, so the percentage of points for the seven categories is provided for convenience in Table N.1.

The second assumption or procedural rule is that no attempt was made to derive implied statements of activity from the original statements. In some cases, it was tempting to imply other activities from the original statements; however, this could not be done consistently. Doing so would have introduced more information loss and been potentially misleading. The intent was to minimize interpretation of the original statements and to allow you to draw any additional conclusions based on your particular experiences.

A third procedural step that became necessary was the grouping of activities. This step was necessary to reduce the "information overload" associated with having over 65 different activities. This step was not always a graceful one and certainly had a degree of subjectivity. However, the intent of this study is to provide you with a context from which to compare the various methodologies. Understanding this context helps you frame your understanding with your own experiences.

# Framework High-Level Comparison

The first dimension of the framework, QMS elements, provides a total quality management context in which to compare the assessment methodologies. [Refer to Figure 16.1.] The QMS elements used are the seven categories of the Malcolm Baldrige National Quality Award. Each of the elements will be discussed separately.

- ✧ *Leadership*. SEI devotes a fair number of statements (over 16%) to this QMS element. Malcolm Baldrige (MB) and ISO 9001 (ISO) follow at 10.3 and 7.5%, respectively. ISO is devoting less than half the number of statements as SEI.

- ✧ *Information and Analysis*. MB places the highest emphasis on this element at 13.2%; however, SEI and ISO are not far behind.

- ✧ *Strategic Planning*. This category highlights the difference in focus of Malcolm Baldrige and the other two assessments. Baldrige assigns 6.6% of its activities to this category. SEI does not address this area in its activities, and ISO devotes an almost negligible number of activities. It should be noted, however, that the overall process of using SEI and ISO to improve an organization's quality management system certainly is part of strategic planning. These methodologies, however, do not integrate this activity into their direct requirements.

- ✧ *Human Resource Development and Management*. MB devotes 12.5% to this category, which is significant. SEI is next at 9.5%, and ISO is half of Baldrige at 6.9%. SEI and ISO also differ from Malcolm Baldrige in that their primary focus is on education and training. Malcolm Baldrige addresses a much broader set of topics such as work and job design, compensation and recognition, and employee well-being and

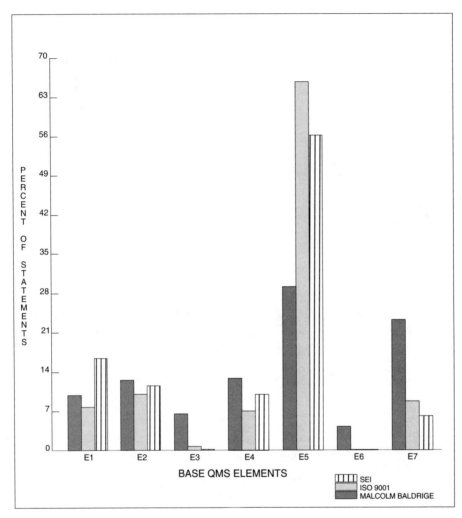

E1 = Leadership
E2 = Information and Analysis
E3 = Strategic Planning
E4 = Human Resource Development and Management
E5 = Process Management
E6 = Business Results
E7 = Customer Focus and Satisfaction

**Fig. 16.1** Quality management system element comparison.

satisfaction. Following the theme of strategic planning, Baldrige also addresses the need for human resource planning.

✧ *Process Management.* ISO and SEI devote the majority of their statements to this area, 66.4 and 56.3%, respectively. MB is also significant at 29.4%, but this is about half that of the other two. The result is a telling comparison of the three methodologies. As would be expected, these high percentages are done at the expense of other areas. It also shows the basic philosophical difference among the assessments methodologies. SEI and ISO have an attention-to-detail approach. Both are very specific about what they are looking for in processes. ISO has many activities that can be classified as "controlling" types of requirements. SEI is even more detailed than ISO about what it is looking for in processes. In contrast, MB is at a higher level and includes product and service production, delivery processes, business processes, and support services.

✧ *Business Results.* MB devotes a little over 4% of its statements to this QMS element. Interestingly, ISO and SEI have no requirements in this category. This highlights another basic philosophical difference between MB and the other two methods. On the one hand, MB devotes only about 4% of its statements to this area, but it puts a heavy emphasis (25% of total points available) on business results in its scoring model. These statements are focused on discussing the results achieved from other areas within Malcolm Baldrige. Baldrige is taking the seemingly simple approach of measuring the quality management system based on what it is achieving. This measurement not only covers more than just product and service quality but also includes productivity and operational effectiveness, supply quality, and financial performance. Financial performance from a business point of view is obviously very important, but it is not something that is traditionally associated with quality. In the final analysis, every business is measured by, and its "quality" is associated with, its financial results. Intuitively, there seems to be a strong link between those companies that are perceived as having superior quality and those that are financially successful. This begs the question; are these companies financially successful because of their quality? Or is the opposite situation true, their financial success breeds high quality? The answer lies more in the fact that their success, financial and quality, is the result of their quality management systems. Unfortunately, the word *quality* can bring a negative connotation to those who are unfamiliar with the concepts behind these assessment models. Many people still associate quality with product and service attributes. This perception brought about the emergence of the term *total quality management.*

✧ *Customer Focus and Satisfaction.* This category also shows a wide contrast in the methodologies. MB is at 23.6%, which is one of its two highest categories. This is in contrast to ISO at 8.9% and SEI at 6.5%. Because ISO and SEI were created in the context of contractual situations between two parties, they do not place as much emphasis on customer focus and satisfaction. However, with many firms now using these assessments for general market products, this is a significant shortcoming.

The second dimension of the framework, QMS activities, provides an action context for comparison. [Refer to Figure 16.2.] The action context addresses the need to understand what the people in the system are doing. The QMS activities chosen represent the broadest range of activities found in the QMS assessment methodologies studied and those judged most representative of quality principles and concepts. Each of the activities is discussed separately.

- ✧ *Planning.* MB puts a significant emphasis on this QMS activity at 23.5% followed by ISO at 15.7% and SEI at 9.7%. SEI is focused on the software aspect of a system.

- ✧ *Implementing.* SEI puts a very significant emphasis on the Do/Implement phase at 38.4%. ISO is also very significant at 32.2%. MB is the lowest of the three but is also significant at almost 20%. This is SEI's highest QMS activities area. ISO's and SEI's emphasis on this area is indicative of their focus on processes and procedures.

- ✧ *Managing.* This Check/Manage phase is ISO's most significant, with over 44% of its requirements devoted to this QMS activity. This result demonstrates ISO's high focus on operational management and control. SEI follows ISO with almost 27% of its statements focused on this area. This is SEI's second highest QMS activity. MB follows third at 17.6%.

- ✧ *Improving.* MB puts heavy emphasis on this Act/Enable activity (at over 30%) and is Baldrige's highest QMS activity. This is in direct contrast to SEI and ISO at 8.5 and 0.7%, respectively. This is another important area where the philosophical differences among the methodologies are readily apparent. MB puts an overwhelmingly strong emphasis on continuous improvement, yet ISO and SEI do have continuous improvement of a different nature incorporated into their assessment models. For ISO, this takes the form of periodic (twice yearly) surveillance audits. For SEI, in addition to some "built-in" emphasis, it also takes the form of periodic reassessments every 12–18 months.

- ✧ *Communicating.* ISO (5.5%), SEI (5.2%), and MB (1.5%) are not very high in general, but ISO and SEI do emphasize this much more than Malcolm Baldrige. As described earlier under the QMS activities introduction, these activities would be termed direct communications between people as opposed to indirect communications such as documenting and reviewing.

- ✧ *Training.* SEI overwhelmingly leads this Act/Enable area with over 11%. SEI emphasizes training in all of its key process areas through its Ability to Perform common feature. These training requirements are generally very specific in the type of train-

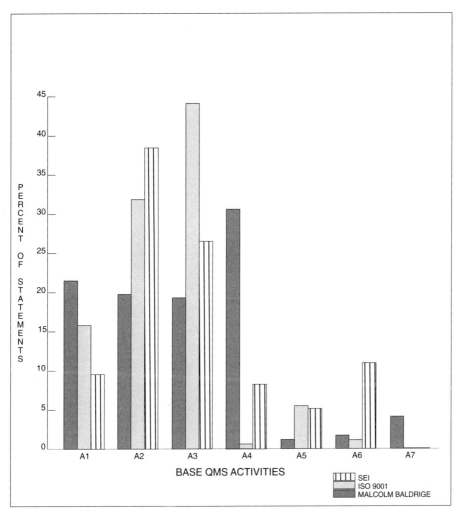

A1 – Planning
A2 = Implementing
A3 = Managing
A4 = Improving
A5 = Communicating
A6 = Training
A7 = Motivating

**Fig. 16.2** Quality management system activity comparison.

ing and the individuals who should be receiving the training. These are in direct contrast to MB and ISO, which are very low at 2.2 and 1.4%, respectively.

❖ *Motivating*. In ISO and SEI there are no activities, but MB at 4.4% does address this Act/Enable QMS activity. Baldrige addresses motivating under its High Performance Work Systems and Employee Well-Being and Satisfaction Examination Items.

# Framework Comparison Summary

The purpose of this book is to compare three primary quality management system assessment methodologies. For the QMS elements, the top three elements (highest percentage) in each methodology are

- ✧ Malcolm Baldrige
    - ✗ Process Management
    - ✗ Customer Focus and Satisfaction
    - ✗ Information and Analysis
- ✧ ISO
    - ✗ Process Management
    - ✗ Information and Analysis
    - ✗ Customer Focus and Satisfaction
- ✧ SEI
    - ✗ Process Management
    - ✗ Leadership
    - ✗ Information and Analysis

Each assessment model emphasizes different aspects of TQM. This can be seen in SEI and ISO, which have an overwhelming focus on Process Management. This is also Baldrige's highest element area. Malcolm Baldrige's second largest element is Customer Focus and Satisfaction, while SEI and ISO also have some activity in this area. MB, SEI, and ISO also have in their top three elements Information and Analysis. All three have this as the second or third highest element.

For the QMS activities, the top three elements (highest percentage) in each methodology are

- ✧ Malcolm Baldrige
  - ✗ Improving
  - ✗ Planning
  - ✗ Implementing

- ✧ ISO
  - ✗ Managing
  - ✗ Implementing
  - ✗ Planning

- ✧ SEI
  - ✗ Implementing
  - ✗ Managing
  - ✗ Training

Malcolm Baldrige, from an activity perspective, puts a large emphasis on Improving. ISO puts an overwhelming emphasis on Managing, which is SEI's second biggest activity area. SEI has its highest emphasis on Implementing, and this is ISO's second biggest activity area. Baldrige also puts emphasis on Implementing. Baldrige and ISO have Planning in their top three activities. In addition, SEI has high activity emphasis on Training.

The process of translating each of the QMS requirements into statements of activity was very informative, because it gave insight into the tone and focus of the assessment methodologies. The use of certain language, such as "establishing and maintaining" or "reviewing and approving," conveyed each assessment's view of quality and the implementation of quality. SEI and ISO are specific in their language. SEI is particularly specific about the kinds of activities it expects to see at the various maturity levels. ISO specifies *what* it expects as opposed to SEI, which specifies more of the *how* it should be implemented. SEI provides flexibility in meeting its requirements by outlining Goals (GO) for each key process area and states that the key practices "describe *what* is to be done, but they should not be interpreted as mandating *how* the goals should be achieved." Malcolm Baldrige is also a *what* type of assessment, but at a higher level than ISO or SEI. As an example, Baldrige does not say that you have to control documents. Instead, Baldrige says, "improving processes to achieve better quality...." This may involve controlling documents, but Baldrige will not tell you to do so. ISO, however, is very specific about what documents need to be controlled and what is required to control them. SEI is also specific about what documents should exist and how they should be controlled.

The QMS framework provides a means by which you can see how your own quality system compares to these three major assessment models. This can simplify the quality practitioner's job of meeting the requirements of SEI CMM, ISO 9001, or Malcolm Baldrige. The number of Quality Management System assessment models is growing. The planned introductions of ISO 14000, an Environmental Management System standard, and ISO SPICE (Software Process Improvement and Capability dEtermination), an internationalization of the SEI CMM, presents a future concern for organizations. The growth in quality management system assessment models means that more resources in the organization will be required for assessments. The cost of assessment is not insignificant and will eventually result in the need for consolidation of these models. Organizations can reduce their cost of assessment by having an in-depth understanding of the assessment models and then structuring their quality management system in such a way that all assessment requirements are more easily accommodated.

# V

---

# Appendixes

*This section provides detailed reference material you can use to gain a thorough understanding of the methodologies. The appendixes are grouped as follows:*

- ✧ *the requirements of MB, SEI, and ISO are contained in Appendixes A, B, and C*
- ✧ *the cross-referenced requirements of MB, SEI, and ISO are contained in Appendixes D, E, F, G, H, and I*
- ✧ *the quality plan requirements of SEI and ISO are contained in Appendix J*
- ✧ *the properties matrixes for MB, SEI, and ISO are contained in Appendixes K, L, and M*
- ✧ *the properties matrix summary for MB, SEI, and ISO is contained in Appendix N*

# QMS Statements of Activity: Malcolm Baldrige

**Table A.1** QMS Statements of Activity: Malcolm Baldrige

| MB Element | QMS Requirement | Statement of Activity |
| --- | --- | --- |
| 1.0 | Leadership | "The Leadership category examines senior executives' personal leadership and involvement in creating and sustaining a customer focus, clear values and expectations, and a leadership system that promotes performance excellence. Also examined is how the values and expectations are integrated into the company's management system, including how the company addresses its public responsibilities and corporate citizenship."[1] |
| 1.1 | Senior Executive Leadership | Setting directions through leadership and personal involvement (senior executives). |
| | | Developing and maintaining a leadership system for performance excellence (senior executives). |
| 1.1.a | | Providing effective leadership and direction in building and improving company competitiveness, performance, and capabilities (senior executives): |
| | | (1) creating and reinforcing values and expectations throughout the company's leadership system; |
| | | (2) setting directions and performance excellence goals through strategic and business planning; |
| | | (3) reviewing overall company performance, including customer-related and operational performance (senior executives). |
| 1.1.b | | Evaluating and improving the effectiveness of the company's leadership system and organization to pursue performance excellence goals (senior executives). |

**Table A.1** QMS Statements of Activity: Malcolm Baldrige (Continued)

| MB Element | QMS Requirement | Statement of Activity |
|---|---|---|
| 1.2 | Leadership System and Organization | Integrating the company's customer focus and performance expectations into the company's leadership system and organization. |
| 1.2.a | | Focusing the company's leadership system, management, and organization on customers and high performance objectives. |
| 1.2.b | | Communicating and reinforcing the values, expectations, and directions of the company throughout the entire work force. |
| 1.2.c | | Reviewing overall company and work unit performance. |
| | | Using the overall company and work unit performance reviews to improve performance. |
| 1.3 | Public Responsibility and Corporate Citizenship | Including the company's responsibilities to the public in its performance improvement practices. |
| | | Leading and contributing as a corporate citizen in its key communities (the company). |
| 1.3.a | | Integrating the company's public responsibilities into its performance improvement efforts: |
| | | (1) addressing the risks and regulatory and other legal requirements in planning and in setting operational requirements and targets; |
| | | (2) looking ahead to anticipate public concerns and to assess possible impacts on society of the company's products, services, and operations; |
| | | (3) promoting legal and ethical conduct in all that the company does. |
| 1.3.b | | Leading as a corporate citizen in the company's key communities. |
| 2.0 | Information and Analysis | "The Information and Analysis category examines the management and effectiveness of the use of data and information to support customer-driven performance excellence and marketplace success."[2] |
| 2.1 | Management of Information and Data | Selecting and managing information and data used for planning, management, and evaluation of overall performance by the company. |
| 2.1.a | | Selecting and managing information and data needed to drive improvement of overall company performance: |
| | | (1) relating how each of the main types of data and information is related to the key business drivers; |
| | | (2) deriving key requirements such as reliability, rapid access, and rapid update from user needs. |

**Table A.1** QMS Statements of Activity: Malcolm Baldrige (Continued)

| MB Element | QMS Requirement | Statement of Activity |
|---|---|---|
| 2.1.b | | Evaluating and improving the selection, analysis, and integration of information and data, aligning them with the company's business priorities (the company): |
| | | (1) considering the scope of information and data; |
| | | (2) using and analyzing information and data to support process management and performance improvement; |
| | | (3) considering feedback from users of information and data. |
| 2.2 | Competitive Comparisons and Benchmarking | Supporting the company's improvement of overall performance by the use of its processes and the use of comparative information and data. |
| 2.2.a | | Selecting and using competitive comparisons and benchmarking information and data to help drive improvement of overall company performance: |
| | | (1) determining needs and priorities; |
| | | (2) seeking appropriate information and data—from within and outside the company's industry; |
| | | (3) improving understanding of processes and process performance by using the information and data within the company; |
| | | (4) setting stretch targets by use of the information and data encouraging breakthrough approaches by use of the information and data. |
| 2.2.b | | Evaluating and improving the company's overall process for selecting and using competitive comparisons and benchmarking information and data to improve planning and overall company performance. |
| 2.3 | Analysis and Use of Company-Level Data | Analyzing data related to quality, customers, and operational performance, together with relevant financial data, to support company-level review, action, and planning. |
| 2.3.a | | Integrating and analyzing information and data from all parts of the company to support reviews, business decisions, and planning: |
| | | (1) using analysis to gain an understanding of customers and markets; |
| | | (2) using analysis to gain an understanding of operational performance and company capabilities; |
| | | (3) using analysis to gain an understanding of competitive performance. |

**Table A.1** QMS Statements of Activity: Malcolm Baldrige (Continued)

| MB Element | QMS Requirement | Statement of Activity |
|---|---|---|
| 2.3.b | | Relating customer and market data, improvements in product/service quality, and improvements in operational performance to changes in financial and/or market indicators of performance (the company). |
| | | Setting priorities for improvement actions by the use of this information. |
| 3.0 | Strategic Planning | "The Strategic Planning category examines how the company sets strategic directions and how it determines key plan requirements. Also examined is how the plan requirements are translated into an effective performance management system."[3] |
| 3.1 | Strategy Development | Planning overall performance and competitive leadership for short term and the longer term (the company). |
| | | Developing key business drivers to serve as the basis for deploying plan requirements throughout the company. |
| 3.1.a | | Developing strategies and business plans to strengthen its customer-related, operational, and financial performance and its competitive position (the company): |
| | | (1) considering customer requirements and expectations and their expected changes; |
| | | (2) considering the competitive environment; |
| | | (3) considering the risks: financial, market, technological, and societal; |
| | | (4) considering company capabilities—human resource, technology, research and development and business processes—to seek new market leadership opportunities and/or to prepare for key new requirements; |
| | | (5) considering supplier and/or partner capabilities. |
| 3.1.b | | Translating strategies and plans into actionable key business drivers which serve as the basis for deploying plan requirements, addressed in Item 3.2. |
| 3.1.c | | Evaluating and improving the company's strategic planning and plan deployment processes. |
| 3.2 | Strategy Deployment | Deploying the company's key business drivers. |
| | | Projecting the company's performance into the future relative to competitors and key benchmarks. |
| 3.2.a | | Deriving specific key business drivers from the company's strategic direction. |
| | | Translating these drivers into an action plan: |

**Table A.1** QMS Statements of Activity: Malcolm Baldrige (Continued)

| MB Element | QMS Requirement | Statement of Activity |
|---|---|---|
| | | (1) deploying key performance requirements and associated operational performance measures and/or indicators; |
| | | (2) aligning work unit and supplier and/or partner plans and targets by the company; |
| | | (3) including productivity and cycle time improvement and reduction in waste in plans and targets; |
| | | (4) committing the principal resources to the accomplishment of plans, noting any important distinctions between short-term plans and longer-term plans. |
| 3.2.b | | Projecting key measures and/or indicators of the company's customer-related and operational performance for 2–5 years. |
| | | Comparing expected projections for product and/or service quality and operational performance with expected projections for key competitors and key benchmarks over this time period. |
| 4.0 | Human Resource Development and Management | "The Human Resource Development and Management category examines how the work force is enabled to develop and utilize its full potential, aligned with the company's performance objectives. Also examined are the company's efforts to build and maintain an environment conducive to performance excellence, full participation, and personal and organizational growth."[4] |
| 4.1 | Human Resource Planning and Evaluation | Aligning the company's human resource planning and evaluation with its strategic and business plans taking into consideration the development and well-being of the entire work force. |
| 4.1.a | | Translating the company's overall requirements from strategic and business planning (Category 3.0) to specific human resource plans: |
| | | (1) improving flexibility, innovation, and rapid response by making changes in the work design; |
| | | (2) developing, educating, and training employees; |
| | | (3) changing compensation, recognition, and benefits; |
| | | (4) recruiting, including expected or planned changes in demographics of the work force. |
| 4.1.b | | Evaluating and improving the company's human resource planning and practices. |
| | | Aligning the plans and practices with the company's strategic and business directions. |
| | | Analyzing and using employee-related data and company performance data for: |

**Table A.1** QMS Statements of Activity: Malcolm Baldrige (Continued)

| MB Element | QMS Requirement | Statement of Activity |
|---|---|---|
| | | (1) assessing the development and well-being of all categories and types of employees using employee-related data and company performance data where appropriate; |
| | | (2) assessing the linkage of the human resource practices to key business results using employee-related data and company performance data where appropriate; |
| | | (3) ensuring that reliable and complete human resource information is available for company strategic and business planning. |
| 4.2 | High Performance Work Systems | Enabling and encouraging all employees to contribute effectively to achieving high performance objectives by use of the company's work and job design and compensation and recognition approaches. |
| 4.2.a | | Promoting high performance through the company's work and job design: |
| | | (1) creating opportunities for initiative and self-directed responsibility through work and job design; |
| | | (2) responding rapidly and with flexibility to changing requirements through work and job design; |
| | | (3) ensuring effective communications across functions or units that need to work together to meet customer and/or operational requirements through work and job design. |
| 4.2.b | | Reinforcing the effectiveness of the work and job design through the company's compensation and recognition approaches for individuals and groups, including managers. |
| 4.3 | Employee Education, Training, and Development | Addressing company plans, including building company capabilities and contributing to employee motivation, progression, and development, through the company's education and training. |
| 4.3.a | | Educating and training as a key vehicle in building company and employee capabilities: |
| | | (1) addressing key performance objectives, including those related to enhancing high performance work units, with education and training; |
| | | (2) addressing progression and development of all employees, with education and training. |
| 4.3.b | | Designing, delivering, reinforcing and evaluating education and training: |
| | | (1) involving employees and line managers in determining specific education and training needs. |

**Table A.1** QMS Statements of Activity: Malcolm Baldrige (Continued)

| MB Element | QMS Requirement | Statement of Activity |
|---|---|---|
| | | Designing education and training (employees and line managers): |
| | | (2) delivering education and training; |
| | | (3) reinforcing knowledge and skills through on-the-job application; |
| | | (4) evaluating and improving education and training. |
| 4.4 | Employee Well-Being and Satisfaction | Maintaining a work environment and a work climate conducive to the well-being and development of all employees (the company). |
| 4.4.a | | Maintaining a safe and healthful work environment (the company): |
| | | (1) including employee well-being factors such as health, safety, and ergonomics in improvement activities; |
| | | (2) measuring and/or indicating principal improvement requirements and targets for each factor relevant and important to the work environment of the company's employees. |
| 4.4.b | | Supporting the employee's overall well-being and satisfaction by the services, facilities, activities, and opportunities that the company makes available. |
| | | Enhancing the employee's work experience and development potential. |
| 4.4.c | | Determining employee satisfaction, well-being, and motivation. |
| | | Using this information to improve satisfaction, well-being, and motivation. |
| 5.0 | Process Management | "The Process Management category examines the key aspects of process management, including customer-focused design, product and service delivery processes, support services and supply management involving all work units, including research and development. The category examines how key processes are designed, effectively managed, and improved to achieve higher performance."[5] |
| 5.1 | Design and Introduction of Products and Services | Designing and introducing new and/or modified products and services to meet both key product and service quality requirements and company operational performance requirements. |
| | | Designing key production/delivery processes to meet both key product and service quality requirements and company operational performance requirements. |
| 5.1.a | | Designing products, services, and production/delivery processes: |

**Table A.1** QMS Statements of Activity: Malcolm Baldrige (Continued)

| MB Element | QMS Requirement | Statement of Activity |
|---|---|---|
| | | (1) translating customer requirements into product and service design requirements; |
| | | (2) translating product and service design requirements into efficient and effective production/delivery processes, including an appropriate measurement plan; |
| | | (3) addressing all requirements associated with products, services, and production/delivery processes early in design by appropriate company units, suppliers, and partners to ensure integration, coordination, and capability. |
| 5.1.b | | Reviewing and/or testing product, service, and production/delivery process designs in detail to ensure trouble-free launch. |
| 5.1.c | | Evaluating and improving designs and design processes so that introductions of new or modified products and services progressively improve in quality and cycle time. |
| 5.2 | Process Management: Product and Service Production and Delivery | Managing the company's key product and service production/delivery processes to ensure that design requirements are met and that both quality and operational performance are continuously improved. |
| 5.2.a | | Maintaining the performance of key production/delivery processes to ensure that such processes meet design requirements addressed in Item 5.1 (the company): |
| | | (1) the key processes and their principal requirements; |
| | | (2) maintaining process performance by use of the measurement plan and measurements and/or observations. |
| 5.2.b | | Evaluating and improving processes to achieve better operational performance, including cycle time: |
| | | (1) using process analysis and research; |
| | | (2) using benchmarking; |
| | | (3) using alternative technology; |
| | | (4) considering information from customers of the processes—within and outside the company. |
| 5.3 | Process Management: Support Services | Designing and managing the company's key support service processes so that current requirements are met and that operational performance is continuously improved. |
| 5.3.a | | Designing key support service processes: |
| | | (1) determining or setting key requirements; |
| | | (2) translating these requirements into efficient and effective processes, including operational requirements and an appropriate measurement plan; |

**Table A.1** QMS Statements of Activity: Malcolm Baldrige (Continued)

| MB Element | QMS Requirement | Statement of Activity |
|---|---|---|
| | | (3) addressing all requirements early in design by all appropriate company units to ensure integration, coordination, and capability. |
| 5.3.b | | Maintaining the performance of key support service processes to ensure that such processes meet design requirements (the company): |
| | | (1) the key processes and their principal requirements; |
| | | (2) maintaining process performance by use of the measurement plan and measurements. |
| 5.3.c | | Evaluating and improving processes to achieve better operational performance, including cycle time: |
| | | (1) using process analysis and research; |
| | | (2) using benchmarking; |
| | | (3) using alternative technology; |
| | | (4) considering information from customers of the processes—within and outside the company. |
| 5.4 | Management of Supplier Performance | Ensuring that materials, components, and services furnished by other businesses meet the company's performance requirements (the company). |
| | | Improving supplier relationships and performance through the company's actions and plans. |
| 5.4.a | | Communicating the company's requirements to suppliers: |
| | | (1) a brief summary of the principal requirements for key suppliers, the measures and/or indicators associated with these requirements, and the expected performance levels; |
| | | (2) determining whether or not the company's requirements are met by suppliers; |
| | | (3) feeding back performance information to suppliers. |
| 5.4.b | | Evaluating and improving the company's management of supplier relationships and performance: |
| | | (1) improving suppliers' abilities to meet requirements; |
| | | (2) improving the company's own procurement processes; seeking and using feedback from suppliers and from other units within the company; |
| | | (3) minimizing costs associated with inspection, test, audit, or other approaches used to verify supplier performance. |

**Table A.1** QMS Statements of Activity: Malcolm Baldrige (Continued)

| MB Element | QMS Requirement | Statement of Activity |
|---|---|---|
| 6.0 | Business Results | "The Business Results category examines the company's performance and improvement in key business areas—product and service quality, productivity and operational effectiveness, supply quality, and financial performance indicators linked to these areas. Also examined are performance levels relative to those of competitors."[6] |
| 6.1 | Product and Service Quality Results | Improving product and service quality by using key measures and/or indicators. |
| 6.1.a | | Using current levels and trends in key measures and/or indicators of product and service quality, including appropriate comparative data. |
| 6.2 | Company Operational and Financial Results | Improving company operational and financial performance by using key measures and/or indicators. |
| 6.2.a | | Using current levels and trends in key measures and/or indicators of company operational and financial performance, including appropriate comparative data. |
| 6.3 | Supplier Performance Results | Improving supplier performance by using key measures and/or indicators of such performance. |
| 6.3.a | | Using current levels and trends in key measures and/or indicators of supplier performance, including appropriate comparative data. |
| 7.0 | Customer Focus and Satisfaction | "The Customer Focus and Satisfaction category examines the company's systems for customer learning and for building and maintaining customer relationships. Also examined are levels and trends in key measures of business success—customer satisfaction and retention, market share, and satisfaction relative to competitors."[7] |
| 7.1 | Customer and Market Knowledge | Determining near-term and longer-term requirements and expectations of customers and markets (the company). |
| | | Developing listening and learning strategies to understand and anticipate needs (the company). |
| 7.1.a | | Determining current and near-term requirements and expectations of customers (the company): |
| | | (1) determining and/or selecting customer groups and/or market segments, considering customers of competitors and other potential customers; |
| | | (2) collecting information, including what information is sought, frequency and methods of collection. |
| | | Ensuring objectivity and validity: |
| | | (3) determining specific product and service features and the relative importance of these features to customer groups or segments; |

**Table A.1** QMS Statements of Activity: Malcolm Baldrige (Continued)

| MB Element | QMS Requirement | Statement of Activity |
| --- | --- | --- |
| | | (4) using other key information and data such as complaints, gains and losses of customers, and product/service performance, to support the determination. |
| 7.1.b | | Addressing future requirements and expectations of customers (the company). |
| | | Using key listening and learning strategies (the company). |
| 7.1.c | | Evaluating and improving the company's processes for determining customer requirements and expectations. |
| 7.2 | Customer Relationship Management | Providing effective management of the company's responses and follow ups with customers to preserve and build relationships and to increase knowledge about specific customers and about general customer expectations. |
| 7.2.a | | Providing information and easy access to enable customers to seek information and assistance, to comment, and to complain (the company). |
| | | Setting, deploying, and tracking contact management performance measures and service standards. |
| 7.2.b | | Resolving formal and informal complaints and feedback received by all company units effectively and promptly (the company). |
| | | Ensuring effective recovery of customer confidence (the company). |
| | | Meeting customer requirements for resolution effectiveness (the company). |
| | | Eliminating causes of complaints (the company). |
| 7.2.c | | Following up with customers on products, services, and recent transactions (the company). |
| | | Determining satisfaction (the company). |
| | | Resolving problems (the company). |
| | | Seeking feedback for improvement (the company). |
| | | Building relationships (the company). |
| 7.2.d | | Evaluating and improving the company's customer relationship management: |
| | | (1) improving service standards, including those related to access and complaint management, based upon customer information; |
| | | (2) Aggregating and using customer comments and complaints throughout the company; |
| | | (3) accumulating knowledge about customers. |

**Table A.1** QMS Statements of Activity: Malcolm Baldrige (Continued)

| MB Element | QMS Requirement | Statement of Activity |
|---|---|---|
| 7.3 | Customer Satisfaction Determination | Determining customer satisfaction, customer repurchase intentions, and customer satisfaction relative to competitors (the company). |
| | | Evaluating and improving determination processes (the company). |
| 7.3.a | | Determining customer satisfaction (the company): |
| | | (1) ensuring objectivity and validity; |
| | | (2) capturing key information that reflects customers' likely future market behavior, such as repurchase intentions and/or positive referrals, by the use of customer satisfaction measurements. |
| 7.3.b | | Determining customer satisfaction relative to that for competitors: |
| | | (1) using company-based comparative studies; |
| | | (2) using comparative studies or evaluations made by independent organizations and/or customers. |
| | | Ensuring objectivity and validity of studies or evaluations. |
| 7.3.c | | Evaluating and improving the company's overall processes and measurement scales for determining customer satisfaction and customer satisfaction relative to that for competitors. |
| | | Using other indicators (such as gains and losses of customers) and customer dissatisfaction indicators (such as complaints) in the improvement process. |
| | | Taking into account the effectiveness of the use of customer satisfaction information and data throughout the company. |
| 7.4 | Customer Satisfaction Results | Determining the company's customer satisfaction and customer dissatisfaction results using key measures and/or indicators of these results. |
| 7.4.a | | Using current levels and trends in key measures and/or indicators of customer satisfaction and customer retention. |
| | | Segmenting results by customer group. |
| 7.4.b | | Using current levels and trends in key measures and/or indicators of customer dissatisfaction. |
| | | Addressing the most relevant and important indicators for the company's products/services. |
| 7.5 | Customer Satisfaction Comparison | Comparing the company's customer satisfaction results with those of competitors. |
| 7.5.a | | Using current levels and trends in key measures and/or indicators of customer satisfaction relative to competitors. |

**Table A.1** QMS Statements of Activity: Malcolm Baldrige (Continued)

| MB Element | QMS Requirement | Statement of Activity |
|---|---|---|
| | | Including gains and losses of customers or customer accounts to competitors. |
| | | Including objective information and/or data from independent organizations, including customers. |
| | | Segmenting results by customer group. |
| 7.5.b | | Determining trends in gaining or losing market share to competitors. |

[1]U.S. Department of Commerce, *The Malcolm Baldrige National Quality Award* (National Institute of Standards and Technology, 1995), p. 21.
[2]Ibid., p. 23.
[3]Ibid., p. 25.
[4]Ibid., p. 27.
[5]Ibid., p. 30.
[6]Ibid., p. 34.
[7]Ibid., p. 36.

P P E N D I X

# B

# QMS Statements of Activity: ISO 9001

**Table B.1** QMS Statements of Activity: ISO 9001 (ANSI/ASQC Q9001–1994)

| ISO Element | QMS Requirement | Statement of Activity |
|---|---|---|
| 4.1 | Management Responsibility | |
| 4.1.1 | Quality Policy | Defining and documenting its policy for quality, including objectives for quality and its commitment to quality (supplier's management with executive responsibility). |
| | | Ensuring relevancy to the supplier's organizational goals and the expectations and needs of its customers (quality policy). |
| | | Ensuring that this policy is understood, implemented, and maintained at all levels of the organization (the supplier). |
| 4.1.2 | Organization | |
| 4.1.2.1 | Responsibility and Authority | Defining and documenting the responsibility, authority, and interrelation of personnel who manage, perform, and verify work affecting quality, particularly for personnel who need the organizational freedom and authority for: |
| | | a) initiating action to prevent the occurrence of any nonconformities relating to product, process, and quality system; |
| | | b) identifying and recording any problems relating to the product, process, and quality system; |
| | | c) initiating, recommending, or providing solutions through designated channels; |
| | | d) verifying the implementation of solutions; |

**Table B.1** QMS Statements of Activity: ISO 9001 (ANSI/ASQC Q9001–1994) (Continued)

| ISO Element | QMS Requirement | Statement of Activity |
|---|---|---|
| | | e) controlling further processing, delivery, or installation of nonconforming product until the deficiency or unsatisfactory condition has been corrected. |
| 4.1.2.2 | Resources | Identifying resource requirements (the supplier). |
| | | Providing adequate resources, including the assignment of trained personnel (see 4.18), for management, performance of work, and verification activities including internal quality audits. |
| 4.1.2.3 | Management Representative | Appointing a member of the supplier's own management who, irrespective of other responsibilities, shall have defined authority for a and b (the supplier's management with executive responsibility): |
| | | a) ensuring that a quality system is established, implemented, and maintained in accordance with this American National Standard, and |
| | | b) reporting on the performance of the quality system to the supplier's management for review and as a basis for improvement of the quality system. |
| 4.1.3 | Management Review | Reviewing the quality system at defined intervals sufficient to ensure its continuing suitability and effectiveness in satisfying the requirements of this American National Standard and the supplier's stated quality policy and objectives (see 4.1.1) (the supplier's management with executive responsibility). |
| | | Maintaining records of such reviews (see 4.16). |
| 4.2 | Quality System | |
| 4.2.1 | General | Establishing, documenting, and maintaining a quality system as a means of ensuring that product conforms to specified requirements (the supplier). The supplier shall prepare a quality manual covering the requirements of this American National Standard. The quality manual shall include or make reference to the quality-system procedures and outline the structure of the documentation used in the quality system: |
| 4.2.2 | Quality-System Procedures | a) preparing documented procedures consistent with the requirements of this American National Standard and the supplier's stated quality policy (the supplier). |
| | | b) implementing the quality system and its documented procedures effectively (the supplier). |
| 4.2.3 | Quality Planning | Defining and documenting how the requirements for quality will be met (the supplier). |
| | | Ensuring consistency with all other requirements of a supplier's quality system (quality planning). |

**Table B.1** QMS Statements of Activity: ISO 9001 (ANSI/ASQC Q9001–1994) (Continued)

| ISO Element | QMS Requirement | Statement of Activity |
|---|---|---|
| | | Documenting in a format to suit the supplier's method of operation (quality planning). |
| | | Considering the following activities, as appropriate, in meeting the specified requirements for products, projects, or contracts: (the supplier) |
| | | a) the preparation of quality plans; |
| | | b) the identification and acquisition of any controls, processes, equipment (including inspection and test equipment), fixtures, resources, and skills that may be needed to achieve the required quality; |
| | | c) ensuring the compatibility of the design, the production process, installation, servicing, inspection and test procedures, and the applicable documentation; |
| | | d) the updating, as necessary, of quality control, inspection, and testing techniques, including the development of new instrumentation; |
| | | e) the identification of any measurement requirement involving capability that exceeds the known state of the art, in sufficient time for the needed capability to be developed; |
| | | f) the identification of suitable verification at appropriate stages in the realization of product; |
| | | g) the clarification of standards of acceptability for all features and requirements, including those that contain a subjective element; |
| | | h) the identification and preparation of quality records (see 4.16). |
| 4.3 | Contract Review | |
| 4.3.1 | General | Establishing and maintaining documented procedures for contract review and for the coordination of these activities (the supplier). |
| 4.3.2 | Review | Reviewing by the supplier, before submission of a tender, or at the acceptance of a contract or order (statement of requirement), the tender, contract, or order to ensure that: |
| | | a) the requirements are adequately defined and documented; where no written statement of requirement is available for an order received by verbal means, the supplier shall ensure that the order requirements are agreed before their acceptance; |
| | | b) any differences between the contract or accepted order requirements and those in the tender are resolved; |

**Table B.1** QMS Statements of Activity: ISO 9001 (ANSI/ASQC Q9001–1994) (Continued)

| ISO Element | QMS Requirement | Statement of Activity |
|---|---|---|
| | | c) the supplier has the capability to meet the contract or accepted order requirements. |
| 4.3.3 | Amendment to Contract | Identifying how an amendment to a contract is made and correctly transferred to the functions concerned within the supplier's organization (the supplier). |
| 4.3.4 | Records | Maintaining records of contract reviews (see 4.16). |
| | | Establishing channels for communication and interfaces with the customer's organization in these contract matters. |
| 4.4 | Design Control | |
| 4.4.1 | General | Establishing and maintaining documented procedures to control and verify the design of the product in order to ensure that the specified requirements are met (the supplier). |
| 4.4.2 | Design and Development Planning | Preparing plans for each design and development activity (the supplier). The plans shall describe or reference these activities, and define responsibility for their implementation. The design and development activities shall be assigned to qualified personnel equipped with adequate resources. The plans shall be updated, as the design evolves. |
| 4.4.3 | Organizational and Technical Interfaces | Defining organizational and technical interfaces between different groups which input into the design process. |
| | | Documenting, transmitting, and reviewing regularly, the necessary information. |
| 4.4.4 | Design Input | Identifying, documenting, and reviewing for adequacy by the supplier, design-input requirements relating to the product, including applicable statutory and regulatory requirements. |
| | | Resolving incomplete, ambiguous, or conflicting requirements with those responsible for imposing these requirements. |
| | | Taking into consideration the results of any contract-review activities (design input). |
| 4.4.5 | Design Output | Documenting and expressing the design output in terms that can be verified against design-input requirements and validated (see 4.4.8). |
| | | Design output shall: |
| | | a) meet the design-input requirements; |
| | | b) contain or make reference to acceptance criteria; |
| | | c) identify those characteristics of the design that are crucial to the safe and proper functioning of the product (e.g., operating, storage, handling, maintenance, and disposal requirements). |
| | | Reviewing the design-output documents before release. |

**Table B.1** QMS Statements of Activity: ISO 9001 (ANSI/ASQC Q9001–1994) (Continued)

| ISO Element | QMS Requirement | Statement of Activity |
| --- | --- | --- |
| 4.4.6 | Design Review | Planning and conducting formal documented reviews of the design results, at appropriate stages of design. Participants at each design review shall include representatives of all functions concerned with the design stage being reviewed, as well as other specialist personnel, as required. |
|  |  | Maintaining records of such reviews (see 4.16). |
| 4.4.7 | Design Verification | Performing design verification to ensure that the design-stage output meets the design-stage input requirements, at appropriate stages of design. |
|  |  | Recording design-verification measures (see 4.16). |
|  |  | NOTE 10 In addition to conducting design reviews (see 4.4.6), design verification may include activities such as: |
|  |  | performing alternative calculations, |
|  |  | comparing the new design with a similar proven design, if available, |
|  |  | undertaking tests and demonstrations, and |
|  |  | reviewing the design-stage documents before release. |
| 4.4.8 | Design Validation | Performing design validation to ensure that product conforms to defined user needs and/or requirements. |
|  |  | NOTES |
|  |  | 11 Design validation follows successful design verification (see 4.4.7). |
|  |  | 12 Validation is normally performed under defined operating conditions. |
|  |  | 13 Validation is normally performed on the final product, but may be necessary in earlier stages prior to product completion. |
|  |  | 14 Multiple validations may be performed if there are different intended uses. |
| 4.4.9 | Design Changes | Identifying, documenting, reviewing, and approving by authorized personnel, all design changes and modifications, before their implementation. |
| 4.5 | Document and Data Control | |
| 4.5.1 | General | Establishing and maintaining documented procedures to control all documents and data that relate to the requirements of this American National Standard including, to the extent applicable, documents of external origin such as standards and customer drawings (the supplier). |

**Table B.1** QMS Statements of Activity: ISO 9001 (ANSI/ASQC Q9001–1994) (Continued)

| ISO Element | QMS Requirement | Statement of Activity |
|---|---|---|
| 4.5.2 | Document and Data Approval and Issue | Reviewing and approving for adequacy by authorized personnel prior to issue (documents and data). |
| | | Establishing and making readily available a master list or equivalent document-control procedure identifying the current revision status of documents, to preclude the use of invalid and/or obsolete documents. |
| | | This control shall ensure that: |
| | | a) the pertinent issues of appropriate documents are available at all locations where operations essential to the effective functioning of the quality system are performed; |
| | | b) invalid and/or obsolete documents are promptly removed from all points of issue or use, or otherwise assured against unintended use; |
| | | c) any obsolete documents retained for legal and/or knowledge-preservation purposes are suitably identified. |
| 4.5.3 | Document and Data Changes | Reviewing and approving changes to documents and data by the same functions/organizations that performed the original review and approval, unless specifically designated otherwise. |
| | | The designated functions/organizations shall have access to pertinent background information upon which to base their review and approval. |
| | | Where practicable, the nature of the change shall be identified in the document or the appropriate attachments. |
| 4.6 | Purchasing | |
| 4.6.1 | General | Establishing and maintaining documented procedures to ensure that purchased product (see 3.1) conforms to specified requirements (the supplier): |
| 4.6.2 | Evaluation of Sub-Contractors | a) evaluating and selecting subcontractors on the basis of their ability to meet subcontract requirements including the quality system and any specific quality-assurance requirements; |
| | | b) defining the type and extent of control exercised by the supplier over subcontractors. |
| | | c) establishing and maintaining quality records of acceptable subcontractors (see 4.16). |
| 4.6.3 | Purchasing Data | Containing data clearly describing the product ordered (purchasing documents): |
| | | a) the type, class, grade, or other precise identification; |

**Table B.1** QMS Statements of Activity: ISO 9001 (ANSI/ASQC Q9001–1994) (Continued)

| ISO Element | QMS Requirement | Statement of Activity |
|---|---|---|
| | | b) the title or other positive identification, and applicable issues of specifications, drawings, process requirements, inspection instructions, and other relevant technical data, including requirements for approval or qualification of product, procedures, process equipment, and personnel; |
| | | c) the title, number, and issue of the quality-system standard to be applied. |
| | | Reviewing and approving purchasing documents for adequacy of the specified requirements prior to release (the supplier). |
| 4.6.4 | Verification of Purchased Product | |
| 4.6.4.1 | Supplier Verification at Subcontractor's Premises | Specifying verification arrangements and the method of product release in the purchasing documents, where the supplier proposes to verify purchased product at the subcontractor's premises. |
| 4.6.4.2 | Customer Verification of Subcontracted Product | Affording the right to verify at the subcontractor's premises and the supplier's premises, by the supplier's customer or the customer's representative, that subcontracted product conforms to specified requirements, where specified in the contract. |
| 4.7 | Control of Customer-Supplied Product | Establishing and maintaining documented procedures for the control of verification, storage, and maintenance of customer-supplied product provided for incorporation into the supplies or for related activities (the supplier). |
| | | Recording and reporting to the customer, any such product that is lost, damaged, or is otherwise unsuitable for use (see 4.16). |
| 4.8 | Product Identification and Traceability | Establishing and maintaining documented procedures for identifying the product by suitable means from receipt and during all stages of production, delivery, and installation (the supplier). |
| | | Establishing and maintaining documented procedures for unique identification of individual product or batches, where and to the extent that traceability is a specified requirement (the supplier). |
| | | Recording this identification (see 4.16). |
| 4.9 | Process Control | Identifying and planning the production, installation, and servicing processes that directly affect quality (the supplier). |
| | | Ensuring that these processes are carried out under controlled conditions. |
| | | Controlled conditions shall include the following: |
| | | a) documented procedures defining the manner of production, installation, and servicing, where the absence of such procedures could adversely affect quality; |

**Table B.1** QMS Statements of Activity: ISO 9001 (ANSI/ASQC Q9001–1994) (Continued)

| ISO Element | QMS Requirement | Statement of Activity |
|---|---|---|
| | | b) use of suitable production, installation, and servicing equipment, and a suitable working environment; |
| | | c) compliance with reference standards/codes, quality plans, and/or documented procedures; |
| | | d) monitoring and control of suitable process parameters and product characteristics; |
| | | e) the approval of processes and equipment, as appropriate; |
| | | f) criteria for workmanship, which shall be stipulated in the clearest practical manner (e.g., written standards, representative samples, or illustrations); |
| | | g) suitable maintenance of equipment to ensure continuing process capability. |
| | | Carrying out the processes by qualified operators, where the results of processes cannot be fully verified by subsequent inspection and testing of the product and where, for example, processing deficiencies may become apparent only after the product is in use. |
| | | Monitoring and controlling process parameters to ensure that the specified requirements are met, where the results of processes cannot be fully verified by subsequent inspection and testing of the product and where, for example, processing deficiencies may become apparent only after the product is in use. |
| | | Specifying the requirements for any qualification of process operations, including associated equipment and personnel (see 4.18). |
| | | Maintaining records for qualified processes, equipment, and personnel, as appropriate (see 4.16). |
| 4.10 | Inspection and Testing | |
| 4.10.1 | General | Establishing and maintaining documented procedures for inspection and testing activities in order to verify that the specified requirements for the product are met (the supplier). |
| | | Detailing the required inspection and testing, and the records to be established, in the quality plan or documented procedures. |
| 4.10.2 | Receiving Inspection and Testing | |
| 4.10.2.1 | | Ensuring that incoming product is not used or processed (except in the circumstances described in 4.10.2.3) until it has been inspected or otherwise verified as conforming to specified requirements (the supplier). |

**Table B.1** QMS Statements of Activity: ISO 9001 (ANSI/ASQC Q9001–1994) (Continued)

| ISO Element | QMS Requirement | Statement of Activity |
|---|---|---|
| | | Verifying that the specified requirements are in accordance with the quality plan and/or documented procedures. |
| 4.10.2.2 | | Determining the amount and nature of receiving inspection, considering the amount of control exercised at the subcontractor's premises and the recorded evidence of conformance provided. |
| 4.10.2.3 | | Identifying and recording incoming product released for urgent production purposes prior to verification, (see 4.16), in order to permit immediate recall and replacement in the event of nonconformity to specified requirements. |
| 4.10.3 | In-Process Inspection and Testing | a) inspecting and testing the product as required by the quality plan and/or documented procedures; |
| | | b) holding product until the required inspection and tests have been completed or necessary reports have been received and verified, except when product is released under positive-recall procedures (see 4.10.2.3). |
| 4.10.4 | Final Inspection and Testing | Carrying out all final inspection and testing in accordance with the quality plan and/or documented procedures to complete the evidence of conformance of the finished product to the specified requirements (the supplier). |
| | | Requiring that all specified inspection and tests, including those specified either on receipt of product or in-process, have been carried out and that the results meet specified requirements, in the quality plan and/or documented procedures for final inspection and testing. |
| | | Completing all the activities specified in the quality plan and/or documented procedures satisfactorily, with the associated data and documentation available and authorized. |
| 4.10.5 | Inspection and Test Records | Establishing and maintaining records which provide evidence that the product has been inspected and/or tested (the supplier). These records shall show clearly whether the product has passed or failed the inspections and/or tests according to defined acceptance criteria. Where the product fails to pass any inspection and/or test, the procedures for control of nonconforming product shall apply (see 4.13). |
| | | Records shall identify the inspection authority responsible for the release of product (see 4.16). |
| 4.11 | Control of Inspection, Measuring, and Test Equipment | |

**Table B.1** QMS Statements of Activity: ISO 9001 (ANSI/ASQC Q9001–1994) (Continued)

| ISO Element | QMS Requirement | Statement of Activity |
|---|---|---|
| 4.11.1 | General | Establishing and maintaining documented procedures to control, calibrate, and maintain inspection, measuring, and test equipment (including test software) used by the supplier to demonstrate the conformance of product to the specified requirements (the supplier). |
| | | Using inspection, measuring, and test equipment in a manner that ensures that the measurement uncertainty is known and is consistent with the required measurement capability. |
| | | Checking where test software or comparative references such as test hardware are used as suitable forms of inspection, to prove that they are capable of verifying the acceptability of product, prior to release for use during production, installation, or servicing. |
| | | Rechecking at prescribed intervals, where test software or comparative references such as test hardware are used as suitable forms of inspection, to prove that they are capable of verifying the acceptability of product, prior to release for use during production, installation, or servicing. |
| | | Establishing the extent and frequency of such checks (the supplier). |
| | | Maintaining records as evidence of control (see 4.16) (the supplier). |
| | | Verifying that the measuring equipment is functionally adequate: |
| 4.11.2 | Control Procedure | a) determining the measurements to be made and the accuracy required. |
| | | Selecting the appropriate inspection, measuring, and test equipment that is capable of the necessary accuracy and precision: |
| | | b) identifying all inspection, measuring, and test equipment that can affect product quality. |
| | | Calibrating and adjusting them at prescribed intervals, or prior to use, against certified equipment having a known valid relationship to internationally or nationally recognized standards. |
| | | Documenting the basis used for calibration, where no such standards exist. |
| | | c) defining the process employed for the calibration of inspection, measuring, and test equipment, including details of equipment type, unique identification, location, frequency of checks, check method, acceptance criteria, and action to be taken when results are unsatisfactory; |

**Table B.1** QMS Statements of Activity: ISO 9001 (ANSI/ASQC Q9001–1994) (Continued)

| ISO Element | QMS Requirement | Statement of Activity |
|---|---|---|
| | | d) identifying inspection, measuring, and test equipment with a suitable indicator or approved identification record to show the calibration status; |
| | | e) maintaining calibration records for inspection, measuring, and test equipment (see 4.16); |
| | | f) assessing and documenting the validity of previous inspection and test results when inspection, measuring, and test equipment is found to be out of calibration; |
| | | g) ensuring that the environmental conditions are suitable for the calibrations, inspections, measurements, and tests being carried out; |
| | | h) ensuring that the handling, preservation, and storage of inspection, measuring, and test equipment is such that the accuracy and fitness for use are maintained; |
| | | i) safeguarding inspection, measuring, and test facilities, including both test hardware and test software, from adjustments which would invalidate the calibration setting. |
| 4.12 | Inspection and Test Status | Identifying the inspection and test status of product, by suitable means, which indicate the conformance or nonconformance of product with regard to inspection and tests performed. |
| | | Maintaining the identification of inspection and test status, as defined in the quality plan and/or documented procedures, throughout production, installation, and servicing of the product to ensure that only product that has passed the required inspections and tests [or released under an authorized concession (see 4.13.2)] is dispatched, used, or installed. |
| 4.13 | Control of Nonconforming Product | |
| 4.13.1 | General | Establishing and maintaining documented procedures to ensure that product that does not conform to specified requirements is prevented from unintended use or installation (the supplier). |
| | | Providing for identification, documentation, evaluation, segregation (when practical), disposition of nonconforming product, and notification to the functions concerned. |
| 4.13.2 | Review and Disposition of Nonconforming Product | Defining the responsibility for review and authority for the disposition of nonconforming product. |
| | | Reviewing the nonconforming product in accordance with documented procedures. It may be |
| | | a) reworked to meet the specified requirements, |

**Table B.1** QMS Statements of Activity: ISO 9001 (ANSI/ASQC Q9001–1994) (Continued)

| ISO Element | QMS Requirement | Statement of Activity |
|---|---|---|
| | | b) accepted with or without repair by concession, |
| | | c) regraded for alternative applications, or |
| | | d) rejected or scrapped. |
| | | Reporting for concession to the customer or customer's representative, where required by the contract, the proposed use or repair of product (see 4.13.2b), which does not conform to specified requirements. |
| | | Recording to denote the actual condition (see 4.16), the description of the nonconformity that has been accepted, and the description of repairs. |
| | | Reinspecting repaired and/or reworked product in accordance with the quality plan and/or documented procedures. |
| 4.14 | Corrective and Preventative Action | |
| 4.14.1 | General | Establishing and maintaining documented procedures for implementing corrective and preventive action (the supplier). |
| | | Taking corrective or preventive action to eliminate the causes of actual or potential nonconformities to the degree appropriate to the magnitude of problems and commensurate with the risks encountered. |
| | | Implementing and recording any changes to the documented procedures resulting from corrective and preventive action (the supplier). |
| 4.14.2 | Corrective Action | The procedures for corrective action shall include: |
| | | a) handling, effectively, customer complaints and reports of product nonconformities; |
| | | b) investigating the cause of nonconformities relating to product, process, and quality system. |
| | | Recording the results of the investigation (see 4.16): |
| | | c) determining the corrective action needed to eliminate the cause of nonconformities; |
| | | d) applying controls to ensure that corrective action is taken and that it is effective. |
| 4.14.3 | Preventative Action | The procedures for preventative action shall include: |
| | | a) using appropriate sources of information such as processes and work operations that affect product quality, concessions, audit results, quality records, service reports, and customer complaints to detect, analyze, and eliminate potential causes of nonconformities; |

**Table B.1** QMS Statements of Activity: ISO 9001 (ANSI/ASQC Q9001–1994) (Continued)

| ISO Element | QMS Requirement | Statement of Activity |
|---|---|---|
| | | b) determining the steps needed to deal with any problems requiring preventive action; |
| | | c) initiating preventive action and application of controls to ensure that it is effective; |
| | | d) confirming that relevant information on actions taken is submitted for management review (see 4.1.3). |
| 4.15 | Handling, Storage, Packaging, Preservation, and Delivery | |
| 4.15.1 | General | Establishing and maintaining documented procedures for handling, storage, packaging, preservation, and delivery of product (the supplier). |
| 4.15.2 | Handling | Providing methods of handling product that prevent damage or deterioration (the supplier). |
| 4.15.3 | Storage | Using designated storage areas or stock rooms to prevent damage or deterioration of product, pending use or delivery (the supplier). |
| | | Stipulating appropriate methods for authorizing receipt to and dispatch from such areas. |
| | | Assessing the condition of product in stock in order to detect deterioration, at appropriate intervals. |
| 4.15.4 | Packaging | Controlling packing, packaging, and marking processes (including materials used) to the extent necessary to ensure conformance to specified requirements (the supplier). |
| 4.15.5 | Preservation | Applying appropriate methods for preservation and segregation of product when the product is under the supplier's control. |
| 4.15.6 | Delivery | Arranging for the protection of the quality of product after final inspection and test (the supplier). |
| | | Extending where contractually specified, this protection to include delivery to destination. |
| 4.16 | Control of Quality Records | Establishing and maintaining documented procedures for identification, collection, indexing, access, filing, storage, maintenance, and disposition of quality records (the supplier). |
| | | Maintaining quality records to demonstrate conformance to specified requirements and the effective operation of the quality system. |
| | | Ensuring that all quality records shall be legible and shall be stored and retained in such a way that they are readily retrievable in facilities that provide a suitable environment to prevent damage or deterioration and to prevent loss. |

**Table B.1** QMS Statements of Activity: ISO 9001 (ANSI/ASQC Q9001–1994) (Continued)

| ISO Element | QMS Requirement | Statement of Activity |
|---|---|---|
| | | Establishing and recording retention times for quality records. |
| | | Ensuring where agreed contractually, that quality records shall be made available for evaluation by the customer or the customer's representative for an agreed period. |
| 4.17 | Internal Quality Audits | Establishing and maintaining documented procedures for planning and implementing internal quality audits to verify whether quality activities and related results comply with planned arrangements and to determine the effectiveness of the quality system (the supplier). |
| | | Scheduling internal quality audits on the basis of the status and importance of the activity to be audited. |
| | | Performing internal quality audits (by personnel independent of those having direct responsibility for the activity being audited). |
| | | Recording and bringing to the attention of the personnel having responsibility in the area audited, the results of the audits (see 4.16). |
| | | Taking timely corrective action on deficiencies found during the audit, by the management personnel responsible for the area. |
| | | Verifying and recording by follow-up audit activities, the implementation and effectiveness of the corrective action taken (see 4.16). |
| 4.18 | Training | Establishing and maintaining documented procedures for identifying training needs and provide for the training of all personnel performing activities affecting quality (the supplier). |
| | | Qualifying personnel performing specific assigned tasks on the basis of appropriate education, training, and/or experience, as required. |
| | | Maintaining appropriate records of training (see 4.16). |
| 4.19 | Servicing | Establishing and maintaining documented procedures for performing, verifying, and reporting that the servicing meets the specified requirements, where servicing is a specified requirement (the supplier). |
| 4.20 | Statistical Techniques | |
| 4.20.1 | Identification of Need | Identifying the need for statistical techniques required for establishing, controlling, and verifying process capability and product characteristics (the supplier). |
| 4.20.2 | Procedures | Establishing and maintaining documented procedures to implement and control the application of the statistical techniques identified in 4.20.1 (the supplier). |

# QMS Statements of Activity: SEI CMM

**Table C.1** QMS Statements of Activity: SEI CMM

| SEI Element | QMS Requirement | Statement of Activity |
|---|---|---|
| LEVEL 1 | INITIAL | "The software process is characterized as ad hoc, and occasionally even chaotic. Few processes are defined, and success depends on individual effort."[1] |
| LEVEL 2 | REPEATABLE | "Basic project management processes are established to track cost, schedule, and functionality. The necessary process discipline is in place to repeat earlier successes on projects with similar applications."[2] |
| RM | Requirements Management | "The purpose of Requirements Management is to establish a common understanding between the customer and the software project of the customer's requirements that will be addressed by the software project."[3] |
| RM.GO.1 | | Controlling system requirements allocated to software to establish a baseline for software engineering and management use. |
| RM.GO.2 | | Keeping software plans, products, and activities consistent with the system requirements allocated to software. |
| RM.CO.1 | | Following a written organizational policy for managing the system requirements allocated to software (the project). |
| RM.AB.1 | | Establishing responsibility for analyzing the system requirements and allocating them to hardware, software, and other system components (for each project). |
| RM.AB.2 | | Documenting the allocated requirements. |

**Table C.1** QMS Statements of Activity: SEI CMM (Continued)

| SEI Element | QMS Requirement | Statement of Activity |
| --- | --- | --- |
| RM.AB.3 | | Providing adequate resources and funding for managing the allocated requirements. |
| RM.AB.4 | | Training members of the software engineering group and other software-related groups to perform their requirements management activities. |
| RM.AC.1 | | Reviewing the allocated requirements before they are incorporated into the software project (the software engineering group). |
| RM.AC.2 | | Using the allocated requirements as the basis for software plans, work products, and activities (the software engineering group). |
| RM.AC.3 | | Reviewing and incorporating, into the software project, changes to the allocated requirements. |
| RM.ME.1 | | Making and using measurements to determine the status of the activities for managing the allocated requirements. |
| RM.VE.1 | | Reviewing the activities for managing the allocated requirements with senior management on a periodic basis. |
| RM.VE.2 | | Reviewing the activities for managing the allocated requirements with the project manager on both a periodic and event-driven basis. |
| RM.VE.3 | | Reviewing and/or auditing the activities and work products for managing the allocated requirements (the software quality assurance group). |
| | | Reporting the results of reviewing and/or auditing the activities and work products for managing the allocated requirements (the software quality assurance group). |
| PP | Software Project Planning | "The purpose of Software Project Planning is to establish reasonable plans for performing the software engineering and for managing the software project."[4] |
| PP.GO.1 | | Documenting software estimates for use in planning and tracking the software project. |
| PP.GO.2 | | Planning and documenting software project activities and commitments. |
| PP.GO.3 | | Agreeing to their commitments related to the software project (affected groups and individuals). |
| PP.CO.1 | | Designating a project software manager to be responsible for negotiating commitments and developing the project's software development plan. |
| PP.CO.2 | | Following a written organizational policy for planning a software project (the project). |

**Table C.1** QMS Statements of Activity: SEI CMM (Continued)

| SEI Element | QMS Requirement | Statement of Activity |
|---|---|---|
| PP.AB.1 | | Documenting and approving a statement of work for the software project. |
| PP.AB.2 | | Assigning responsibilities for developing the software development plan. |
| PP.AB.3 | | Providing adequate resources and funding for planning the software project. |
| PP.AB.4 | | Training the software managers, software engineers, and other individuals involved in the software project planning in software estimating and planning procedures applicable to their areas of responsibility. |
| PP.AC.1 | | Participating on the project proposal team (the software engineering group). |
| PP.AC.2 | | Initiating software project planning in the early stages of, and in parallel with, the overall project planning. |
| PP.AC.3 | | Participating with other affected groups in the overall project planning throughout the project's life (the software engineering group). |
| PP.AC.4 | | Reviewing with senior management, according to a documented procedure, software project commitments made to individuals and groups external to the organization. |
| PP.AC.5 | | Identifying or defining a software life cycle with predefined stages of manageable size. |
| PP.AC.6 | | Developing the project's software development plan according to a documented procedure. |
| PP.AC.7 | | Documenting the plan for the software project. |
| PP.AC.8 | | Identifying software work products that are needed to establish and maintain control of the software project. |
| PP.AC.9 | | Deriving estimates for the size of the software work products (or changes to the size of software work products), according to a documented procedure. |
| PP.AC.10 | | Deriving estimates for the software project's effort and costs, according to a documented procedure. |
| PP.AC.11 | | Deriving estimates for the project's critical computer resources, according to a documented procedure. |
| PP.AC.12 | | Deriving the project's software schedule, according to a documented procedure. |
| PP.AC.13 | | Identifying, assessing, and documenting the software risks associated with the cost, resource, schedule, and technical aspects of the project. |

**Table C.1** QMS Statements of Activity: SEI CMM (Continued)

| SEI Element | QMS Requirement | Statement of Activity |
|---|---|---|
| PP.AC.14 | | Preparing plans for the project's software engineering facilities and support tools. |
| PP.AC.15 | | Recording software planning data. |
| PP.ME.1 | | Measuring the software planning activities to determine their status. |
| PP.VE.1 | | Reviewing the activities for software project planning with senior management on a periodic basis. |
| PP.VE.2 | | Reviewing the activities for software project planning with the project manager on both a periodic and event-driven basis. |
| PP.VE.3 | | Reviewing and/or auditing the activities and work products for software project planning (the software quality assurance group). |
| | | Reporting the results of reviewing and/or auditing the activities and work products for software project planning (the software quality assurance group). |
| PT | Software Project Tracking and Oversight | "The purpose of Software Project Tracking and Oversight is to provide adequate visibility into actual progress so that management can take effective actions when the software project's performance deviates significantly from the software plans."[5] |
| PT.GO.1 | | Tracking actual results and performances against the software plans. |
| PT.GO.2 | | Taking and managing corrective actions to closure when actual results and performance deviate significantly from the software plans. |
| PT.GO.3 | | Agreeing to changes to software commitments by the affected groups and individuals. |
| PT.CO.1 | | Designating a project software manager to be responsible for the project's software activities and results. |
| PT.CO.2 | | Following a written organizational policy for managing the software project (the project). |
| PT.AB.1 | | Documenting and approving a software development plan for the software project. |
| PT.AB.2 | | Assigning responsibility explicitly by the project software manager for software work products and activities. |
| PT.AB.3 | | Providing adequate resources and funding for tracking the software project. |
| PT.AB.4 | | Training the software managers in managing the technical and personnel aspects of the software project. |

**Table C.1** QMS Statements of Activity: SEI CMM (Continued)

| SEI Element | QMS Requirement | Statement of Activity |
|---|---|---|
| PT.AB.5 | | Orienting first-line software managers in the technical aspects of the software project. |
| PT.AC.1 | | Tracking the software activities by use of a documented software development plan. |
| | | Communicating the status of the software activities by use of a documented software development plan. |
| PT.AC.2 | | Revising the project's software development plan according to a documented procedure. |
| PT.AC.3 | | Reviewing software project commitments and changes to commitments made to individuals and groups external to the organization with senior management according to a documented procedure. |
| PT.AC.4 | | Communicating approved changes to commitments that affect the software project to the members of the software engineering group and other software-related groups. |
| PT.AC.5 | | Tracking the size of the software work products (or size of the changes to the software work products). |
| | | Taking corrective actions as necessary. |
| PT.AC.6 | | Tracking the project's software effort and costs. |
| | | Taking corrective actions as necessary. |
| PT.AC.7 | | Tracking the project's critical computer resources. |
| | | Taking corrective actions as necessary. |
| PT.AC.8 | | Tracking the project's software schedule. |
| | | Taking corrective actions as necessary. |
| PT.AC.9 | | Tracking software engineering technical activities. |
| | | Taking corrective actions as needed. |
| PT.AC.10 | | Tracking the software risks associated with cost, resource, schedule, and technical aspects of the project. |
| PT.AC.11 | | Recording actual measurement data and replanning data for the software project. |
| PT.AC.12 | | Conducting periodic internal reviews to track technical progress, plans, performance, and issues against the software development plan (the software engineering group). |
| PT.AC.13 | | Conducting formal reviews to address the accomplishments and results of the software project at selected project milestones according to a documented procedure. |
| PT.ME.1 | | Measuring the software tracking and oversight activities to determine their status. |

**Table C.1** QMS Statements of Activity: SEI CMM (Continued)

| SEI Element | QMS Requirement | Statement of Activity |
|---|---|---|
| PT.VE.1 | | Reviewing the activities for software project tracking and oversight with senior management on a periodic basis. |
| PT.VE.2 | | Reviewing the activities for software project tracking and oversight with the project manager on both a periodic and event-driven basis. |
| PT.VE.3 | | Reviewing and/or auditing the activities and work products for software project tracking and oversight (the software quality assurance group). |
| | | Reporting the results of reviewing and/or auditing the activities and work products for software project tracking and oversight (the software quality assurance group). |
| SM | Software Subcontract Management | "The purpose of Software Subcontract Management is to select qualified software subcontractors and manage them effectively."[6] |
| SM.GO.1 | | Selecting qualified software subcontractors (the prime contractor). |
| SM.GO.2 | | Agreeing to their commitments to each other (the prime contractor and the software subcontractor). |
| SM.GO.3 | | Maintaining ongoing communications (the prime contractor and the software subcontractor). |
| SM.GO.4 | | Tracking the software subcontractor's actual results and performance against its commitments (the prime contractor). |
| SM.CO.1 | | Following a written organizational policy for managing the software subcontract (the project). |
| SM.CO.2 | | Designating a subcontract manager to be responsible for establishing and managing the software subcontract. |
| SM.AB.1 | | Providing adequate resources and funding for selecting the software subcontractor and managing the subcontract. |
| SM.AB.2 | | Training software managers and other individuals who are involved in establishing and managing the software subcontract to perform these activities. |
| SM.AB.3 | | Orienting software managers and other individuals who are involved in managing the software subcontract in the technical aspects of the subcontract. |
| SM.AC.1 | | Defining and planning the work to be subcontracted according to a documented procedure. |
| SM.AC.2 | | Selecting the software subcontractor, based on an evaluation of the subcontract bidders' ability to perform the work, according to a documented procedure. |

**Table C.1** QMS Statements of Activity: SEI CMM (Continued)

| SEI Element | QMS Requirement | Statement of Activity |
|---|---|---|
| SM.AC.3 | | Using the contractual agreement between the prime contractor and the software subcontractor as the basis for managing the subcontract. |
| SM.AC.4 | | Reviewing and approving a documented subcontractor's software development plan by the prime contractor. |
| SM.AC.5 | | Tracking the software activities by use of a documented and approved subcontractor's software development plan. |
| | | Communicating the status of the software activities by use of a documented and approved subcontractor's software development plan. |
| SM.AC.6 | | Resolving changes to the software subcontractor's statement of work, subcontract terms and conditions, and other commitments, according to a documented procedure. |
| SM.AC.7 | | Conducting periodic status/coordination reviews with the software subcontractor's management (the prime contractor's management). |
| SM.AC.8 | | Holding periodic technical reviews and interchanges with the software subcontractor. |
| SM.AC.9 | | Conducting formal reviews to address the subcontractor's software engineering accomplishments and results at selected milestones, according to a documented procedure. |
| SM.AC.10 | | Monitoring the subcontractor's software quality assurance activities according to a documented procedure (the prime contractor's software quality assurance group). |
| SM.AC.11 | | Monitoring the subcontractor's activities for software configuration management according to a documented procedure (the prime contractor's software configuration management group). |
| SM.AC.12 | | Conducting acceptance testing as part of the delivery of the subcontractor's software products according to a documented procedure (the prime contractor). |
| SM.AC.13 | | Evaluating the software subcontractor's performance on a periodic basis. |
| | | Reviewing the evaluation with the subcontractor. |
| SM.ME.1 | | Measuring the activities for managing the software subcontract to determine their status. |
| SM.VE.1 | | Reviewing the activities for managing the software subcontract with senior management on a periodic basis. |

**Table C.1** QMS Statements of Activity: SEI CMM (Continued)

| SEI Element | QMS Requirement | Statement of Activity |
|---|---|---|
| SM.VE.2 | | Reviewing the activities for managing the software subcontract with the project manager on both a periodic and event-driven basis. |
| SM.VE.3 | | Reviewing and/or auditing the activities and work products for managing the software subcontract (the software quality assurance group). |
| | | Reporting the results of reviewing and/or auditing the activities and work products for managing the software subcontract (the software quality assurance group). |
| QA | Software Quality Assurance | "The purpose of Software Quality Assurance is to provide management with appropriate visibility into the process being used by the software project and of the products being built."[7] |
| QA.GO.1 | | Planning software quality assurance activities. |
| QA.GO.2 | | Verifying adherence of software products and activities to the applicable standards, procedures, and requirements, objectively. |
| QA.GO.3 | | Informing affected groups and individuals of software quality assurance activities and results. |
| QA.GO.4 | | Addressing noncompliance issues that cannot be resolved within the software project (senior management). |
| QA.CO.1 | | Following a written organizational policy for implementing software quality assurance (SQA) (the project). |
| QA.AB.1 | | Establishing a group that is responsible for coordinating and implementing SQA for the project (i.e., the SQA group). |
| QA.AB.2 | | Providing adequate resources and funding for performing the SQA activities. |
| QA.AB.3 | | Training members of the SQA group to perform their SQA activities. |
| QA.AB.4 | | Orienting the members of the software project on the role, responsibilities, authority, and value of the SQA group. |
| QA.AC.1 | | Preparing a SQA plan for the software project according to a documented procedure. |
| QA.AC.2 | | Performing the SQA group's activities in accordance with the SQA plan. |
| QA.AC.3 | | Participating in the preparation and review of the project's software development plan, standards, and procedures (the SQA group). |
| QA.AC.4 | | Reviewing the software engineering activities to verify compliance (the SQA group). |

**Table C.1** QMS Statements of Activity: SEI CMM (Continued)

| SEI Element | QMS Requirement | Statement of Activity |
|---|---|---|
| QA.AC.5 | | Auditing designated software work products to verify compliance (the SQA group). |
| QA.AC.6 | | Reporting the results of its activities to the software engineering group periodically (the SQA group). |
| QA.AC.7 | | Documenting and handling deviations identified in the software activities and software work products, according to a documented procedure. |
| QA.AC.8 | | Conducting periodic reviews of its activities and findings with the customer's SQA personnel, as appropriate (the SQA group). |
| QA.ME.1 | | Measuring the SQA activities in order to determine their cost and schedule status. |
| QA.VE.1 | | Reviewing the SQA activities with senior management on a periodic basis. |
| QA.VE.2 | | Reviewing the SQA activities with the project manager on both a periodic and event-driven basis. |
| QA.VE.3 | | Reviewing periodically the activities and software work products of the project's SQA group (experts independent of the SQA group). |
| CM | Software Configuration Management | "The purpose of Software Configuration Management is to establish and maintain the integrity of the products of the software project throughout the project's software life cycle."[8] |
| CM.GO.1 | | Planning software configuration management activities. |
| CM.GO.2 | | Identifying, controlling, and making available selected software work products. |
| CM.GO.3 | | Controlling changes to identified software work products. |
| CM.GO.4 | | Informing affected groups and individuals of the status and content of software baselines. |
| CM.CO.1 | | Following a written organizational policy for implementing software configuration management (SCM) (the project). |
| CM.AB.1 | | Establishing a board having the authority for managing the project's software baselines (i.e., a software configuration control board—SCCB). |
| CM.AB.2 | | Establishing a group that is responsible for coordinating and implementing SCM for the project (i.e., the SCM group). |
| CM.AB.3 | | Providing adequate resources and funding for performing the SCM activities. |
| CM.AB.4 | | Training members of the SCM group in the objectives, procedures, and methods for performing their SCM activities. |

**Table C.1** QMS Statements of Activity: SEI CMM (Continued)

| SEI Element | QMS Requirement | Statement of Activity |
|---|---|---|
| CM.AB.5 | | Training members of the software engineering group and other software-related groups to perform their SCM activities. |
| CM.AC.1 | | Preparing a SCM plan for each software project according to a documented procedure. |
| CM.AC.2 | | Using a documented and approved SCM plan as the basis for performing the SCM activities. |
| CM.AC.3 | | Establishing a configuration management library system as a repository for the software baselines. |
| CM.AC.4 | | Identifying the software work products to be placed under configuration management. |
| CM.AC.5 | | Initiating, recording, reviewing, approving, and tracking change requests and problem reports for all configuration items/units according to a documented procedure. |
| CM.AC.6 | | Controlling changes to baselines according to a documented procedure. |
| CM.AC.7 | | Creating and controlling the release of products from the software baseline library, according to a documented procedure. |
| CM.AC.8 | | Recording the status of configuration items/units according to a documented procedure. |
| CM.AC.9 | | Developing and making available to affected groups and individuals, standard reports documenting the SCM activities and the contents of the software baseline. |
| CM.AC.10 | | Conducting software baseline audits according to a documented procedure. |
| CM.ME.1 | | Measuring the SCM activities to determine their status. |
| CM.VE.1 | | Reviewing the SCM activities with senior management on a periodic basis. |
| CM.VE.2 | | Reviewing the SCM activities with the project manager on both a periodic and event-driven basis. |
| CM.VE.3 | | Auditing software baselines to verify that they conform to the documentation that defines them, periodically (the SCM group). |
| CM.VE.4 | | Reviewing and/or auditing the activities and work products for SCM (the software quality assurance group). |
| | | Reporting the results of reviewing and/or auditing the activities and work products for SCM (the software quality assurance group). |

**Table C.1** QMS Statements of Activity: SEI CMM (Continued)

| SEI Element | QMS Requirement | Statement of Activity |
|---|---|---|
| LEVEL 3 | DEFINED | "The software process for both management and engineering activities is documented, standardized, and integrated into a standard software process for the organization. All projects use an approved, tailored version of the organization's standard software process for developing and maintaining software."[9] |
| PF | Organization Process Focus | "The purpose of Organization Process Focus is to establish the organizational responsibility for software process activities that improve the organization's overall software process capability."[10] |
| PF.GO.1 | | Coordinating software process development and improvement activities across the organization. |
| PF.GO.2 | | Identifying the strengths and weaknesses of the software processes used relative to a process standard. |
| PF.GO.3 | | Planning organization-level process development and improvement activities. |
| PF.CO.1 | | Following a written organizational policy for coordinating software process development and improvement activities across the organization. |
| PF.CO.2 | | Sponsoring the organization's activities for software process development and improvement (senior management). |
| PF.CO.3 | | Overseeing the organization's activities for software process development and improvement (senior management). |
| PF.AB.1 | | Establishing a group that is responsible for the organization's software process activities. |
| PF.AB.2 | | Providing adequate resources and funding for the organization's software process activities. |
| PF.AB.3 | | Training members of the group responsible for the organization's software process activities to perform these activities. |
| PF.AB.4 | | Orienting members of the software engineering group and other software-related groups on the organization's software process activities and their roles in those activities. |
| PF.AC.1 | | Assessing the software process periodically. |
| | | Developing action plans to address the software process assessment findings. |
| PF.AC.2 | | Developing and maintaining a plan for its software process development and improvement activities (the organization). |
| PF.AC.3 | | Coordinating at the organization level, the organization's and projects' activities for developing and improving their software processes. |
| PF.AC.4 | | Coordinating the use of the organization's software process database at the organizational level. |

**Table C.1** QMS Statements of Activity: SEI CMM (Continued)

| SEI Element | QMS Requirement | Statement of Activity |
|---|---|---|
| PF.AC.5 | | Monitoring and evaluating new processes, methods, and tools. |
| | | Transferring to other parts of the organization, new processes, methods, and tools. |
| PF.AC.6 | | Coordinating training for the organization's and projects' software processes across the organization. |
| PF.AC.7 | | Informing the groups involved in implementing the software processes of the organization's and projects' activities for software process development and improvement. |
| PF.ME.1 | | Measuring the organization's process development and improvement activities in order to determine their status. |
| PF.VE.1 | | Reviewing the activities for software process development and improvement with senior management on a periodic basis. |
| PD | Organization Process Definition | "The purpose of Organization Process Definition is to develop and maintain a usable set of software process assets that improve process performance across the projects and provide a basis for cumulative, long-term benefits to the organization."[11] |
| PD.GO.1 | | Developing and maintaining a standard software process for the organization. |
| PD.GO.2 | | Collecting, reviewing and making available information related to the use of the organization's standard software process by the software projects. |
| PD.CO.1 | | Following a written policy for developing and maintaining a standard software process and related process assets (the organization). |
| PD.AB.1 | | Providing adequate resources and funding for developing and maintaining the organization's standard software process and related process assets. |
| PD.AB.2 | | Training the individuals who develop and maintain the organization's standard software process and related process assets to perform these activities. |
| PD.AC.1 | | Developing and maintaining the organization's standard software process according to a documented procedure. |
| PD.AC.2 | | Documenting the organization's standard software process according to established organization standards. |
| PD.AC.3 | | Documenting and maintaining descriptions of software life cycles that are approved for use by the projects. |
| PD.AC.4 | | Developing and maintaining guidelines and criteria for the projects' tailoring of the organization's standard software process. |
| PD.AC.5 | | Establishing and maintaining the organization's software process database. |

**Table C.1** QMS Statements of Activity: SEI CMM (Continued)

| SEI Element | QMS Requirement | Statement of Activity |
|---|---|---|
| PD.AC.6 | | Establishing and maintaining a library of software process-related documentation. |
| PD.ME.1 | | Measuring the organization's process definition activities to determine their status. |
| PD.VE.1 | | Reviewing and/or auditing the organization's activities and work products for developing and maintaining the organization's standard software process and related process assets (the software quality assurance group). |
| | | Reporting the results of reviewing and/or auditing the organization's activities and work products for developing and maintaining the organization's standard software process and related process assets (the software quality assurance group). |
| TP | Training Program | "The purpose of Training Program key process area is to develop the skills and knowledge of individuals so they can perform their roles effectively and efficiently."[12] |
| TP.GO.1 | | Planning training activities. |
| TP.GO.2 | | Providing training for developing the skills and knowledge needed to perform software management and technical roles. |
| TP.GO.3 | | Training individuals in the software engineering group and software-related groups to perform their roles. |
| TP.CO.1 | | Following a written policy for meeting its training needs (the organization). |
| TP.AB.1 | | Establishing a group responsible for fulfilling the training needs of the organization. |
| TP.AB.2 | | Providing adequate resources and funding for implementing the training program. |
| TP.AB.3 | | Having the necessary skills and knowledge to perform their training activities (members of the training group). |
| TP.AB.4 | | Orienting software managers on the training program. |
| TP.AC.1 | | Developing and maintaining a training plan that specifies its training needs (each software project). |
| TP.AC.2 | | Developing and revising the organization's training plan according to a documented procedure. |
| TP.AC.3 | | Performing the training for the organization in accordance with the organization's training plan. |
| TP.AC.4 | | Developing and maintaining training courses prepared at the organization level according to organization standards. |

**Table C.1** QMS Statements of Activity: SEI CMM (Continued)

| SEI Element | QMS Requirement | Statement of Activity |
|---|---|---|
| TP.AC.5 | | Establishing and using a waiver procedure for required training to determine whether individuals already possess the knowledge and skills required to perform in their designated roles. |
| TP.AC.6 | | Maintaining records of training. |
| TP.ME.1 | | Measuring the training program activities to determine their status. |
| TP.ME.2 | | Measuring the training program to determine its quality. |
| TP.VE.1 | | Reviewing the training program activities with senior management on a periodic basis. |
| TP.VE.2 | | Evaluating the training program independently on a periodic basis for consistency with, and relevance to, the organization's needs. |
| TP.VE.3 | | Reviewing and/or auditing the training program activities and work products. |
| | | Reporting the results of reviewing and/or auditing the training program activities and work products. |
| IM | Integrated Software Management | "The purpose of Integrated Software Management is to integrate the software engineering and management activities into a coherent, defined software process that is tailored from the organization's standard software process and related process assets, which are described in Organization Process Definition."[13] |
| IM.GO.1 | | Tailoring the organization's standard software process to create a version for use as the project's defined software process. |
| IM.GO.2 | | Planning and managing the project according to the project's defined software process. |
| IM.CO.1 | | Following a written organizational policy requiring that the software project be planned and managed using the organization's standard software process and related process assets (the project). |
| IM.AB.1 | | Providing adequate resources and funding for managing the software project using the project's defined software process. |
| IM.AB.2 | | Training the individuals responsible for developing the project's defined software process in how to tailor the organization's standard software process and use the related process assets. |
| IM.AB.3 | | Training the software managers in managing the technical, administrative, and personnel aspects of the software project based on the project's defined software process. |
| IM.AC.1 | | Developing the project's defined software process by tailoring the organization's standard software process according to a documented procedure. |

**Table C.1** QMS Statements of Activity: SEI CMM (Continued)

| SEI Element | QMS Requirement | Statement of Activity |
| --- | --- | --- |
| IM.AC.2 | | Revising each project's defined software process according to a documented procedure. |
| IM.AC.3 | | Developing and revising the project's software development plan, which describes the use of the project's defined software process, according to a documented procedure. |
| IM.AC.4 | | Managing the software project in accordance with the project's defined software process. |
| IM.AC.5 | | Planning and estimating software by using the organization's software process database. |
| IM.AC.6 | | Managing the size of the software work products (or size of changes to the software work products) according to a documented procedure. |
| IM.AC.7 | | Managing the project's software effort and costs according to a documented procedure. |
| IM.AC.8 | | Managing the project's critical computer resources according to a documented procedure. |
| IM.AC.9 | | Managing the critical dependencies and critical paths of the project's software schedule according to a documented procedure. |
| IM.AC.10 | | Identifying, assessing, documenting, and managing the project's software risks according to a documented procedure. |
| IM.AC.11 | | Performing reviews of the software project periodically to determine the actions needed to bring the software project's performance and results in line with the current and projected needs of the business, customer, and end users, as appropriate. |
| IM.ME.1 | | Measuring the integrated software management activities to determine their effectiveness. |
| IM.VE.1 | | Reviewing the activities for managing the software project with senior management on a periodic basis. |
| IM.VE.2 | | Reviewing the activities for managing the software project with the project manager on both a periodic and event-driven basis. |
| IM.VE.3 | | Reviewing and/or auditing the activities and work products for managing the software project by the software quality assurance group. |
| | | Reporting the results of reviewing and/or auditing the activities and work products for managing the software project by the software quality assurance group. |

**Table C.1** QMS Statements of Activity: SEI CMM (Continued)

| SEI Element | QMS Requirement | Statement of Activity |
|---|---|---|
| PE | Software Product Engineering | "The purpose of Software Product Engineering is to consistently perform a well-defined engineering process that integrates all the software engineering activities to produce correct, consistent software products effectively and efficiently" [14] |
| PE.GO.1 | | Defining, integrating and performing consistently the software engineering tasks to produce the software. |
| PE.GO.2 | | Keeping software work products consistent with each other. |
| PE.CO.1 | | Following a written organizational policy for performing the software engineering activities (the project). |
| PE.AB.1 | | Providing adequate resources and funding for performing the software engineering tasks. |
| PE.AB.2 | | Training members of the software engineering technical staff to perform their technical assignments. |
| PE.AB.3 | | Orienting members of the software engineering technical staff in related software engineering disciplines. |
| PE.AB.4 | | Orienting the project manager and all software managers in the technical aspects of the software project. |
| PE.AC.1 | | Integrating appropriate software engineering methods and tools into the project's defined software process. |
| PE.AC.2 | | Analyzing the allocated requirements systematically in order to develop, maintain, document, and verify the software requirements according to the project's defined software process. |
| PE.AC.3 | | Developing, maintaining, documenting, and verifying the software design according to the project's defined software process, to accommodate the software requirements and to form the framework for coding. |
| PE.AC.4 | | Implementing the software requirements and software design by developing, maintaining, documenting, and verifying the software code, according to the project's defined software process. |
| PE.AC.5 | | Performing software testing according to the project's defined software process. |
| PE.AC.6 | | Planning and performing integration testing of the software according to the project's defined software process. |
| PE.AC.7 | | Planning and performing system and acceptance testing of the software to demonstrate that the software satisfies its requirements. |
| PE.AC.8 | | Developing and maintaining the documentation that will be used to operate and maintain the software according to the project's defined software process. |

**Table C.1** QMS Statements of Activity: SEI CMM (Continued)

| SEI Element | QMS Requirement | Statement of Activity |
| --- | --- | --- |
| PE.AC.9 | | Collecting and analyzing data on defects identified in peer reviews and testing according to the project's defined software process. |
| PE.AC.10 | | Maintaining consistency across software work products, including the software plans, process descriptions, allocated requirements, software requirements, software design, code, test plans, and test procedures. |
| PE.ME.1 | | Measuring the software products in order to determine their functionality and quality. |
| PE.ME.2 | | Measuring the software product engineering activities in order to determine their status. |
| PE.VE.1 | | Reviewing the activities for software product engineering with senior management on a periodic basis. |
| PE.VE.2 | | Reviewing the activities for software product engineering with the project manager on both a periodic and event-driven basis. |
| PE.VE.3 | | Reviewing and/or auditing the activities and work products for software product engineering (the software quality assurance group). |
| | | Reporting the results of reviewing and/or auditing the activities and work products for software product engineering (the software quality assurance group). |
| IC | Intergroup Coordination | "The purpose of Intergroup Coordination is to establish a means for the software engineering group to participate actively with the other engineering groups so the project is better able to satisfy the customer's needs effectively and efficiently."[15] |
| IC.GO.1 | | Agreeing to the customer's requirements by all affected groups. |
| IC.GO.2 | | Agreeing to the commitments between the engineering groups by the affected groups. |
| IC.GO.3 | | Identifying, tracking and resolving intergroup issues (the engineering groups). |
| IC.CO.1 | | Following a written organizational policy for establishing interdisciplinary engineering teams (the project). |
| IC.AB.1 | | Providing adequate resources and funding for coordinating the software engineering activities with other engineering groups. |
| IC.AB.2 | | Enabling effective communication and coordination by ensuring that the support tools used by the different engineering groups are compatible. |
| IC.AB.3 | | Training all managers in the organization in teamwork. |

**Table C.1** QMS Statements of Activity: SEI CMM (Continued)

| SEI Element | QMS Requirement | Statement of Activity |
|---|---|---|
| IC.AB.4 | | Orienting all task leaders in each engineering group in the processes, methods, and standards used by the other engineering groups. |
| IC.AB.5 | | Orienting the members of the engineering groups in working as a team. |
| IC.AC.1 | | Participating with the customer and end users, as appropriate, to establish the system requirements (the software engineering group and the other engineering groups). |
| IC.AC.2 | | Monitoring and coordinating technical activities by having representatives of the project's software engineering group work with representatives of the other engineering groups. |
| | | Resolving technical issues by having representatives of the project's software engineering group work with representatives of the other engineering groups. |
| IC.AC.3 | | Communicating intergroup commitments by using a documented plan. |
| | | Coordinating and tracking the work performed by using a documented plan. |
| IC.AC.4 | | Identifying, negotiating, and tracking critical dependencies among engineering groups according to a documented procedure. |
| IC.AC.5 | | Reviewing work products produced as input to other engineering groups to ensure that the work products meet their needs (representatives of the receiving groups). |
| IC.AC.6 | | Handling intergroup issues not resolvable by the individual representatives of the project engineering groups according to a documented procedure. |
| IC.AC.7 | | Conducting periodic technical reviews and interchanges (representatives of the project engineering groups). |
| IC.ME.1 | | Measuring the intergroup coordination activities in order to determine their status. |
| IC.VE.1 | | Reviewing the activities for intergroup coordination with senior management on a periodic basis. |
| IC.VE.2 | | Reviewing the activities for intergroup coordination with the project manager on both a periodic and even-driven basis. |
| IC.VE.3 | | Reviewing and/or auditing the activities and work products for intergroup coordination (the software quality assurance group). |
| | | Reporting the results of reviewing and/or auditing the activities and work products for intergroup coordination (the software quality assurance group). |

**Table C.1** QMS Statements of Activity: SEI CMM (Continued)

| SEI Element | QMS Requirement | Statement of Activity |
|---|---|---|
| PR | Peer Reviews | "The purpose of Peer Reviews is to remove defects from the software work products early and efficiently. An important corollary effect is to develop a better understanding of the software work products and of defects that might be prevented."[16] |
| PR.GO.1 | | Planning peer review activities. |
| PR.GO.2 | | Identifying and removing defects in the software work products. |
| PR.CO.1 | | Following a written organizational policy for performing peer reviews (the project). |
| PR.AB.1 | | Providing adequate resources and funding for performing peer reviews on each software work product to be reviewed. |
| PR.AB.2 | | Training peer review leaders in how to lead peer reviews. |
| PR.AB.3 | | Training reviewers who participate in peer reviews in the objectives, principles, and methods of peer reviews. |
| PR.AC.1 | | Planning peer reviews. |
| | | Documenting the plans for peer reviews. |
| PR.AC.2 | | Performing peer reviews according to a documented procedure. |
| PR.AC.3 | | Recording data on the conduct and results of the peer reviews. |
| PR.ME.1 | | Measuring the peer review activities to determine their status. |
| PR.VE.1 | | Reviewing and/or auditing the activities and work products for peer reviews (the software quality assurance group). |
| | | Reporting the results of reviewing and/or auditing the activities and work products for peer reviews (the software quality assurance group). |
| LEVEL 4 | MANAGED | "Detailed measures of the software process and product quality are collected. Both the software process and products are quantitatively understood and controlled."[17] |
| QP | Quantitative Process Management | "The purpose of Quantitative Process Management is to control the process performance of the software project quantitatively. Software process performance represents the actual results achieved from following a software process."[18] |
| QP.GO.1 | | Planning the quantitative process management activities. |
| QP.GO.2 | | Controlling quantitatively, the process performance of the project's defined software process. |
| QP.GO.3 | | Knowing, in quantitative terms, the process capability of the organization's standard software process. |

**Table C.1** QMS Statements of Activity: SEI CMM (Continued)

| SEI Element | QMS Requirement | Statement of Activity |
|---|---|---|
| QP.CO.1 | | Following a written organizational policy for measuring and quantitatively controlling the performance of the project's defined software process. |
| QP.CO.2 | | Following a written policy for analyzing the process capability of the organization's standard software process. |
| QP.AB.1 | | Establishing a group that is responsible for coordinating the quantitative process management activities for the organization. |
| QP.AB.2 | | Providing adequate resources and funding for the quantitative process management activities. |
| QP.AB.3 | | Establishing support for collecting, recording, and analyzing data for selected process and product measurements. |
| QP.AB.4 | | Training the individuals implementing or supporting quantitative process management to perform these activities. |
| QP.AB.5 | | Orienting the members of the software engineering group and other software-related groups on the goals and value of quantitative process management. |
| QP.AC.1 | | Developing the software project's plan for quantitative process management according to a documented procedure. |
| QP.AC.2 | | Performing quantitative process management activities in accordance with the project's quantitative process management plan. |
| QP.AC.3 | | Determining the strategy for the data collection and the quantitative analyses to be performed based on the project's defined software process. |
| QP.AC.4 | | Collecting the measurement data used to control the project's defined software process quantitatively according to a documented procedure. |
| QP.AC.5 | | Analyzing and controlling the project's defined software process, according to a documented procedure. |
| QP.AC.6 | | Preparing and distributing reports documenting the results of the software project's quantitative process management activities. |
| QP.AC.7 | | Establishing and maintaining the process capability baseline for the organization's standard software process according to a documented procedure. |
| QP.ME.1 | | Measuring the activities for quantitative process management in order to determine their status. |
| QP.VE.1 | | Reviewing the activities for quantitative process management with senior management on a periodic basis. |

**Table C.1** QMS Statements of Activity: SEI CMM (Continued)

| SEI Element | QMS Requirement | Statement of Activity |
|---|---|---|
| QP.VE.2 | | Reviewing the software project's activities for quantitative process management with the project manager on both a periodic and event-driven basis. |
| QP.VE.3 | | Reviewing and/or auditing the activities and work products for quantitative process management (the software quality assurance group). |
| | | Reporting the results of reviewing and/or auditing the activities and work products for quantitative process management (the software quality assurance group). |
| QM | Software Quality Management | "The purpose of Software Quality Management is to develop a quantitative understanding of the quality of the project's software products and achieve specific quality goals."[19] |
| QM.GO.1 | | Planning the project's software quality management activities. |
| QM.GO.2 | | Defining measurable goals for software product quality and their priorities. |
| QM.GO.3 | | Quantifying and managing actual progress toward achieving the quality goals for the software products. |
| QM.CO.1 | | Following a written organizational policy for managing software quality (the project). |
| QM.AB.1 | | Providing adequate resources and funding for managing the quality of the software products. |
| QM.AB.2 | | Training the individuals implementing and supporting software quality management to perform their activities. |
| QM.AB.3 | | Training the members of the software engineering group and other software-related groups in software quality management. |
| QM.AC.1 | | Developing and maintaining the project's software quality plan according to a documented procedure. |
| QM.AC.2 | | Basing the project's activities for software quality management on the project's software quality plan. |
| QM.AC.3 | | Defining, monitoring, and revising the project's quantitative quality goals for the software products throughout the software life cycle. |
| QM.AC.4 | | Measuring, analyzing, and comparing the quality of the project's software products to the products' quantitative quality goals on an event-driven basis. |
| QM.AC.5 | | Allocating the software project's quantitative quality goals for the products appropriately to the subcontractors delivering software products to the project. |
| QM.ME.1 | | Measuring the software quality management activities in order to determine their status. |

**Table C.1** QMS Statements of Activity: SEI CMM (Continued)

| SEI Element | QMS Requirement | Statement of Activity |
|---|---|---|
| QM.VE.1 | | Reviewing the activities for software quality management with senior management on a periodic basis. |
| QM.VE.2 | | Reviewing the activities for software quality management with the project manager on both a periodic and event-driven basis. |
| QM.VE.3 | | Reviewing and/or auditing the activities and work products for software quality management (the software quality assurance group). |
| | | Reporting the results of reviewing and/or auditing the activities and work products for software quality management (the software quality assurance group). |
| LEVEL 5 | OPTIMIZING | "Continuous process improvement is enabled by quantitative feedback from the process and from piloting innovative ideas and technologies."[20] |
| DP | Defect Prevention | "The purpose of Defect Prevention is to identify the cause of defects and prevent them from recurring."[21] |
| DP.GO.1 | | Planning defect prevention activities. |
| DP.GO.2 | | Seeking and identifying common causes of defects. |
| DP.GO.3 | | Prioritizing and eliminating systematically, common causes of defects. |
| DP.CO.1 | | Following a written policy for defect prevention activities (the organization). |
| DP.CO.2 | | Following a written organizational policy for defect prevention activities (the project). |
| DP.AB.1 | | Establishing an organization-level team to coordinate defect prevention activities. |
| DP.AB.2 | | Establishing a team to coordinate defect prevention activities for the software project. |
| DP.AB.3 | | Providing adequate resources and funding for defect prevention activities at the project and organization levels. |
| DP.AB.4 | | Training members of the software engineering group and other software-related groups to perform their defect prevention activities. |
| DP.AC.1 | | Developing and maintaining a plan for its defect prevention activities (the software project). |
| DP.AC.2 | | Preparing at the beginning of a software task, for the activities of that task and the related defect prevention activities (the members of the team performing the task). |
| DP.AC.3 | | Conducting causal analysis meetings according to a documented procedure. |

**Table C.1** QMS Statements of Activity: SEI CMM (Continued)

| SEI Element | QMS Requirement | Statement of Activity |
|---|---|---|
| DP.AC.4 | | Reviewing and coordinating implementation, on a periodic basis, of action proposals from causal analysis meetings (each of the teams assigned to coordinate defect prevention activities). |
| DP.AC.5 | | Documenting and tracking defect prevention data across the teams coordinating defect prevention activities. |
| DP.AC.6 | | Incorporating revisions to the organization's standard software process resulting from defect prevention actions, according to a documented procedure. |
| DP.AC.7 | | Incorporating revisions to the project's defined software process resulting from defect prevention actions, according to a documented procedure. |
| DP.AC.8 | | Receiving feedback on the status and results of the organization's and project's defect prevention activities on a periodic basis (members of the software engineering group and software-related groups). |
| DP.ME.1 | | Measuring the defect prevention activities in order to determine their status. |
| DP.VE.1 | | Reviewing the organization's activities for defect prevention with senior management on a periodic basis. |
| DP.VE.2 | | Reviewing the software project's activities for defect prevention with the project manager on both a periodic and event-driven basis. |
| DP.VE.3 | | Reviewing and/or auditing the activities and work products for defect prevention (the software quality assurance group). |
| | | Reporting the results of reviewing and/or auditing the activities and work products for defect prevention (the software quality assurance group). |
| TM | Technology Change Management | "The purpose of Technology Change Management is to identify new technologies (i.e., tools, methods, and processes) and track them into the organization in an orderly manner."[22] |
| TM.GO.1 | | Planning incorporation of technology changes. |
| TM.GO.2 | | Evaluating new technologies to determine their effect on quality and productivity. |
| TM.GO.3 | | Transferring appropriate new technologies into normal practice across the organization. |
| TM.CO.1 | | Following a written policy for improving its technology capability (the organization). |
| TM.CO.2 | | Sponsoring the organization's activities for technology change management (senior management). |

**Table C.1** QMS Statements of Activity: SEI CMM (Continued)

| SEI Element | QMS Requirement | Statement of Activity |
|---|---|---|
| TM.CO.3 | | Overseeing the organization's technology change management activities (senior management). |
| TM.AB.1 | | Establishing a group responsible for the organization's technology change management activities. |
| TM.AB.2 | | Providing adequate resources and funding to establish and staff a group responsible for the organization's technology change management activities. |
| TM.AB.3 | | Establishing support for collecting and analyzing data needed to evaluate technology changes. |
| TM.AB.4 | | Providing appropriate data on the software processes and software work products to support analyses performed to evaluate and select technology changes. |
| TM.AB.5 | | Training members of the group responsible for the organization's technology change management activities to perform these activities. |
| TM.AC.1 | | Developing and maintaining a plan for technology change management (the organization). |
| TM.AC.2 | | Identifying areas of technology change by working with the software projects (the group responsible for the organization's technology change management activities). |
| TM.AC.3 | | Informing software managers and technical staff of new technologies. |
| TM.AC.4 | | Analyzing the organization's standard software process systematically to identify areas that need or could benefit from new technology (the group responsible for the organization's technology change management). |
| TM.AC.5 | | Selecting and acquiring technologies for the organization and software projects according to a documented procedure. |
| TM.AC.6 | | Conducting pilot efforts for improving technology, where appropriate, before a new technology is introduced into normal practice. |
| TM.AC.7 | | Incorporating appropriate new technologies into the organization's standard software process according to a documented procedure. |
| TM.AC.8 | | Incorporating appropriate new technologies into the project's defined software processes, according to a documented procedure. |
| TM.ME.1 | | Measuring the organization's activities for technology change management in order to determine their status. |

**Table C.1** QMS Statements of Activity: SEI CMM (Continued)

| SEI Element | QMS Requirement | Statement of Activity |
|---|---|---|
| TM.VE.1 | | Reviewing the organization's activities for technology change management with senior management on a periodic basis. |
| TM.VE.2 | | Reviewing and/or auditing the activities and work products for technology change management (the software quality assurance group). |
| | | Reporting the results of reviewing and/or auditing the activities and work products for technology change management (the software quality assurance group). |
| PC | Process Change Management | "The purpose of Process Change Management is to continually improve the software processes used in the organization with the intent of improving software quality, increasing productivity, and decreasing the cycle time for product development."[23] |
| PC.GO.1 | | Planning continuous process improvement. |
| PC.GO.2 | | Participating organization wide in the organization's software process improvement activities. |
| PC.GO.3 | | Improving continuously the organization's standard software process and the projects' defined software processes. |
| PC.CO.1 | | Following a written policy for implementing software process improvements (the organization). |
| PC.CO.2 | | Sponsoring the organization's activities for software process improvement (senior management). |
| PC.AB.1 | | Providing adequate resources and funding for software process improvement activities. |
| PC.AB.2 | | Training software managers in software process improvement. |
| PC.AB.3 | | Training the managers and technical staff of the software engineering group and other software-related groups in software process improvement. |
| PC.AB.4 | | Training senior management in software process improvement. |
| PC.AC.1 | | Establishing a software process improvement program that empowers the members of the organization to improve the processes of the organization. |
| PC.AC.2 | | Coordinating software process improvement activities [the group responsible for the organization's software process activities (e.g., software engineering process group)]. |
| PC.AC.3 | | Developing and maintaining a plan for software process improvement, according to a documented procedure (the organization). |
| PC.AC.4 | | Performing the software process improvement activities in accordance with the software process improvement plan. |

**Table C.1** QMS Statements of Activity: SEI CMM (Continued)

| SEI Element | QMS Requirement | Statement of Activity |
|---|---|---|
| PC.AC.5 | | Handling software process improvement proposals, according to a documented procedure. |
| PC.AC.6 | | Participating actively in teams to develop software process improvements for assigned process areas (members of the organization). |
| | | Developing software process improvement for assigned process areas (members of the organization). |
| PC.AC.7 | | Installing where appropriate, the software process improvements on a pilot basis to determine their benefits and effectiveness before they are introduced into normal practice. |
| PC.AC.8 | | Implementing a software process improvement into normal practice, according to a documented procedure. |
| PC.AC.9 | | Maintaining records of software process improvement activities. |
| PC.AC.10 | | Receiving feedback on the status and results of the software process improvement activities on an event-driven basis (software managers and technical staff). |
| PC.ME.1 | | Measuring the software process improvement activities in order to determine their status. |
| PC.VE.1 | | Reviewing the activities for software process improvement with senior management on a periodic basis. |
| PC.VE.2 | | Reviewing and/or auditing the activities and work products for software process improvement (the software quality assurance group). |
| | | Reporting the results of reviewing and/or auditing the activities and work products for software process improvement (the software quality assurance group). |

[1]Software Engineering Institute, CMU/SEI-93-TR-24, Capability Maturity Model for Software, Version 1.1 (Carnegie Mellon University, 1993), pp. 8–9.

[2]Ibid.

[3]Software Engineering Institute, CMU/SEI-93-TR-25, Key Practices of the Capability Maturity Model, Version 1.1 (Carnegie Mellon University, 1993), p. O-20.

[4]Ibid.

[5]Ibid.

[6]Ibid.

[7]Ibid., p. O-21.

[8]Ibid.

[9]Software Engineering Institute, CMU/SEI-93-TR-24, Capability Maturity Model for Software, Version 1.1 (Carnegie Mellon University, 1993), pp. 8–9.

[10]Software Engineering Institute, CMU/SEI-93-TR-25, Key Practices of the Capability Maturity Model, Version 1.1 (Carnegie Mellon University, 1993), p. O-21.

[11]Ibid.

[12]Ibid., p. O-22.

[13]Ibid.

[14]Ibid.

[15]Ibid.

[16]Ibid., pp. O-22–O-23.

[17]Software Engineering Institute, *CMU/SEI-93-TR-24*, *Capability Maturity Model for Software, Version 1.1* (Carnegie Mellon University, 1993), pp. 8–9.

[18]Software Engineering Institute, *CMU/SEI-93-TR-25*, *Key Practices of the Capability Maturity Model, Version 1.1* (Carnegie Mellon University, 1993), p. O-23.

[19]Ibid.

[20]Software Engineering Institute, *CMU/SEI-93-TR-24*, *Capability Maturity Model for Software, Version 1.1* (Carnegie Mellon University, 1993), pp. 8–9.

[21]Software Engineering Institute, *CMU/SEI-93-TR-25*, *Key Practices of the Capability Maturity Model, Version 1.1* (Carnegie Mellon University, 1993), p. O-24.

[22]Ibid.

[23]Ibid.

# Correlated Statements of Activity: Malcolm Baldrige to ISO 9001

**Table D.1** Malcolm Baldrige Statements Correlated to ISO 9001

| MB Requirement | ISO 9001 Correlated Requirements |
| --- | --- |
| 1.1 Senior Executive Leadership | 4.1 Management Responsibility |
| | 4.1.1 Quality Policy |
| | 4.1.2.1 Responsibility and Authority |
| | 4.1.2.2 Resources |
| | 4.1.2.3 Management Representative |
| | 4.1.3 Management Review |
| 1.2 Leadership System and Organization | 4.1 Management Responsibility |
| | 4.1.1 Quality Policy |
| | 4.1.2.1 Responsibility and Authority |
| | 4.1.2.2 Resources |
| | 4.1.3 Management Review |
| 1.3 Public Responsibility and Corporate Citizenship | |
| 2.1 Management of Information and Data | 4.5 Document and Data Control |
| | 4.5.1 General |
| | 4.5.2 Document and Data Approval and Issue |
| | 4.5.3 Document and Data Changes |
| | 4.6 Purchasing |
| | 4.6.3 Purchasing Data |

**Table D.1** Malcolm Baldrige Statements Correlated to ISO 9001 (Continued)

| MB Requirement | ISO 9001 Correlated Requirements |
| --- | --- |
| | 4.10 Inspection and Testing |
| | 4.10.5 Inspection and Test Records |
| | 4.16 Control of Quality Records |
| | 4.20 Statistical Techniques |
| | 4.20.2 Procedures |
| 2.2 Competitive Comparisons and Benchmarking | |
| 2.3 Analysis and Use of Company-Level Data | 4.14 Corrective and Preventative Action |
| | 4.14.3 Preventative Action |
| | 4.20 Statistical Techniques |
| 3.1 Strategy Development | 4.2 Quality System |
| 3.2 Strategy Deployment | |
| 4.1 Human Resource Planning and Evaluation | |
| 4.2 High Performance Work Systems | 4.4 Design Control |
| | 4.4.3 Organizational and Technical Interfaces |
| 4.3 Employee Education, Training, and Development | 4.18 Training |
| 4.4 Employee Well-Being and Satisfaction | |
| 5.1 Design and Introduction of Products and Services | 4.4 Design Control |
| | 4.4.1 General |
| | 4.4.2 Design and Development Planning |
| | 4.4.3 Organizational and Technical Interfaces |
| | 4.4.4 Design Input |
| | 4.4.5 Design Output |
| | 4.4.6 Design Review |
| | 4.4.7 Design Verification |
| | 4.4.8 Design Validation |
| | 4.4.9 Design Changes |
| | 4.5 Document and Data Control |
| | 4.5.1 General |
| | 4.10 Inspection and Testing |
| | 4.10.1 General |
| | 4.10.2.1 |

**Table D.1** Malcolm Baldrige Statements Correlated to ISO 9001 (Continued)

| MB Requirement | ISO 9001 Correlated Requirements |
|---|---|
| | 4.10.2.2 |
| | 4.10.2.3 |
| | 4.10.3 In-Process Inspection and Testing |
| | 4.10.4 Final Inspection and Testing |
| | 4.10.5 Inspection and Test Records |
| | 4.14 Corrective and Preventative Action |
| | 4.14.1 General |
| | 4.14.2 Corrective Action |
| | 4.14.3 Preventative Action |
| | 4.15 Handling, Storage, Packaging, Preservation, and Delivery |
| | 4.15.1 General |
| | 4.15.2 Handling |
| | 4.15.3 Storage |
| | 4.15.4 Packaging |
| | 4.15.5 Preservation |
| | 4.15.6 Delivery |
| | 4.19 Servicing |
| 5.2 Process Management: Product and Service Production and Delivery | 4.4 Design Control |
| | 4.4.1 General |
| | 4.5 Document and Data Control |
| | 4.5.1 General |
| | 4.6 Purchasing |
| | 4.6.1 General |
| | 4.7 Control of Customer-Supplied Product |
| | 4.8 Product Identification and Traceability |
| | 4.9 Process Control |
| | 4.10 Inspection and Testing |
| | 4.10.1 General |
| | 4.10.2.1 |
| | 4.10.2.2 |
| | 4.10.2.3 |

**Table D.1**  Malcolm Baldrige Statements Correlated to ISO 9001 (Continued)

| MB Requirement | ISO 9001 Correlated Requirements |
| --- | --- |
| | 4.10.3 In-Process Inspection and Testing |
| | 4.10.4 Final Inspection and Testing |
| | 4.10.5 Inspection and Test Records |
| | 4.11 Control of Inspection, Measuring, and Test Equipment |
| | 4.11.1 General |
| | 4.11.2 Control Procedure |
| | 4.12 Inspection and Test Status |
| | 4.13 Control of Nonconforming Product |
| | 4.13.1 General |
| | 4.13.2 Review and Disposition of Nonconforming Product |
| | 4.14 Corrective and Preventative Action |
| | 4.14.1 General |
| | 4.14.2 Corrective Action |
| | 4.14.3 Preventative Action |
| | 4.15 Handling, Storage, Packaging, Preservation, and Delivery |
| | 4.15.1 General |
| | 4.15.2 Handling |
| | 4.15.3 Storage |
| | 4.15.4 Packaging |
| | 4.15.5 Preservation |
| | 4.15.6 Delivery |
| | 4.16 Control of Quality Records |
| | 4.17 Internal Quality Audits |
| | 4.19 Servicing |
| | 4.20 Statistical Techniques |
| | 4.20.2 Procedures |
| 5.3 Process Management: Support Services | 4.9 Process Control |
| | 4.14 Corrective and Preventative Action |
| 5.4 Management of Supplier Performance | 4.6 Purchasing |
| | 4.6.1 General |

**Table D.1**  Malcolm Baldrige Statements Correlated to ISO 9001 (Continued)

| MB Requirement | ISO 9001 Correlated Requirements |
| --- | --- |
| | 4.6.2 Evaluation of Sub-Contractors |
| | 4.6.3 Purchasing Data |
| | 4.6.4 Verification of Purchased Product |
| | 4.6.4.1 Supplier Verification at Subcontractor's Premises |
| | 4.6.4.2 Customer Verification of Subcontracted Product |
| | 4.7 Control of Customer-Supplied Product |
| | 4.8 Product Identification and Traceability |
| | 4.10 Inspection and Testing |
| | 4.10.2 Receiving Inspection and Testing |
| | 4.10.2.1 |
| | 4.10.2.2 |
| | 4.10.2.3 |
| | 4.10.4 Final Inspection and Testing |
| | 4.10.5 Inspection and Test Records |
| | 4.13 Control of Nonconforming Product |
| | 4.13.1 General |
| | 4.13.2 Review and Disposition of Nonconforming Product |
| | 4.14 Corrective and Preventative Action |
| | 4.14.1 General |
| | 4.14.2 Corrective Action |
| | 4.14.3 Preventative Action |
| 6.1 Product and Service Quality Results | |
| 6.2 Company Operational and Financial Results | |
| 6.3 Supplier Performance Results | |
| 7.1 Customer and Market Knowledge | 4.3 Contract Review |
| | 4.3.1 General |
| | 4.3.2 Review |
| | 4.3.3 Amendment to Contract |
| | 4.3.4 Records |
| 7.2 Customer Relationship Management | 4.3 Contract Review |

**Table D.1**  Malcolm Baldrige Statements Correlated to ISO 9001 (Continued)

| MB Requirement | ISO 9001 Correlated Requirements |
|---|---|
| | 4.3.1 General |
| | 4.3.2 Review |
| | 4.3.4 Records |
| | 4.6 Purchasing |
| | 4.6.4.2 Customer Verification of Subcontracted Product |
| | 4.14 Corrective and Preventative Action |
| | 4.14.2 Corrective Action |
| | 4.14.3 Preventative Action |
| 7.3 Customer Satisfaction Determination | 4.19 Servicing |
| 7.4 Customer Satisfaction Results | 4.19 Servicing |
| 7.5 Customer Satisfaction Comparison | |

# E

# Correlated Statements of Activity: Malcolm Baldrige to SEI CMM

**Table E.1** Malcolm Baldrige Statements Correlated to SEI CMM

| MB Requirement | SEI CMM Correlated Requirements |
|---|---|
| 1.1 Senior Executive Leadership | Requirements Management<br>RM.VE.1 |
| | Software Project Planning<br>PP.AC.4, PP.VE.1 |
| | Software Project Tracking and Oversight<br>PT.AC.3, PT.VE.1 |
| | Software Subcontract Management<br>SM.VE.1 |
| | Software Quality Assurance<br>QA.GO.4, QA.VE.1 |
| | Software Configuration Management<br>CM.VE.1 |
| | Organization Process Focus<br>PF.CO.2, PF.CO.3, PF.VE.1 |
| | Training Program<br>TP.VE.1 |
| | Integrated Software Management<br>IM.VE.1 |
| | Software Product Engineering<br>PE.VE.1 |

**Table E.1** Malcolm Baldrige Statements Correlated to SEI CMM (Continued)

| MB Requirement | SEI CMM Correlated Requirements |
| --- | --- |
| | Intergroup Coordination<br>IC.VE.1 |
| | Quantitative Process Management<br>QP.VE.1 |
| | Software Quality Management<br>QM.VE.1 |
| | Defect Prevention<br>DP.VE.1 |
| | Technology Change Management<br>TM.CO.2, TM.CO.3 |
| | Process Change Management<br>PC.AB.4, PC.CO.2, PC.VE.1 |
| 1.2 Leadership System and Organization | Requirements Management<br>RM.VE.1, RM.VE.2 |
| | Software Project Planning<br>PP.AC.4, PP.VE.1, PP.VE.2 |
| | Software Project Tracking and Oversight<br>PT.AC.3, PT.VE.1, PT.VE.2 |
| | Software Subcontract Management<br>SM.VE.1, SM.VE.2 |
| | Software Quality Assurance<br>QA.VE.1, QA.VE.2 |
| | Software Configuration Management<br>CM.VE.1, CM.VE.2 |
| | Organization Process Focus<br>PF.VE.1 |
| | Training Program<br>TP.VE.1 |
| | Integrated Software Management<br>IM.VE.1, IM.VE.2 |
| | Software Product Engineering<br>PE.VE.1, PE.VE.2 |
| | Intergroup Coordination<br>IC.VE.1, IC.VE.2 |
| | Quantitative Process Management<br>QP.VE.1, QP.VE.2 |

**Table E.1** Malcolm Baldrige Statements Correlated to SEI CMM (Continued)

| MB Requirement | SEI CMM Correlated Requirements |
|---|---|
|  | Software Quality Management<br>QM.VE.1, QM.VE.2 |
|  | Defect Prevention<br>DP.VE.1, DP.VE.2 |
|  | Technology Change Management<br>TM.VE.1 |
|  | Process Change Management<br>PC.VE.1 |
| 1.3 Public Responsibility and Corporate Citizenship |  |
| 2.1 Management of Information and Data | Software Project Planning<br>PP.AC.15 |
|  | Software Project Tracking and Oversight<br>PT.AC.11 |
|  | Organization Process Focus<br>PF.AC.4 |
|  | Software Configuration Management<br>CM.AC.8 |
|  | Organization Process Definition<br>PD.GO.2, PD.AC.5, PD.AC.6 |
|  | Training Program<br>TP.AC.6 |
|  | Integrated Software Management<br>IM.AC.5 |
|  | Software Product Engineering<br>PE.AC.9 |
|  | Peer Reviews<br>PR.AC.3 |
|  | Quantitative Process Management<br>QP.AB.3, QP.AC.3, QP.AC.4 |
|  | Software Quality Management<br>QM.AC.4 |
|  | Defect Prevention<br>DP.AC.5 |
|  | Technology Change Management<br>TM.AB.3, TM.AB.4 |

**Table E.1** Malcolm Baldrige Statements Correlated to SEI CMM (Continued)

| MB Requirement | SEI CMM Correlated Requirements |
|---|---|
| | Process Change Management<br>PC.AC.9 |
| | Requirements Management<br>RM.ME.1 |
| | Software Project Planning<br>PP.ME.1 |
| | Software Project Tracking and Oversight<br>PT.ME.1 |
| | Software Subcontract Management<br>SM.ME.1 |
| | Software Quality Assurance<br>QA.ME.1 |
| | Software Configuration Management<br>CM.ME.1 |
| | Organization Process Focus<br>PF.ME.1 |
| | Organization Process Definition<br>PD.ME.1 |
| | Training Program<br>TP.ME.1, TP.ME.2 |
| | Integrated Software Management<br>IM.ME.1 |
| | Software Product Engineering<br>PE.ME.1, PE.ME.2 |
| | Intergroup Coordination<br>IC.ME.1 |
| | Peer Reviews<br>PR.ME.1 |
| | Quantitative Process Management<br>QP.ME.1 |
| | Software Quality Management<br>QM.ME.1 |
| | Defect Prevention<br>DP.ME.1 |
| | Technology Change Management<br>TM.ME.1 |

**Table E.1** Malcolm Baldrige Statements Correlated to SEI CMM (Continued)

| MB Requirement | SEI CMM Correlated Requirements |
|---|---|
| | Process Change Management<br>PC.ME.1 |
| 2.2 Competitive Comparisons and Benchmarking | Organization Process Focus<br>PF.GO.1, PF.GO.2, PF.GO.3, PF.CO.1, PF.CO.2, PF.CO.3, PF.AB.1, PF.AB.2, PF.AC.1, PF.AC.2, PF.AC.3, PF.AC.4, PF.AC.5, PF.AC.6, PF.AC.7, PF.ME.1, PF.VE.1 |
| | Organization Process Definition<br>PD.GO.1, PD.GO.2, PD.CO.1, PD.AB.1, PD.AB.2, PD.AC.1, PD.AC.2, PD.AC.3, PD.AC.4, PD.AC.5, PD.AC.6, PD.ME.1, PD.VE.1 |
| | Technology Change Management<br>TM.GO.1, TM.GO.2, TM.GO.3, TM.CO.1, TM.CO.2, TM.CO.3, TM.AB.3, TM.AB.4, TM.AC.1, TM.AC.2, TM.AC.3, TM.AC.4, TM.AC.5, TM.AC.6, TM.AC.7, TM.AC.8, TM.ME.1 |
| | Process Change Management<br>PC.GO.1, PC.GO.2, PC.GO.3, PC.CO.1, PC.CO.2, PC.AB.1, PC.AC.1, PC.AC.2, PC.AC.3, PC.AC.4, PC.AC.5, PC.AC.6, PC.AC.7, PC.AC.8, PC.AC.9, PC.AC.10, PC.ME.1, PC.VE.1, PC.VE.2 |
| 2.3 Analysis and Use of Company-Level Data | Software Configuration Management<br>CM.ME.1 |
| | Defect Prevention<br>DP.AC.3, DP.ME.1 |
| | Intergroup Coordination<br>IC.ME.1 |
| | Integrated Software Management<br>IM.ME.1 |
| | Process Change Management<br>PC.ME.1 |
| | Organization Process Definition<br>PD.ME.1 |
| | Software Product Engineering<br>PE.AC.2, PE.AC.9, PE.ME.1, PE.ME.2 |
| | Organization Process Focus<br>PF.ME.1 |
| | Software Project Planning<br>PP.ME.1 |
| | Peer Reviews<br>PR.ME.1 |

**Table E.1** Malcolm Baldrige Statements Correlated to SEI CMM (Continued)

| MB Requirement | SEI CMM Correlated Requirements |
| --- | --- |
| | Software Project Tracking and Oversight<br>PT.ME.1 |
| | Software Quality Assurance<br>QA.ME.1 |
| | Software Quality Management<br>QM.ME.1 |
| | Quantitative Process Management<br>QP.AB.1, QP.AB.2, QP.AB.3, QP.AC.1, QP.AC.2, QP.AC.3, QP.AC.4, QP.AC.5, QP.AC.6, QP.AC.7, QP.CO.1, QP.CO.2, QP.GO.1, QP.GO.2, QP.GO.3, QP.ME.1, QP.VE.1, QP.VE.2, QP.VE.3 |
| | Requirements Management<br>RM.AB.1, RM.ME.1 |
| | Software Subcontract Management<br>SM.ME.1 |
| | Technology Change Management<br>TM.AB.3, TM.AB.4, TM.AC.4, TM.ME.1 |
| | Training Program<br>TP.ME.1 TP.ME.2 |
| 3.1 Strategy Development | |
| 3.2 Strategy Deployment | |
| 4.1 Human Resource Planning and Evaluation | |
| 4.2 High Performance Work Systems | Intergroup Coordination<br>IC.GO.1, IC.GO.2, IC.GO.3, IC.CO.1, IC.AB.1, IC.AB.2, IC.AB.3, IC.AB.4, IC.AB.5, IC.AC.1, IC.AC.2, IC.AC.3, IC.AC.4, IC.AC.5, IC.AC.6, IC.AC.7, IC.ME.1, IC.VE.1, IC.VE.2, IC.VE.3 |
| 4.3 Employee Education, Training, and Development | Training Program<br>TP.GO.1, TP.GO.2, TP.GO.3, TP.CO.1, TP.AB.1, TP.AB.2, TP.AB.3, TP.AB.4, TP.AC.1, TP.AC.2, TP.AC.3, TP.AC.4, TP.AC.5, TP.AC.6, TP.ME.1, TP.ME.2, TP.VE.1, TP.VE.2, TP.VE.3 |
| | Requirements Management<br>RM.AB.4 |
| | Software Project Planning<br>PP.AB.4 |
| | Software Project Tracking and Oversight<br>PT.AB.4, PT.AB.5 |

**Table E.1** Malcolm Baldrige Statements Correlated to SEI CMM (Continued)

| MB Requirement | SEI CMM Correlated Requirements |
|---|---|
| | Software Subcontract Management<br>SM.AB.2, SM.AB.3 |
| | Software Quality Assurance<br>QA.AB.3, QA.AB.4 |
| | Software Configuration Management<br>CM.AB.4, CM.AB.5 |
| | Organization Process Focus<br>PF.AB.3 PF.AB.4 |
| | Organization Process Definition<br>PD.AB.2 |
| | Integrated Software Management<br>IM.AB.2, IM.AB.3 |
| | Software Product Engineering<br>PE.AB.2, PE.AB.3, PE.AB.4 |
| | Intergroup Coordination<br>IC.AB.3, IC.AB.4, IC.AB.5 |
| | Peer Reviews<br>PR.AB.2, PR.AB.3 |
| | Quantitative Process Management<br>QP.AB.4 |
| | Software Quality Management<br>QM.AB.2, QM.AB.3 |
| | Defect Prevention<br>DP.AB.4 |
| | Technology Change Management<br>TM.AB.5 |
| | Process Change Management<br>PC.AB.2, PC.AB.3, PC.AB.4 |
| 4.4 Employee Well-Being and Satisfaction | |
| 5.1 Design and Introduction of Products and Services | Requirements Management<br>RM.GO.1, RM.GO.2, RM.CO.1, RM.AC.1, RM.AC.2, RM.AC.3, RM.ME.1, RM.VE.1, RM.VE.2, RM.VE.3 |
| | Software Product Engineering<br>PE.GO.1, PE.GO.2, PE.CO.1, PE.AC.1, PE.AC.2, PE.AC.3, PE.AC.4, PE.AC.5, PE.AC.6, PE.AC.7, PE.AC.8, PE.AC.9, PE.AC.10, PE.ME.1, PE.ME.2, PE.VE.1, PE.VE.2, PE.VE.3 |

**Table E.1** Malcolm Baldrige Statements Correlated to SEI CMM (Continued)

| MB Requirement | SEI CMM Correlated Requirements |
|---|---|
| | Intergroup Coordination<br>IC.CO.1, IC.AC.1, IC.AC.2, IC.AC.3, IC.AC.4, IC.AC.5, IC.AC.6, IC.AC.7 |
| | Peer Reviews<br>PR.GO.2, PR.CO.1, PR.AC.1, PR.AC.2, PR.ME.1, PR.VE.1 |
| | Software Quality Management<br>QM.GO.3, QM.CO.1, QM.AC.1, QM.AC.2, QM.AC.3, QM.AC.4, QM.AC.5, QM.ME.1, QM.VE.1, QM.VE.2, QM.VE.3 |
| 5.2 Process Management: Product and Service Production and Delivery | Requirements Management<br>RM.ME.1, RM.VE.1, RM.VE.2, RM.VE.3 |
| | Software Project Planning<br>PP.ME.1, PP.VE.1, PP.VE.2, PP.VE.3 |
| | Software Project Tracking and Oversight<br>PT.GO.1, PT.GO.2, PT.CO.2, PT.ME.1, PT.VE.1, PT.VE.2, PT.VE.3 |
| | Software Quality Assurance<br>QA.GO.2, QA.GO.4, QA.ME.1, QA.VE.1, QA.VE.2, QA.VE.3 |
| | Software Configuration Management<br>CM.GO.2, CM.GO.3, CM.ME.1, CM.VE.1, CM.VE.2, CM.VE.3, CM.VE.4 |
| | Organization Process Focus<br>PF.GO.1, PF.GO.2, PF.GO.3, PF.CO.1, PF.AB.1, PF.AB.2, PF.AC.1, PF.AC.2, PF.AC.3, PF.AC.4, PF.AC.5, PF.AC.6, PF.ME.1, PF.VE.1 |
| | Organization Process Definition<br>PD.GO.1, PD.GO.2, PD.CO.1, PD.AB.1, PD.AC.1, PD.AC.2, PD.AC.3, PD.AC.4, PD.AC.5, PD.AC.6, PD.ME.1, PD.VE.1 |
| | Integrated Software Management<br>IM.GO.2, IM.ME.1, IM.VE.1, IM.VE.2, IM.VE.3 |
| | Defect Prevention<br>DP.ME.1, DP.VE.1, DP.VE.2, DP.VE.3 |
| | Technology Change Management<br>TM.ME.1, TM.VE.1, TM.VE.2 |
| | Process Change Management<br>PC.GO.1, PC.GO.2, PC.GO.3, PC.CO.1, PC.CO.2, PC.AB.1, PC.AC.1, PC.AC.2, PC.AC.3, PC.AC.4, PC.AC.5, PC.AC.6, PC.AC.7, PC.AC.8, PC.AC.9, PC.AC.10, PC.ME.1, PC.VE.1, PC.VE.2 |
| 5.3 Process Management: Support Services | |

**Table E.1** Malcolm Baldrige Statements Correlated to SEI CMM (Continued)

| MB Requirement | SEI CMM Correlated Requirements |
|---|---|
| 5.4 Management of Supplier Performance | Software Subcontract Management<br>SM.GO.3, SM.GO.4, SM.CO.1, SM.AC.5, SM.ME.1, SM.VE.1, SM.VE.2, SM.VE.3 |
| 6.1 Product and Service Quality Results | |
| 6.2 Company Operational and Financial Results | |
| 6.3 Supplier Performance Results | |
| 7.1 Customer and Market Knowledge | Requirements Management<br>RM.AB.1, RM.AB.2, RM.AB.3, RM.CO.1, RM.AC.1, RM.AC.2, RM.AC.3, RM.GO.1, RM.GO.2, RM.ME.1, RM.VE.1, RM.VE.2, RM.VE.3, |
| 7.2 Customer Relationship Management | Software Quality Assurance<br>QA.AC.8<br><br>Integrated Software Management<br>IM.AC.11<br><br>Intergroup Coordination<br>IC.AC.1 |
| 7.3 Customer Satisfaction Determination | |
| 7.4 Customer Satisfaction Results | |
| 7.5 Customer Satisfaction Comparison | |

# Correlated Statements of Activity: ISO 9001 to Malcolm Baldrige

**Table F.1** ISO 9001 Statements Correlated to Malcolm Baldrige

| ISO 9001 Requirement | Malcolm Baldrige Correlated Requirements |
|---|---|
| 4.1 Management Responsibility | 1.1 Senior Executive Leadership |
| | 1.1.a |
| | 1.2 Leadership System and Organization |
| | 1.2.c |
| 4.2 Quality System | 3.1 Strategy Development |
| | 3.1.a |
| | 3.1.b |
| | 3.1.c |
| 4.3 Contract Review | 7.1 Customer and Market Knowledge |
| | 7.1.a |
| | 7.1.b |
| | 7.2 Customer Relationship Management |
| | 7.2.a |
| | 7.2.b |
| | 7.2.c |
| | 7.2.d |
| 4.4 Design Control | 4.2 High Performance Work Systems |
| | 4.2.a |

**Table F.1** ISO 9001 Statements Correlated to Malcolm Baldrige (Continued)

| ISO 9001 Requirement | Malcolm Baldrige Correlated Requirements |
|---|---|
| | 5.1 Design and Introduction of Products and Services |
| | 5.1.a |
| | 5.1.b |
| | 5.2 Process Management: Product and Service Production and Delivery |
| 4.5 Document and Data Control | 2.1 Management of Information and Data |
| | 5.1 Design and Introduction of Products and Services |
| | 5.2 Process Management: Product and Service Production and Delivery |
| 4.6 Purchasing | 2.1 Management of Information and Data |
| | 5.2 Process Management: Product and Service Production and Delivery |
| | 5.4 Management of Supplier Performance |
| | 5.4.a |
| | 7.2 Customer Relationship Management |
| 4.7 Control of Customer-Supplied Product | 5.2 Process Management: Product and Service Production and Delivery |
| | 5.4 Management of Supplier Performance |
| 4.8 Product Identification and Traceability | 5.2 Process Management: Product and Service Production and Delivery |
| | 5.4 Management of Supplier Performance |
| 4.9 Process Control | 5.2 Process Management: Product and Service Production and Delivery |
| | 5.2.a |
| | 5.2.b |
| | 5.3 Process Management: Support Services |
| | 5.3.b |
| | 5.3.c |
| 4.10 Inspection and Testing | 2.1 Management of Information and Data |
| | 5.1 Design and Introduction of Products and Services |
| | 5.1.b |
| | 5.2 Process Management: Product and Service Production and Delivery |
| | 5.4 Management of Supplier Performance |

**Table F.1** ISO 9001 Statements Correlated to Malcolm Baldrige (Continued)

| ISO 9001 Requirement | Malcolm Baldrige Correlated Requirements |
|---|---|
| 4.11 Control of Inspection, Measuring, and Test Equipment | 5.2 Process Management: Product and Service Production and Delivery |
| 4.12 Inspection and Test Status | 5.2 Process Management: Product and Service Production and Delivery |
| 4.13 Control of Nonconforming Product | 5.2 Process Management: Product and Service Production and Delivery |
| | 5.4 Management of Supplier Performance |
| 4.14 Corrective and Preventative Action | 2.3 Analysis and Use of Company-Level Data |
| | 2.3.b |
| | 5.1 Design and Introduction of Products and Services |
| | 5.1.c |
| | 5.2 Process Management: Product and Service Production and Delivery |
| | 5.2.b |
| | 5.3 Process Management: Support Services |
| | 5.3.c |
| | 5.4 Management of Supplier Performance |
| | 5.4.b |
| | 7.2 Customer Relationship Management |
| | 7.2.b |
| | 7.2.c |
| | 7.2.d |
| 4.15 Handling, Storage, Packaging, Preservation, and Delivery | 5.1 Design and Introduction of Products and Services |
| | 5.2 Process Management: Product and Service Production and Delivery |
| 4.16 Control of Quality Records | 2.1 Management of Information and Data |
| | 5.2 Process Management: Product and Service Production and Delivery |
| 4.17 Internal Quality Audits | 5.2 Process Management: Product and Service Production and Delivery |
| 4.18 Training | 4.3 Employee Education, Training, and Development |
| | 4.3.a |
| | 4.3.b |
| 4.19 Servicing | 5.1 Design and Introduction of Products and Services |

**Table F.1** ISO 9001 Statements Correlated to Malcolm Baldrige (Continued)

| ISO 9001 Requirement | Malcolm Baldrige Correlated Requirements |
|---|---|
| | 5.2 Process Management: Product and Service Production and Delivery |
| | 7.3 Customer Satisfaction Determination |
| | 7.4 Customer Satisfaction Results |
| 4.20 Statistical Techniques | 2.1 Management of Information and Data |
| | 2.1.a |
| | 2.3 Analysis and Use of Company-Level Data |
| | 2.3.a |
| | 2.3.b |
| | 5.2 Process Management: Product and Service Production and Delivery |

# Correlated Statements of Activity: ISO 9001 to SEI CMM

**Table G.1** ISO 9001 Statements Correlated to SEI CMM

| ISO 9001 Requirement | SEI CMM Correlated Requirements |
|---|---|
| 4.1 Management Responsibility<br>4.1.1 Quality Policy | Software Quality Assurance<br>QA.CO.1 |
| | Software Quality Management<br>QM.CO.1 |
| 4.1.2 Organization<br>4.1.2.1. Responsibility and Authority | Requirements Management<br>RM.AB.1 |
| | Software Project Planning<br>PP.GO.3, PP.CO.1, PP.AB.2, PP.AC.1, PP.AC.3 |
| | Software Project Tracking and Oversight<br>PT.GO.3, PT.CO.1, PT.AB.2, PT.AB.3 |
| | Software Subcontract Management<br>SM.CO.2 |
| | Software Quality Assurance<br>QA.AB.1 |
| | Software Configuration Management<br>CM.AB.1, CM.AB.2 |
| | Organization Process Focus<br>PF.AB.1 |
| | Training Program<br>TP.AB.1 |

**Table G.1** ISO 9001 Statements Correlated to SEI CMM (Continued)

| ISO 9001 Requirement | SEI CMM Correlated Requirements |
|---|---|
| | Intergroup Coordination<br>IC.GO.1, IC.GO.2, IC.GO.3, IC.CO.1, IC.AB.1, IC.AB.2, IC.AB.3, IC.AB.4, IC.AB.5, IC.AC.1, IC.AC.2, IC.AC.3, IC.AC.4, IC.AC.5, IC.AC.6, IC.AC.7, IC.ME.1, IC.VE.1, IC.VE.2, IC.VE.3 |
| | Quantitative Process Management<br>QP.AB.1 |
| | Defect Prevention<br>DP.AB.1, DP.AB.2 |
| | Technology Change Management<br>TM.AB.1 |
| 4.1.2.2. Resources | Requirements Management<br>RM.AB.3 |
| | Software Project Planning<br>PP.AB.3, PP.AC.9, PP.AC.10, PP.AC.11 |
| | Software Project Tracking and Oversight<br>PT.AB.3 |
| | Software Subcontract Management<br>SM.AB.1 |
| | Software Quality Assurance<br>QA.AB.2 |
| | Software Configuration Management<br>CM.AB.3 |
| | Organization Process Focus<br>PF.AB.2 |
| | Organization Process Definition<br>PD.AB.1 |
| | Training Program<br>TP.AB.2 |
| | Integrated Software Management<br>IM.AB.1 |
| | Software Product Engineering<br>PE.AB.1 |
| | Intergroup Coordination<br>IC.AB.1 |
| | Peer Reviews<br>PR.AB.1 |

**Table G.1** ISO 9001 Statements Correlated to SEI CMM (Continued)

| ISO 9001 Requirement | SEI CMM Correlated Requirements |
| --- | --- |
| | Quantitative Process Management<br>QP.AB.2 |
| | Software Quality Management<br>QM.AB.1 |
| | Defect Prevention<br>DP.AB.3 |
| | Technology Change Management<br>TM.AB.2 |
| | Process Change Management<br>PC.AB.1 |
| 4.1.3 Management Review | Requirements Management<br>RM.VE.1, RM.VE.2, RM.VE.3 |
| | Software Project Planning<br>PP.AC.4, PP.VE.1, PP.VE.2, PP.VE.3 |
| | Software Project Tracking and Oversight<br>PT.VE.1, PT.VE.2, PT.VE.3 |
| | Software Subcontract Management<br>SM.VE.1, SM.VE.2, SM.VE.3 |
| | Software Quality Assurance<br>QA.VE.1, QA.VE.2, QA.VE.3 |
| | Software Configuration Management<br>CM.VE.1, CM.VE.2, CM.VE.3, CM.VE.4 |
| | Organization Process Focus<br>PF.VE.1 |
| | Organization Process Definition<br>PD.VE.1 |
| | Training Program<br>TP.VE.1, TP.VE.3 |
| | Integrated Software Management<br>IM.VE.1, IM.VE.2, IM.VE.3 |
| | Software Product Engineering<br>PE.VE.1, PE.VE.2, PE.VE.3 |
| | Intergroup Coordination<br>IC.VE.1, IC.VE.2, IC.VE.3 |
| | Peer Reviews<br>PR.VE.1 |

**Table G.1** ISO 9001 Statements Correlated to SEI CMM (Continued)

| ISO 9001 Requirement | SEI CMM Correlated Requirements |
| --- | --- |
| | Quantitative Process Management<br>QP.VE.1, QP.VE.2, QP.VE.3 |
| | Software Quality Management<br>QM.VE.1, QM.VE.2, QM.VE.3 |
| | Defect Prevention<br>DP.VE.1, DP.VE.2, DP.VE.3 |
| | Technology Change Management<br>TM.VE.1, TM.VE.2 |
| | Process Change Management<br>PC.VE.1, PC.VE.2 |
| | Software Project Tracking and Oversight<br>PT.AC.3, PT.AC.12, PT.AC.13 |
| | Software Quality Assurance<br>QA.AC.4, QA.AC.5, QA.AC.8 |
| 4.2 Quality System<br>4.2.2 Quality-System Procedures | Software Project Planning<br>PP.AC.4, PP.AC.6, PP.AC.9, PP.AC.10, PP.AC.11, PP.AC.12 |
| | Software Project Tracking and Oversight<br>PT.AC.2, PT.AC.3, PT.AC.13 |
| | Software Subcontract Management<br>SM.AC.1, SM.AC.2, SM.AC.6, SM.AC.9, SM.AC.10, SM.AC.11, SM.AC.12 |
| | Software Quality Assurance<br>QA.AC.1, QA.AC.7 |
| | Software Configuration Management<br>CM.AC.1, CM.AC.5, CM.AC.6, CM.AC.7, CM.AC.8, CM.AC.10 |
| | Organization Process Definition<br>PD.AC.1, PD.AC.2, PD.AC.3, PD.AC.4, PD.AC.5, PD.AC.6 |
| | Training Program<br>TP.AC.2, TP.AC.4, TP.AC.5 |
| | Integrated Software Management<br>IM.AC.1, IM.AC.2, IM.AC.3, IM.AC.6, IM.AC.7, IM.AC.8, IM.AC.9, IM.AC.10 |
| | Intergroup Coordination<br>IC.AC.4, IC.AC.6 |
| | Peer Reviews<br>PR.AC.2 |

**Table G.1** ISO 9001 Statements Correlated to SEI CMM (Continued)

| ISO 9001 Requirement | SEI CMM Correlated Requirements |
|---|---|
| | Quantitative Process Management<br>QP.AC.1, QP.AC.4, QP.AC.5, QP.AC.7 |
| | Software Quality Management<br>QM.AC.1 |
| | Defect Prevention<br>DP.AC.3, DP.AC.6, DP.AC.7 |
| | Technology Change Management<br>TM.AC.5, TM.AC.7, TM.AC.8 |
| | Process Change Management<br>PC.AC.3, PC.AC.5, PC.AC.8 |
| | Requirements Management<br>RM.VE.1, RM.VE.2, RM.VE.3 |
| | Software Project Planning<br>PP.VE.1, PP.VE.2, PP.VE.3 |
| | Software Project Tracking and Oversight<br>PT.VE.1, PT.VE.2, PT.VE.3 |
| | Software Subcontract Management<br>SM.VE.1, SM.VE.2, SM.VE.3 |
| | Software Quality Assurance<br>QA.VE.1, QA.VE.2, QA.VE.3 |
| | Software Configuration Management<br>CM.VE.1, CM.VE.2, CM.VE.3, CM.VE.4 |
| | Organization Process Focus<br>PF.VE.1 |
| | Organization Process Definition<br>PD.VE.1 |
| | Training Program<br>TP.VE.1, TP.VE.2, TP.VE.3 |
| | Integrated Software Management<br>IM.VE.1, IM.VE.2, IM.VE.3 |
| | Software Product Engineering<br>PE.VE.1, PE.VE.2, PE.VE.3 |
| | Intergroup Coordination<br>IC.VE.1, IC.VE.2, IC.VE.3 |
| | Peer Reviews<br>PR.VE.1 |

**Table G.1** ISO 9001 Statements Correlated to SEI CMM (Continued)

| ISO 9001 Requirement | SEI CMM Correlated Requirements |
|---|---|
| | Quantitative Process Management<br>QP.VE.1, QP.VE.2, QP.VE.3 |
| | Software Quality Management<br>QM.VE.1, QM.VE.2, QM.VE.3 |
| | Defect Prevention<br>DP.VE.1, DP.VE.2, DP.VE.3 |
| | Technology Change Management<br>TM.VE.1, TM.VE.2 |
| | Process Change Management<br>PC.VE.1, PC.VE.2 |
| 4.2.3 Quality Planning | Software Project Planning<br>PP.AC.6, PP.AC.7 |
| | Software Subcontract Management<br>SM.AC.4, SM.AC.5 |
| | Software Quality Assurance<br>QA.AC.1, QA.AC.2, QA.AC.3 |
| | Software Configuration Management<br>CM.AC.1, CM.AC.2 |
| | Intergroup Coordination<br>IC.AC.3 |
| | Peer Reviews<br>PR.AC.1 |
| | Quantitative Process Management<br>QP.AC.1, QP.AC.2 |
| | Software Quality Management<br>QM.AC.1, QM.AC.2 |
| | Defect Prevention<br>DP.AC.1 |
| | Technology Change Management<br>TM.AC.1 |
| | Process Change Management<br>PC.AC.3, PC.AC.4 |
| 4.3 Contract Review | Requirements Management<br>RM.GO.1, RM.GO.2, RM.CO.1, RM.AB.1, RM.AB.2, RM.AB.3,<br>RM.AC.1, RM.AC.2, RM.AC.3, RM.ME.1, RM.VE.1, RM.VE.2,<br>RM.VE.3 |

**Table G.1** ISO 9001 Statements Correlated to SEI CMM (Continued)

| ISO 9001 Requirement | SEI CMM Correlated Requirements |
|---|---|
|  | Software Project Planning<br>PP.GO.1, PP.GO.2, PP.GO.3, PP.CO.1, PP.CO.2, PP.AB.1, PP.AB.2, PP.AB.3, PP.AC.1, PP.AC.2, PP.AC.3, PP.AC.4, PP.AC.5, PP.AC.6, PP.AC.7, PP.AC.8, PP.AC.9, PP.AC.10, PP.AC.11, PP.AC.12, PP.AC.13, PP.AC.14, PP.AC.15, PP.ME.1, PP.VE.1, PP.VE.2, PP.VE.3 |
|  | Software Project Tracking and Oversight<br>PT.AC.2, PT.AC.3, PT.AC.4 |
| 4.4 Design Control | Requirements Management<br>RM.GO.1, RM.GO.2, RM.CO.1, RM.AB.1, RM.AB.2, RM.AB.3, RM.AC.1, RM.AC.2, RM.AC.3, RM.ME.1, RM.VE.1, RM.VE.2, RM.VE.3 |
|  | Software Project Planning<br>PP.GO.1, PP.GO.2, PP.CO.1, PP.CO.2, PP.AB.1, PP.AB.2, PP.AB.3, PP.AB.4, PP.AC.1, PP.AC.2, PP.AC.3, PP.AC.4, PP.AC.5, PP.AC.6, PP.AC.7, PP.AC.8, PP.AC.9, PP.AC.10, PP.AC.11, PP.AC.12, PP.AC.13, PP.AC.14, PP.AC.15, PP.ME.1, PP.VE.1, PP.VE.2, PP.VE.3 |
|  | Software Project Tracking and Oversight<br>PT.GO.1, PT.GO.2, PT.GO.3, PT.CO.1, PT.CO.2, PT.AB.1, PT.AB.2, PT.AB.3, PT.AC.1, PT.AC.2, PT.AC.3, PT.AC.4, PT.AC.5, PT.AC.6, PT.AC.7, PT.AC.8, PT.AC.9, PT.AC.10, PT.AC.11, PT.AC.12, PT.AC.13, PT.ME.1, PT.VE.1, PT.VE.2, PT.VE.3 |
|  | Software Configuration Management<br>CM.GO.1, CM.GO.2, CM.GO.3, CM.GO.4, CM.CO.1, CM.AB.1, CM.AB.2, CM.AB.3, CM.AC.1, CM.AC.2, CM.AC.3, CM.AC.4, CM.AC.5, CM.AC.6, CM.AC.7, CM.AC.8, CM.AC.9, CM.AC.10, CM.ME.1, CM.VE.1, CM.VE.2, CM.VE.3, CM.VE.4 |
|  | Software Product Engineering<br>PE.GO.1, PE.GO.2, PE.CO.1, PE.AB.1, PE.AC.1, PE.AC.2, PE.AC.3, PE.AC.4, PE.AC.5, PE.AC.6, PE.AC.7, PE.AC.8, PE.AC.9, PE.AC.10, PE.ME.1, PE.ME.2, PE.VE.1, PE.VE.2, PE.VE.3 |
|  | Intergroup Coordination<br>IC.GO.1, IC.GO.2, IC.GO.3, IC.CO.1, IC.AB.1, IC.AB.2, IC.AC.1, IC.AC.2, IC.AC.3, IC.AC.4, IC.AC.5, IC.AC.6, IC.AC.7, IC.ME.1, IC.VE.1, IC.VE.2, IC.VE.3 |
|  | Peer Reviews<br>PR.GO.1, PR.GO.2, PR.CO.1, PR.AB.1, PR.AC.1, PR.AC.2, PR.AC.3, PR.ME.1, PR.VE.1 |

**Table G.1** ISO 9001 Statements Correlated to SEI CMM (Continued)

| ISO 9001 Requirement | SEI CMM Correlated Requirements |
|---|---|
| 4.5 Document and Data Control | Software Configuration Management<br>CM.GO.2, CM.GO.3, CM.CO.1, CM.AB.1, CM.AB.2, CM.AB.3, CM.AC.1, CM.AC.2, CM.AC.3, CM.AC.4, CM.AC.5, CM.AC.6, CM.AC.7, CM.AC.8, CM.AC.9, CM.AC.10, CM.ME.1, CM.VE.1, CM.VE.2, CM.VE.3, CM.VE.4 |
| 4.6 Purchasing | Software Subcontract Management<br>SM.GO.1, SM.GO.2, SM.GO.4, SM.CO.1, SM.CO.2, SM.AB.1, SM.AC.1, SM.AC.2, SM.AC.3, SM.AC.4, SM.AC.5, SM.AC.6, SM.AC.7, SM.AC.8, SM.AC.9, SM.AC.10, SM.AC.11, SM.AC.12, SM.AC.13, SM.ME.1, SM.VE.1, SM.VE.2, SM.VE.3<br><br>Software Quality Management<br>QM.AC.5 |
| 4.7 Control of Customer-Supplied Product | |
| 4.8 Product Identification and Traceability | Software Configuration Management<br>CM.GO.2, CM.GO.3, CM.CO.1, CM.AB.1, CM.AB.2, CM.AC.1, CM.AC.2, CM.AC.3, CM.AC.4, CM.AC.5, CM.AC.6, CM.AC.7, CM.AC.8, CM.AC.9, CM.AC.10, CM.ME.1, CM.VE.1, CM.VE.2, CM.VE.3, CM.VE.4 |
| 4.9 Process Control | Software Project Planning<br>PP.GO.1, PP.GO.2, PP.CO.1, PP.CO.2, PP.AB.1, PP.AB.2, PP.AB.3, PP.AB.4, PP.AC.1, PP.AC.2, PP.AC.3, PP.AC.4, PP.AC.5, PP.AC.6, PP.AC.7, PP.AC.8, PP.AC.9, PP.AC.10, PP.AC.11, PP.AC.12, PP.AC.13, PP.AC.14, PP.AC.15, PP.ME.1, PP.VE.1, PP.VE.2, PP.VE.3<br><br>Software Project Tracking and Oversight<br>PT.GO.1, PT.GO.2, PT.CO.1, PT.CO.2, PT.AB.1, PT.AB.2, PT.AB.3, PT.AB.4, PT.AB.5, PT.AC.1, PT.AC.2, PT.AC.3, PT.AC.5, PT.AC.6, PT.AC.7, PT.AC.8, PT.AC.9, PT.AC.10, PT.AC.11, PT.AC.12, PT.AC.13, PT.ME.1, PT.VE.1, PT.VE.2, PT.VE.3<br><br>Software Subcontract Management<br>SM.GO.1, SM.GO.2, SM.GO.4, SM.CO.1, SM.CO.2, SM.AB.1, SM.AC.1, SM.AC.2, SM.AC.3, SM.AC.4, SM.AC.5, SM.AC.6, SM.AC.7, SM.AC.8, SM.AC.9, SM.AC.10, SM.AC.11, SM.AC.12, SM.AC.13, SM.ME.1, SM.VE.1, SM.VE.2, SM.VE.3<br><br>Software Quality Assurance<br>QA.GO.1, QA.GO.2, QA.GO.4, QA.CO.1, QA.AB.1, QA.AB.2, QA.AB.3, QA.AB.4, QA.AC.1, QA.AC.2, QA.AC.3, QA.AC.4, QA.AC.5, QA.AC.6, QA.AC.7, QA.AC.8, QA.ME.1, QA.VE.1, QA.VE.2, QA.VE.3 |

**Table G.1** ISO 9001 Statements Correlated to SEI CMM (Continued)

| ISO 9001 Requirement | SEI CMM Correlated Requirements |
|---|---|
| | Software Configuration Management<br>CM.GO.1, CM.GO.2, CM.GO.3, CM.CO.1, CM.AB.1, CM.AB.2, CM.AB.3, CM.AB.4, CM.AB.5, CM.AC.1, CM.AC.2, CM.AC.3, CM.AC.4, CM.AC.5, CM.AC.6, CM.AC.7, CM.AC.8, CM.AC.9, CM.AC.10, CM.ME.1, CM.VE.1, CM.VE.2, CM.VE.3, CM.VE.4 |
| | Organization Process Definition<br>PD.GO.1, PD.GO.2, PD.CO.1, PD.AB.1, PD.AB.2, PD.AC.1, PD.AC.2, PD.AC.3, PD.AC.4, PD.AC.5, PD.AC.6, PD.ME.1, PD.VE.1 |
| | Integrated Software Management<br>IM.GO.1, IM.GO.2, IM.CO.1, IM.AB.1, IM.AB.2, IM.AB.3, IM.AC.1, IM.AC.2, IM.AC.3, IM.AC.4, IM.AC.5, IM.AC.6, IM.AC.7, IM.AC.8, IM.AC.9, IM.AC.10, IM.AC.11, IM.ME.1, IM.VE.1, IM.VE.2, IM.VE.3 |
| | Software Product Engineering<br>PE.GO.1, PE.GO.2, PE.CO.1, PE.AB.1, PE.AB.2, PE.AB.3, PE.AB.4, PE.AC.1, PE.AC.2, PE.AC.3, PE.AC.4, PE.AC.5, PE.AC.6, PE.AC.7, PE.AC.8, PE.AC.9, PE.AC.10, PE.ME.1, PE.ME.2, PE.VE.1, PE.VE.2, PE.VE.3 |
| | Peer Reviews<br>PR.GO.1, PR.GO.2, PR.CO.1, PR.AB.1, PR.AB.2, PR.AB.3, PR.AC.1, PR.AC.2, PR.AC.3, PR.ME.1, PR.VE.1 |
| | Quantitative Process Management<br>QP.GO.1, QP.GO.2, QP.GO.3, QP.CO.1, QP.CO.2, QP.AB.1, QP.AB.2, QP.AB.3, QP.AB.4, QP.AB.5, QP.AC.1, QP.AC.2, QP.AC.3, QP.AC.4, QP.AC.5, QP.AC.6, QP.AC.7, QP.ME.1, QP.VE.1, QP.VE.2, QP.VE.3 |
| | Software Quality Management<br>QM.GO.1, QM.GO.2, QM.GO.3, QM.CO.1, QM.AB.1, QM.AB.2, QM.AB.3, QM.AC.1, QM.AC.2, QM.AC.3, QM.AC.4, QM.AC.5, QM.ME.1, QM.VE.1, QM.VE.2, QM.VE.3 |
| | Technology Change Management<br>TM.GO.1, TM.GO.2, TM.GO.3, TM.CO.1, TM.AB.1, TM.AB.2, TM.AB.3, TM.AB.4, TM.AB.5, TM.AC.1, TM.AC.2, TM.AC.4, TM.AC.5, TM.AC.6, TM.AC.7, TM.AC.8, TM.ME.1, TM.VE.1, TM.VE.2 |
| 4.10 Inspection and Testing | Software Subcontract Management<br>SM.AC.12 |
| | Software Product Engineering<br>PE.AC.3, PE.AC.4, PE.AC.5, PE.AC.6, PE.AC.7, PE.AC.9, PE.ME.1 |

**Table G.1** ISO 9001 Statements Correlated to SEI CMM (Continued)

| ISO 9001 Requirement | SEI CMM Correlated Requirements |
|---|---|
| | Peer Reviews<br>PR.GO.1, PR.GO.2, PR.CO.1, PR.AB.1, PR.AC.1, PR.AC.2, PR.AC.3, PR.ME.1 |
| 4.11 Control of Inspection, Measuring, and Test Equipment | |
| 4.12 Inspection and Test Status | Software Configuration Management<br>CM.GO.2, CM.GO.4, CM.CO.1, CM.AC.4, CM.AC.5, CM.AC.6, CM.AC.7, CM.AC.8, CM.AC.9 |
| 4.13 Control of Nonconforming Product | Software Configuration Management<br>CM.GO.2, CM.GO.3, CM.GO.4, CM.CO.1, CM.AB.1, CM.AB.2, CM.AC.1, CM.AC.2, CM.AC.3, CM.AC.4, CM.AC.5, CM.AC.6, CM.AC.7, CM.AC.8, CM.AC.9 |
| | Software Product Engineering<br>PE.AC.9 |
| 4.14 Corrective and Preventative Action | Software Project Tracking and Oversight<br>PT.AC.5, PT.AC.6, PT.AC.7, PT.AC.8, PT.AC.9 |
| | Defect Prevention<br>DP.GO.1, DP.GO.2, DP.GO.3, DP.CO.1, DP.CO.2, DP.AB.1, DP.AB.2, DP.AB.3, DP.AC.1, DP.AC.2, DP.AC.3, DP.AC.4, DP.AC.5, DP.AC.6, DP.AC.7, DP.AC.8, DP.ME.1, DP.VE.1, DP.VE.2, DP.VE.3 |
| 4.15 Handling, Storage, Packaging, Preservation, and Delivery | |
| 4.16 Control of Quality Record | Software Configuration Management<br>CM.GO.1, CM.GO.2, CM.GO.3, CM.CO.1, CM.AB.1, CM.AB.2, CM.AC.1, CM.AC.2, CM.AC.3, CM.AC.4, CM.AC.5, CM.AC.6, CM.AC.7, CM.AC.8, CM.AC.9, CM.VE.4 |
| 4.17 Internal Quality Audits | Software Quality Assurance<br>QA.GO.1, QA.GO.2, QA.GO.3, QA.GO.4, QA.CO.1, QA.AB.1, QA.AB.2, QA.AC.1, QA.AC.2, QA.AC.3, QA.AC.4, QA.AC.5, QA.AC.6, QA.AC.7, QA.AC.8, QA.ME.1, QA.VE.1, QA.VE.2, QA.VE.3 |
| 4.18 Training | Training Program<br>TP.GO.1, TP.GO.2, TP.GO.3, TP.CO.1, TP.AB.1, TP.AB.2, TP.AB.3, TP.AB.4, TP.AC.1, TP.AC.2, TP.AC.3, TP.AC.4, TP.AC.5, TP.AC.6, TP.ME.1, TP.ME.2, TP.VE.1, TP.VE.2, TP.VE.3 |
| | Requirements Management<br>RM.AB.4 |
| | Software Project Planning<br>PP.AB.4 |

**Table G.1** ISO 9001 Statements Correlated to SEI CMM (Continued)

| ISO 9001 Requirement | SEI CMM Correlated Requirements |
|---|---|
| | Software Project Tracking and Oversight<br>PT.AB.4, PT.AB.5 |
| | Software Subcontract Management<br>SM.AB.2, SM.AB.3 |
| | Software Quality Assurance<br>QA.AB.3, QA.AB.4 |
| | Software Configuration Management<br>CM.AB.4, CM.AB.5 |
| | Organization Process Focus<br>PF.AB.3, PF.AB.4 |
| | Organization Process Definition<br>PD.AB.2 |
| | Integrated Software Management<br>IM.AB.2, IM.AB.3 |
| | Software Product Engineering<br>PE.AB.2, PE.AB.3, PE.AB.4 |
| | Intergroup Coordination<br>IC.AB.3, IC.AB.4, IC.AB.5 |
| | Peer Reviews<br>PR.AB.2, PR.AB.3 |
| | Quantitative Process Management<br>QP.AB.4 |
| | Software Quality Management<br>QM.AB.2, QM.AB.3 |
| | Defect Prevention<br>DP.AB.4 |
| | Technology Change Management<br>TM.AB.5 |
| | Process Change Management<br>PC.AB.2, PC.AB.3, PC.AB.4 |
| 4.19 Servicing | |
| 4.20 Statistical Techniques | Quantitative Process Management<br>QP.GO.1, QP.GO.2, QP.GO.3, QP.CO.1, QP.CO.2, QP.AB.1,<br>QP.AB.2, QP.AC.1, QP.AC.2, QP.AC.3, QP.AC.4, QP.AC.5,<br>QP.AC.6, QP.AC.7, QP.ME.1, QP.VE.1, QP.VE.2, QP.VE.3 |
| | Software Quality Management<br>QM.GO.3, QM.AC.3, QM.AC.4 |

**Table G.1** ISO 9001 Statements Correlated to SEI CMM (Continued)

| ISO 9001 Requirement | SEI CMM Correlated Requirements |
|---|---|
| | Requirements Management<br>RM.ME.1 |
| | Software Project Planning<br>PP.ME.1 |
| | Software Project Tracking and Oversight<br>PT.ME.1 |
| | Software Subcontract Management<br>SM.ME.1 |
| | Software Quality Assurance<br>QA.ME.1 |
| | Software Configuration Management<br>CM.ME.1 |
| | Organization Process Focus<br>PF.ME.1 |
| | Organization Process Definition<br>PD.ME.1 |
| | Training Program<br>TP.ME.1, TP.ME.2 |
| | Integrated Software Management<br>IM.ME.1 |
| | Software Product Engineering<br>PE.ME.1, PE.ME.2 |
| | Intergroup Coordination<br>IC.ME.1 |
| | Peer Reviews<br>PR.ME.1 |
| | Quantitative Process Management<br>QP.ME.1 |
| | Software Quality Management<br>QM.ME.1 |
| | Defect Prevention<br>DP.ME.1 |
| | Technology Change Management<br>TM.ME.1 |
| | Process Change Management<br>PC.ME.1 |

# Correlated Statements of Activity: SEI CMM to Malcolm Baldrige

**Table H.1** SEI CMM Statements Correlated to Malcolm Baldrige

| SEI CMM Requirement | Malcolm Baldrige Correlated Requirements |
|---|---|
| Goals | 1.1 Senior Executive Leadership |
| | 2.1 Management of Information and Data |
| | 5.2 Process Management: Product and Service Production and Delivery |
| Commitment to Perform | 1.1 Senior Executive Leadership |
| Ability to Perform | 1.1 Senior Executive Leadership |
| | 2.1 Management of Information and Data |
| | 4.3 Employee Education, Training, and Development |
| Activities Performed | 2.1 Management of Information and Data |
| Measurement and Analysis | 2.1 Management of Information and Data |
| | 2.3 Analysis and Use of Company-Level Data |
| | 5.2 Process Management: Product and Service Production and Delivery |
| Verifying Implementation | 1.1 Senior Executive Leadership |
| | 1.2 Leadership System and Organization |
| | 5.2 Process Management: Product and Service Production and Delivery |
| Requirements Management | 1.1 Senior Executive Leadership |
| | 1.2 Leadership System and Organization |

**Table H.1** SEI CMM Statements Correlated to Malcolm Baldrige (Continued)

| SEI CMM Requirement | Malcolm Baldrige Correlated Requirements |
|---|---|
| | 2.1 Management of Information and Data |
| | 2.3 Analysis and Use of Company-Level Data |
| | 5.1 Design and Introduction of Products and Services |
| | 5.2 Process Management: Product and Service Production and Delivery |
| | 7.1 Customer and Market Knowledge |
| Software Project Planning | 1.1 Senior Executive Leadership |
| | 1.2 Leadership System and Organization |
| | 2.1 Management of Information and Data |
| | 2.3 Analysis and Use of Company-Level Data |
| | 4.3 Employee Education, Training, and Development |
| | 5.2 Process Management: Product and Service Production and Delivery |
| Software Project Tracking and Oversight | 1.1 Senior Executive Leadership |
| | 1.2 Leadership System and Organization |
| | 2.1 Management of Information and Data |
| | 2.3 Analysis and Use of Company-Level Data |
| | 4.3 Employee Education, Training, and Development |
| | 5.2 Process Management: Product and Service Production and Delivery |
| Software Subcontract Management | 1.1 Senior Executive Leadership |
| | 1.2 Leadership System and Organization |
| | 2.1 Management of Information and Data |
| | 2.3 Analysis and Use of Company-Level Data |
| | 4.3 Employee Education, Training, and Development |
| | 5.4 Management of Supplier Performance |
| Software Quality Assurance | 1.1 Senior Executive Leadership |
| | 1.2 Leadership System and Organization |
| | 2.1 Management of Information and Data |
| | 2.3 Analysis and Use of Company-Level Data |
| | 4.3 Employee Education, Training, and Development |
| | 5.2 Process Management: Product and Service Production and Delivery |

**Table H.1** SEI CMM Statements Correlated to Malcolm Baldrige (Continued)

| SEI CMM Requirement | Malcolm Baldrige Correlated Requirements |
| --- | --- |
| | 7.2 Customer Relationship Management |
| Software Configuration Management | 1.1 Senior Executive Leadership |
| | 1.2 Leadership System and Organization |
| | 2.1 Management of Information and Data |
| | 2.3 Analysis and Use of Company-Level Data |
| | 4.3 Employee Education, Training, and Development |
| | 5.2 Process Management: Product and Service Production and Delivery |
| Organization Process Focus | 1.1 Senior Executive Leadership |
| | 1.2 Leadership System and Organization |
| | 2.1 Management of Information and Data |
| | 2.2 Competitive Comparisons and Benchmarking |
| | 4.3 Employee Education, Training, and Development |
| | 5.2 Process Management: Product and Service Production and Delivery |
| Organization Process Definition | 1.1 Senior Executive Leadership |
| | 1.2 Leadership System and Organization |
| | 2.1 Management of Information and Data |
| | 2.2 Competitive Comparisons and Benchmarking |
| | 2.3 Analysis and Use of Company-Level Data |
| | 4.3 Employee Education, Training, and Development |
| | 5.2 Process Management: Product and Service Production and Delivery |
| | 7.2 Customer Relationship Management |
| Training Program | 1.1 Senior Executive Leadership |
| | 1.2 Leadership System and Organization |
| | 2.1 Management of Information and Data |
| | 2.3 Analysis and Use of Company-Level Data |
| | 4.3 Employee Education, Training, and Development |
| Integrated Software Management | 1.1 Senior Executive Leadership |
| | 1.2 Leadership System and Organization |
| | 2.1 Management of Information and Data |
| | 4.3 Employee Education, Training, and Development |

**Table H.1** SEI CMM Statements Correlated to Malcolm Baldrige (Continued)

| SEI CMM Requirement | Malcolm Baldrige Correlated Requirements |
| --- | --- |
| | 5.2 Process Management: Product and Service Production and Delivery |
| | 7.2 Customer Relationship Management |
| Software Product Engineering | 1.1 Senior Executive Leadership |
| | 1.2 Leadership System and Organization |
| | 2.1 Management of Information and Data |
| | 2.3 Analysis and Use of Company-Level Data |
| | 4.3 Employee Education, Training, and Development |
| | 5.1 Design and Introduction of Products and Services |
| Intergroup Coordination | 1.1 Senior Executive Leadership |
| | 1.2 Leadership System and Organization |
| | 2.1 Management of Information and Data |
| | 4.2 High Performance Work Systems |
| | 4.3 Employee Education, Training, and Development |
| | 5.1 Design and Introduction of Products and Services |
| | 7.2 Customer Relationship Management |
| Peer Reviews | 2.1 Management of Information and Data |
| | 2.3 Analysis and Use of Company-Level Data |
| | 4.3 Employee Education, Training, and Development |
| | 5.1 Design and Introduction of Products and Services |
| Quantitative Process Management | 1.1 Senior Executive Leadership |
| | 1.2 Leadership System and Organization |
| | 2.1 Management of Information and Data |
| | 2.3 Analysis and Use of Company-Level Data |
| | 4.3 Employee Education, Training, and Development |
| Software Quality Management | 1.1 Senior Executive Leadership |
| | 1.2 Leadership System and Organization |
| | 2.1 Management of Information and Data |
| | 2.3 Analysis and Use of Company-Level Data |
| | 4.3 Employee Education, Training, and Development |
| | 5.1 Design and Introduction of Products and Services |
| Defect Prevention | 1.1 Senior Executive Leadership |

**Table H.1** SEI CMM Statements Correlated to Malcolm Baldrige (Continued)

| SEI CMM Requirement | Malcolm Baldrige Correlated Requirements |
| --- | --- |
| | 1.2 Leadership System and Organization |
| | 2.1 Management of Information and Data |
| | 2.3 Analysis and Use of Company-Level Data |
| | 4.3 Employee Education, Training, and Development |
| | 5.2 Process Management: Product and Service Production and Delivery |
| Technology Change Management | 1.1 Senior Executive Leadership |
| | 1.2 Leadership System and Organization |
| | 2.1 Management of Information and Data |
| | 2.2 Competitive Comparisons and Benchmarking |
| | 2.3 Analysis and Use of Company-Level Data |
| | 4.3 Employee Education, Training, and Development |
| | 5.2 Process Management: Product and Service Production and Delivery |
| Process Change Management | 1.1 Senior Executive Leadership |
| | 1.2 Leadership System and Organization |
| | 2.1 Management of Information and Data |
| | 2.2 Competitive Comparisons and Benchmarking |
| | 2.3 Analysis and Use of Company-Level Data |
| | 4.3 Employee Education, Training, and Development |
| | 5.2 Process Management: Product and Service Production and Delivery |

# I

# Correlated Statements of Activity: SEI CMM to ISO 9001

**Table I.1**  SEI CMM Statements Correlated to ISO 9001

| SEI CMM Requirement | ISO 9001 Correlated Requirements |
| --- | --- |
| Goals | 4.1 Management Responsibility |
|  | 4.1.1 Quality Policy |
| Commitment to Perform | 4.1 Management Responsibility |
|  | 4.1.1 Quality Policy |
| Ability to Perform | 4.1 Management Responsibility |
|  | 4.1.2 Organization |
|  | 4.1.2.2 Resources |
|  | 4.18 Training |
| Activities Performed | 4.1 Management Responsibility |
|  | 4.1.3 Management Review |
|  | 4.2 Quality System |
|  | 4.2.2 Quality-System Procedures |
|  | 4.9 Process Control |
|  | 4.16 Control of Quality Records |
| Measurement and Analysis | 4.20 Statistical Techniques |
| Verifying Implementation | 4.1 Management Responsibility |
|  | 4.1.3 Management Review |
|  | 4.2 Quality System |

**Table I.1** SEI CMM Statements Correlated to ISO 9001 (Continued)

| SEI CMM Requirement | ISO 9001 Correlated Requirements |
|---|---|
| | 4.2.2 Quality-System Procedures |
| Requirements Management | 4.1 Management Responsibility |
| | 4.1.2 Organization |
| | 4.1.2.1 Responsibility and Authority |
| | 4.1.2.2 Resources |
| | 4.1.3 Management Review |
| | 4.2 Quality System |
| | 4.2.2 Quality-System Procedures |
| | 4.3 Contract Review |
| | 4.4 Design Control |
| | 4.4.4 Design Input |
| | 4.18 Training |
| | 4.20 Statistical Techniques |
| Software Project Planning | 4.1 Management Responsibility |
| | 4.1.2 Organization |
| | 4.1.2.1 Responsibility and Authority |
| | 4.1.2.2 Resources |
| | 4.1.3 Management Review |
| | 4.2 Quality System |
| | 4.2.2 Quality-System Procedures |
| | 4.2.3 Quality Planning |
| | 4.3 Contract Review |
| | 4.4 Design Control |
| | 4.4.2 Design and Development Planning |
| | 4.9 Process Control |
| | 4.18 Training |
| | 4.20 Statistical Techniques |
| Software Project Tracking and Oversight | 4.1 Management Responsibility |
| | 4.1.2 Organization |
| | 4.1.2.1 Responsibility and Authority |
| | 4.1.2.2 Resources |
| | 4.1.3 Management Review |

**Table I.1** SEI CMM Statements Correlated to ISO 9001 (Continued)

| SEI CMM Requirement | ISO 9001 Correlated Requirements |
| --- | --- |
| | 4.2 Quality System |
| | 4.2.2 Quality-System Procedures |
| | 4.3 Contract Review |
| | 4.4 Design Control |
| | 4.9 Process Control |
| | 4.14 Corrective and Preventative Action |
| | 4.14.1 General |
| | 4.14.2 Corrective Action |
| | 4.18 Training |
| | 4.20 Statistical Techniques |
| | 4.20.1 Identification of Need |
| | 4.20.2 Procedures |
| Software Subcontract Management | 4.1 Management Responsibility |
| | 4.1.2 Organization |
| | 4.1.2.1 Responsibility and Authority |
| | 4.1.2.2 Resources |
| | 4.1.3 Management Review |
| | 4.2 Quality System |
| | 4.2.2 Quality-System Procedures |
| | 4.6 Purchasing |
| | 4.6.1 General |
| | 4.6.2 Evaluation of Sub-Contractors |
| | 4.6.3 Purchasing Data |
| | 4.6.4 Verification of Purchased Product |
| | 4.10 Inspection and Testing |
| | 4.10.2 Receiving Inspection and Testing |
| | 4.18 Training |
| | 4.20 Statistical Techniques |
| Software Quality Assurance | 4.1 Management Responsibility |
| | 4.1.1 Quality Policy |
| | 4.1.2 Organization |
| | 4.1.2.1 Responsibility and Authority |

**Table I.1** SEI CMM Statements Correlated to ISO 9001 (Continued)

| SEI CMM Requirement | ISO 9001 Correlated Requirements |
| --- | --- |
| | 4.1.2.2 Resources |
| | 4.1.3 Management Review |
| | 4.2 Quality System |
| | 4.2.2 Quality-System Procedures |
| | 4.9 Process Control |
| | 4.17 Internal Quality Audits |
| | 4.18 Training |
| | 4.20 Statistical Techniques |
| Software Configuration Management | 4.1 Management Responsibility |
| | 4.1.2 Organization |
| | 4.1.2.1 Responsibility and Authority |
| | 4.1.2.2 Resources |
| | 4.1.3 Management Review |
| | 4.2 Quality System |
| | 4.2.2 Quality-System Procedures |
| | 4.4 Design Control |
| | 4.4.1 General |
| | 4.4.9 Design Changes |
| | 4.5 Document and Data Control |
| | 4.8 Product Identification and Traceability |
| | 4.9 Process Control |
| | 4.12 Inspection and Test Status |
| | 4.13 Control of Nonconforming Product |
| | 4.16 Control of Quality Records |
| | 4.18 Training |
| | 4.20 Statistical Techniques |
| Organization Process Focus | 4.1 Management Responsibility |
| | 4.1.2 Organization |
| | 4.1.2.1 Responsibility and Authority |
| | 4.1.2.2 Resources |
| | 4.1.3 Management Review |
| | 4.2 Quality System |
| | 4.2.2 Quality-System Procedures |

**Table I.1**  SEI CMM Statements Correlated to ISO 9001 (Continued)

| SEI CMM Requirement | ISO 9001 Correlated Requirements |
| --- | --- |
| Organization Process Definition | 4.18 Training |
| | 4.20 Statistical Techniques |
| | 4.1 Management Responsibility |
| | 4.1.2 Organization |
| | 4.1.2.2 Resources |
| | 4.1.3 Management Review |
| | 4.2 Quality System |
| | 4.2.2 Quality-System Procedures |
| | 4.9 Process Control |
| | 4.18 Training |
| | 4.20 Statistical Techniques |
| Training Program | 4.1 Management Responsibility |
| | 4.1.2 Organization |
| | 4.1.2.1 Responsibility and Authority |
| | 4.1.2.2 Resources |
| | 4.1.3 Management Review |
| | 4.2 Quality System |
| | 4.2.2 Quality-System Procedures |
| | 4.18 Training |
| | 4.20 Statistical Techniques |
| Integrated Software Management | 4.1 Management Responsibility |
| | 4.1.2 Organization |
| | 4.1.2.2 Resources |
| | 4.1.3 Management Review |
| | 4.2 Quality System |
| | 4.2.2 Quality-System Procedures |
| | 4.9 Process Control |
| | 4.18 Training* |
| | 4.20 Statistical Techniques |
| Software Product Engineering | 4.1 Management Responsibility |
| | 4.1.2 Organization |
| | 4.1.2.2 Resources |
| | 4.1.3 Management Review |

**Table I.1** SEI CMM Statements Correlated to ISO 9001 (Continued)

| SEI CMM Requirement | ISO 9001 Correlated Requirements |
|---|---|
| | 4.2 Quality System |
| | 4.2.2 Quality-System Procedures |
| | 4.4 Design Control |
| | 4.4.1 General |
| | 4.4.4 Design Input |
| | 4.4.5 Design Output |
| | 4.4.6 Design Review |
| | 4.4.7 Design Verification |
| | 4.4.8 Design Validation |
| | 4.9 Process Control |
| | 4.10 Inspection and Testing |
| | 4.10.1 General |
| | 4.10.3 In-Process Inspection and Testing |
| | 4.10.4 Final Inspection and Testing |
| | 4.10.5 Inspection and Test Records |
| | 4.13 Control of Nonconforming Product |
| | 4.18 Training |
| | 4.20 Statistical Techniques |
| Intergroup Coordination | 4.1 Management Responsibility |
| | 4.1.2 Organization |
| | 4.1.2.1 Responsibility and Authority |
| | 4.1.2.2 Resources |
| | 4.1.3 Management Review |
| | 4.2 Quality System |
| | 4.2.2 Quality-System Procedures |
| | 4.4 Design Control |
| | 4.4.3 Organizational and Technical Interfaces |
| | 4.18 Training |
| | 4.20 Statistical Techniques |
| | 4.20.1 Identification of Need |
| | 4.20.2 Procedures |
| Peer Reviews | 4.1 Management Responsibility |
| | 4.1.2 Organization |

**Table I.1** SEI CMM Statements Correlated to ISO 9001 (Continued)

| SEI CMM Requirement | ISO 9001 Correlated Requirements |
|---|---|
| | 4.1.2.2 Resources |
| | 4.1.3 Management Review |
| | 4.2 Quality System |
| | 4.2.2 Quality-System Procedures |
| | 4.4 Design Control |
| | 4.4.6 Design Review |
| | 4.9 Process Control |
| | 4.10 Inspection and Testing |
| | 4.10.1 General |
| | 4.10.4 Final Inspection and Testing |
| | 4.10.5 Inspection and Test Records |
| | 4.18 Training |
| | 4.20 Statistical Techniques |
| Quantitative Process Management | 4.1 Management Responsibility |
| | 4.1.2 Organization |
| | 4.1.2.1 Responsibility and Authority |
| | 4.1.2.2 Resources |
| | 4.1.3 Management Review |
| | 4.2 Quality System |
| | 4.2.2 Quality-System Procedures |
| | 4.9 Process Control |
| | 4.18 Training |
| | 4.20 Statistical Techniques |
| | 4.20.1 Identification of Need |
| | 4.20.2 Procedures |
| Software Quality Management | 4.1 Management Responsibility |
| | 4.1.1 Quality Policy |
| | 4.1.2 Organization |
| | 4.1.2.2 Resources |
| | 4.1.3 Management Review |
| | 4.2 Quality System |
| | 4.2.2 Quality-System Procedures |
| | 4.6 Purchasing |

**Table I.1** SEI CMM Statements Correlated to ISO 9001 (Continued)

| SEI CMM Requirement | ISO 9001 Correlated Requirements |
|---|---|
| | 4.18 Training |
| | 4.20 Statistical Techniques |
| Defect Prevention | 4.1 Management Responsibility |
| | 4.1.2 Organization |
| | 4.1.2.1 Responsibility and Authority |
| | 4.1.2.2 Resources |
| | 4.1.3 Management Review |
| | 4.2 Quality System |
| | 4.2.2 Quality-System Procedures |
| | 4.14 Corrective and Preventative Action |
| | 4.14.3 Preventative Action |
| | 4.18 Training |
| | 4.20 Statistical Techniques |
| Technology Change Management | 4.1 Management Responsibility |
| | 4.1.2 Organization |
| | 4.1.2.1 Responsibility and Authority |
| | 4.1.2.2 Resources |
| | 4.1.3 Management Review |
| | 4.2 Quality System |
| | 4.2.2 Quality-System Procedures |
| | 4.9 Process Control |
| | 4.18 Training |
| | 4.20 Statistical Techniques |
| Process Change Management | 4.1 Management Responsibility |
| | 4.1.2 Organization |
| | 4.1.2.2 Resources |
| | 4.1.3 Management Review |
| | 4.2 Quality System |
| | 4.2.2 Quality-System Procedures |
| | 4.18 Training |
| | 4.20 Statistical Techniques |

# J

# Quality Plans

SEI and ISO both address quality plans. The specific details for quality plans that these methodologies outline follow. Malcolm Baldrige does not provide this level of detail in its requirements for quality plans.

## ▦ J.1 SEI QUALITY PLANS

As part of its subpractices, SEI addresses quality planning in the following key process areas:

- ✧ Software Subcontract Management, by the requirement for a subcontractor's software development plan.
- ✧ Software Quality Assurance, by the requirement for a software quality assurance plan.
- ✧ Software Configuration Management, by the requirement for a software configuration plan.
- ✧ Intergroup Coordination, by the requirement for a documented plan that is used as a baseline for the project schedule, contractual/technical aspects of the project, and assignment of responsibilities to the engineering groups.
- ✧ Peer Reviews, by the requirement for documenting plans for peer reviews.
- ✧ Quantitative Process Management, by the requirement for a quantified process management plan, which, among other important aspects, includes identifying tasks or other activities that need to be measured and analyzed.

✧  Software Quality Management, by the requirement for a software quality plan.

✧  Defect Prevention, by the requirement for a defect prevention plan.

✧  Technology Change Management, by the requirement for a technology change management plan.

✧  Process Change Management, by the requirement for a software process improvement plan.

The details of each plan are outlined next.

### SEI's Software Development Plan[1] covers

1. The software project's purpose, scope, goals, and objectives.
2. Selection of software life cycle.
3. Identification of the selected procedures, methods, and standards for developing and/or maintaining the software.

   Examples of software standards and procedures include

   ✗  software development planning,

   ✗  software configuration management,

   ✗  software quality assurance,

   ✗  software design,

   ✗  problem tracking and resolution, and

   ✗  software measurement.

4. Identification of software work products to be developed.
5. Size estimates of the software work products and any changes to the software work products.
6. Estimates of the software project's effort and costs.
7. Estimated use of critical computer resources.
8. The software project's schedules, including identification of milestones and reviews.
9. Identification and assessment of the project's software risks.
10. Plans for the project's software engineering facilities and support tools.

   SEI's Subcontractor's Software Development Plan covers the same content as the Software Project Planning's software development plan.

---

1. Software Engineering Institute, CMU/SEI-93-TR-25, *Key Practices of the Capability Maturity Model, Version 1.1* (Carnegie Mellon University, 1993), pp. L2-19–L2-20.

## SEI's Software Quality Assurance (SQA) Plan[2] covers

1. Responsibilities and authority of the SQA group.
2. Resource requirements for the SQA group (including staff, tools, and facilities).
3. Schedule and funding of the project's SQA group activities.
4. The SQA group's participation in establishing the software development plan, standards, and procedures for the project.
5. Evaluations to be performed by the SQA group. Examples of products and activities to be evaluated include

    ✘ operational software and support software,

    ✘ deliverable and nondeliverable products,

    ✘ software and nonsoftware products (e.g., documents),

    ✘ product development and product verification activities (e.g., executing test cases), and

    ✘ the activities followed in creating the product.

6. Audits and reviews to be conducted by the SQA group.
7. Project standards and procedures to be used as the basis for the SQA group's reviews and audits.
8. Procedures for documenting and tracking noncompliance issues to closure.
9. Documentation that the SQA group is required to produce.
10. Method and frequency of providing feedback to the software engineering group and other software-related groups on SQA activities.

## SEI's Software Configuration Management (SCM) Plan[3] covers

1. The SCM activities to be performed, the schedule of activities, the assigned responsibilities, and the resources required (including staff, tools, and computer facilities).
2. The SCM requirement and activities to be performed by the software engineering group and other software-related groups.

## SEI's Intergroup Coordination Plan[4] is

1. The baseline for

    ✘ the project schedule,

---

2. Ibid., pp. L2-64–L2-65.
3. Ibid., p. L2-77.
4. Ibid., pp. L3-88–L3-89.

    ✗ the contractual and technical aspects of the project, and

    ✗ the assignment of responsibilities to the engineering groups.

2. Used to coordinate activities among the different engineering groups.
3. Readily available to the members of all engineering groups.
4. Updated to incorporate all intergroup commitments and changes to these commitments.
5. Updated as the work progresses to reflect progress and plan changes at the project level, particularly when major project milestones are completed and when plans change significantly.
6. Reviewed and agreed to by all engineering groups and the project manager.

## SEI's Peer Reviews Plans[5]

1. Identify the software work products that will undergo peer review.
2. Specify the schedule of peer reviews.

## SEI's Quantitative Process Management Plan[6] covers

1. The goals and objectives of the quantitative process management activities.
2. The software tasks or other software activities that will be measured and analyzed.
3. The instrumentation of the project's defined software process. The instrumentation is based on the organization's measurement program, the description of the organization's standard software process, and the description of the project's defined software process.
4. The quantitative process management activities to be performed and the schedule for these activities.
5. The groups and individuals responsible for the quantitative process management activities.
6. The resources required to perform the quantitative process management activities, including staff and tools.
7. The procedures to be followed in performing the quantitative process management activities.

---

5. Ibid., p. L3-97.
6. Ibid., pp. L4-7–L4-8.

## SEI's Software Quality Management software quality plan[7] covers

1. The points in the process where software quality is measured.

2. The high-leverage quality goals for the software products. High-leverage quality goals for the software products are those that provide the greatest customer satisfaction at the least cost, or the "must haves" from the customer or end user.

3. The actions that the software project will implement to improve on past quality performance.

4. Quality goals for software work products, as appropriate. Examples of quality goals for software products that are appropriate to document in the project's software quality plan include

   ✘ the characteristics that are planned to be met and

   ✘ the critical characteristics that, if not met, would make the product undesirable or not needed by the customers or end user.

5. The actions that will be taken when the software product quality is projected not to meet the quality goals.

## SEI's Defect Prevention Plan[8]

1. Identifies the defect prevention activities (e.g., task kick-off and causal analysis meetings) that will be held.

2. Specifies the schedule of defect prevention activities.

3. Covers the assigned responsibilities and resources required, including staff and tools.

4. Undergoes peer review.

## SEI's Technology Change Management Plan[9]

1. Covers the assigned responsibilities and resources required, including staff and tools.

2. Defines the long-term technical strategy for automating and improving the organization's standard software process and enhancing the organization's market position.

3. Identifies the procedures to be followed in performing the organization's technology change management activities.

4. Describes the approach for introducing new technologies to address specific needs of the organization and projects.

---

7. Ibid., p. L4-26.
8. Ibid., pp. L5-23–L5-24.
9. Ibid., pp. L5-38–L5-39.

✗ Process areas that are potential areas for technology changes are identified.

✗ Approaches for identifying opportunities for technology changes are identified.

✗ The specific planned or candidate technologies are identified.

✗ Where appropriate, the life span for the planned technologies is estimated, from introduction to replacement.

✗ The make/buy trade-off studies are documented.

✗ Approaches for assessing unproven candidate technologies are defined.

✗ The acquisition and installation procedures are defined.

✗ The initial training, continuing training, and consultation support are defined.

5. Undergoes peer review.

6. Is reviewed by the affected managers.

## SEI's Process Change Management Plan[10] covers

1. The resources required, including staff and tools.

2. The highest priority process areas for improvement.

3. Measurable short-term and long-term goals for the software process performance and improvement.

4. Teams and their assignments for addressing improvements for specific process areas.

5. The procedures for

✗ the senior managers overseeing the software process improvement activities;

✗ the software managers planning and coordinating the software process improvement activities;

✗ individuals and teams identifying, evaluating, and introducing appropriate software process improvements; and

✗ the teams developing software process improvements for assigned process areas.

6. The administrative and support plans required to maintain continuous process improvement.

✗ Appropriate administrative procedures are included to encourage participation in and facilitate the software process improvement activities.

✗ The roles and contributions of employees to continuous process improvement are recognized.

---

10. Ibid., pp. L5-38–L5-39.

# ■ J.2 ISO QUALITY PLANS

ISO outlines quality plans in two of its Guidelines, ISO 9004-1 and ISO 9000-3. These are not considered part of the auditable standards such as ISO 9001, but they do give the user a good idea of the types of items that are looked for during certification.

### ISO 9004-1 QMS Guidelines suggest that the quality plan should define

1. the quality objectives to be attained (e.g., characteristics or specifications, uniformity, effectiveness, aesthetics, cycle time, cost, natural resources, utilization, yield, and dependability);
2. the steps in the processes that constitute the operating practice of the organization (a flowchart or similar diagram can be used to demonstrate the elements of the process);
3. the specific allocation of responsibilities, authority, and resources during the different phases of the project;
4. the specific documented procedures and instructions to be applied;
5. suitable testing, inspection, examination, and audit programs at appropriate stages (e.g., design and development);
6. a documented procedure for changes and modifications in a quality plan as projects proceed;
7. a method for measuring the achievement of the quality objectives;
8. other actions necessary to meet the objectives.

### ISO 9000-3 Software Guidelines suggest that the quality plan should specify or reference

1. quality objectives, expressed in measurable terms whenever possible.
2. defined input and output criteria for each development phase.
3. identification of types of test, verification and validation activities to be carried out.
4. detailed planning of test, verification and validation activities to be carried out, including schedules, resources, and approval authorities.
5. specific responsibilities for quality activities such as
   - ✘ reviews and tests,
   - ✘ configuration management and change control, and
   - ✘ defect control and corrective action.

# K

# Malcolm Baldrige—Properties Matrix

**Table K.1** QMS Properties Matrix: Malcolm Baldrige

| Base QMS Activities | Leadership | Information and Analysis | Strategic Planning | Human Resource Development and Management | Process Management | Business Results | Customer Focus and Satisfaction |
|---|---|---|---|---|---|---|---|
| Planning | 1.1 | 2.2.a, 2.3, 2.3.a, 2.3.b | 3.1, 3.1.b, 3.2, 3.2.a, 3.2.b | 4.1, 4.1.a, 4.3 | 7.3.a, 7.4, 7.4.a, 7.4.b, 7.5, 7.5.a, 7.5.b | | 7.1, 7.1.a, 7.1.b, 7.3, 7.3.a, 7.3.b, 7.4, 7.4.a, 7.4.b, 7.5, 7.5.a, 7.5.b |
| Implementing | 1.1, 1.2 | 2.1.a, 2.2.a, 2.3.a | 3.1, 3.1.a, 3.2 | 4.2.a, 4.3, 4.3.b | 5.1, 5.1.a, 5.3, 5.3.a, 7.2 | | 7.1, 7.1.b, 7.2.a, 7.3, 7.3.a, 7.4, 7.4.a, 7.4.b, 7.5, 7.5.a, 7.5.b |
| Managing | 1.1, 1.1.a, 1.2.a, 1.2.c, 1.3, 1.3.b | 2.1, 2.1.a, 2.3, 2.3.a | | 4.3.b | 5.1.b, 5.2, 5.2.a, 5.2.b, 5.3, 5.3.b, 5.4, 5.4.a | | 7.1.a, 7.2, 7.2.b, 7.2.c, 7.3.b |
| Improving | 1.1.b, 1.2.c, 1.3, 1.3.a | 2.1.b, 2.2, 2.2.a, 2.2.b, 2.3.b | 3.1.c | 4.1.b, 4.3.b, 4.4.c | 1.1.b, 2.1.b, 2.2.b, 3.1.c, 5.1.c, 5.2.b, 5.3.c, 5.4, 5.4.b, 6.1, 6.1.a, 6.2, 6.2.a, 6.3, 6.3.a, 7.1.c, 7.2.d, 7.3, 7.3.c | 6.1, 6.1.a, 6.2, 6.2.a, 6.3, 6.3.a | 7.1.c, 7.2.d, 7.3, 7.3.c |
| Communicating | 1.2.b | | | | | | |
| Training | | 2.1.a, 2.3.b | | 4.3.a | 5.4.a | | |
| Motivating | | | | 4.2, 4.2.a, 4.2.b, 4.4, 4.4.a, 4.4.b | | | |

**Table K.2** QMS Properties Matrix Summary: Malcolm Baldrige

| Base QMS Activities | Base QMS Elements | | | | | | | Total | % |
|---|---|---|---|---|---|---|---|---|---|
| | E1 | E2 | E3 | E4 | E5 | E6 | E7 | | |
| A1 | 1 | 4 | 5 | 3 | 7 | 0 | 12 | 32 | 23.5 |
| A2 | 2 | 3 | 3 | 3 | 5 | 0 | 11 | 27 | 19.9 |
| A3 | 6 | 4 | 0 | 1 | 8 | 0 | 5 | 24 | 17.6 |
| A4 | 4 | 5 | 1 | 3 | 19 | 6 | 4 | 42 | 30.9 |
| A5 | 1 | 0 | 0 | 0 | 1 | 0 | 0 | 2 | 1.5 |
| A6 | 0 | 2 | 0 | 1 | 0 | 0 | 0 | 3 | 2.2 |
| A7 | 0 | 0 | 0 | 6 | 0 | 0 | 0 | 6 | 4.4 |
| Total | 14 | 18 | 9 | 17 | 40 | 6 | 32 | 136 | |
| % | 10.3 | 13.2 | 6.6 | 12.5 | 29.4 | 4.4 | 23.6 | | |

**Note:**

A1 = Planning
A2 = Implementing
A3 = Managing
A4 = Improving
A5 = Communicating
A6 = Training
A7 = Motivating

E1 = Leadership
E2 = Information and Analysis
E3 = Strategic Planning
E4 = Human Resource Development and Management
E5 = Process Management
E6 = Business Results
E7 = Customer Focus and Satisfaction

# L

# ISO 9001—Properties Matrix

**Table L.1** QMS Properties Matrix: ISO 9001

| Base QMS Activities | Base QMS Elements | | | | | | |
|---|---|---|---|---|---|---|---|
| | Leadership | Information and Analysis | Strategic Planning | Human Resource Development and Management | Process Management | Business Results | Customer Focus and Satisfaction |
| Planning | 4.1.1, 4.1.2.1, 4.1.2.2, 4.1.2.3 | 4.20.1 | 4.2.3 | 4.1.2.1, 4.4.3, 4.18 | 4.2.3, 4.4.2, 4.4.4, 4.4.6, 4.4.9, 4.6.2, 4.6.4.1, 4.9, 4.10.1, 4.11.2, 4.13.2, 4.14.3, 4.17 | | 4.3.3 |
| Implementing | 4.1.1, 4.1.2.1, 4.1.2.2 | 4.5.1, 4.5.2, 4.6.3, 4.14.3, 4.16, 4.20.2 | | 4.1.2.2, 4.4.3, 4.18 | 4.2.1, 4.2.2, 4.2.3, 4.4.1, 4.4.4, 4.4.5, 4.4.6, 4.4.9, 4.5.1, 4.5.2, 4.6.1, 4.6.2, 4.7, 4.8, 4.9, 4.10.1, 4.10.3, 4.10.4, 4.10.5, 4.11, 4.11.1, 4.11.2, 4.13.1, 4.14.1, 4.14.2, 4.14.3, 4.15.1, 4.15.2, 4.15.3, 4.15.5, 4.16, 4.17, 4.19 | | 4.3.1, 4.19 |

**Table L.1** QMS Properties Matrix: ISO 9001 (Continued)

| Base QMS Activities | Leadership | Information and Analysis | Strategic Planning | Human Resource Development and Management | Process Management | Business Results | Customer Focus and Satisfaction |
|---|---|---|---|---|---|---|---|
| | | | Base QMS Elements | | | | |
| Managing | 4.1.1, 4.1.3 | 4.5.1, 4.5.2, 4.5.3, 4.6.3, 4.10.5, 4.16, 4.20.2 | | 4.4.3, 4.18 | 4.2.1, 4.2.2, 4.4.1, 4.4.2, 4.4.3, 4.4.4, 4.4.5, 4.4.6, 4.4.7, 4.4.8, 4.4.9, 4.5.1, 4.6.1, 4.6.2, 4.6.3, 4.6.4.1, 4.6.4.2, 4.7, 4.8, 4.9, 4.10.1, 4.10.2.1, 4.10.2.2, 4.10.2.3, 4.10.3, 4.10.4, 4.10.5, 4.11, 4.11.1, 4.11.2, 4.12, 4.13.1, 4.13.2, 4.14.1, 4.14.2, 4.14.3, 4.15.1, 4.15.2, 4.15.3, 4.15.4, 4.15.5, 4.15.6, 4.16, 4.17, 4.19, 4.20.2 | | 4.3.1, 4.3.2, 4.3.4, 4.6.4.2, 4.14.2, 4.14.3, 4.16, 4.19 |
| Improving | | | | | 4.14.3 | | |
| Communicating | 4.1.1, 4.1.2.3 | | | 4.4.3 | 4.4.3, 4.7, 4.17 | | 4.3.4, 4.13.2 |
| Training | | | | 4.18 | 4.9 | | |
| Motivating | | | | | | | |

**Table L.2** QMS Properties Matrix Summary: ISO 9001

| Base QMS Activities | Base QMS Elements | | | | | | | Total | % |
|---|---|---|---|---|---|---|---|---|---|
| | E1 | E2 | E3 | E4 | E5 | E6 | E7 | | |
| A1 | 4 | 1 | 1 | 3 | 13 | 0 | 1 | 23 | 15.7 |
| A2 | 3 | 6 | 0 | 3 | 33 | 0 | 2 | 47 | 32.2 |
| A3 | 2 | 7 | 0 | 2 | 46 | 0 | 8 | 65 | 44.5 |
| A4 | 0 | 0 | 0 | 0 | 1 | 0 | 0 | 1 | 0.7 |
| A5 | 2 | 0 | 0 | 1 | 3 | 0 | 2 | 8 | 5.5 |
| A6 | 0 | 0 | 0 | 1 | 1 | 0 | 0 | 2 | 1.4 |
| A7 | 0 | 0 | 0 | 0 | 0 | 0 | 0 | 0 | 0 |
| Total | 11 | 14 | 1 | 10 | 97 | 0 | 13 | 146 | |
| % | 7.5 | 9.6 | 0.7 | 6.9 | 66.4 | 0 | 8.9 | | |

Note:

A1 = Planning
A2 = Implementing
A3 = Managing
A4 = Improving
A5 = Communicating
A6 = Training
A7 = Motivating

E1 = Leadership
E2 = Information and Analysis
E3 = Strategic Planning
E4 = Human Resource Development and Management
E5 = Process Management
E6 = Business Results
E7 = Customer Focus and Satisfaction

# SEI CMM—Properties Matrix

**Table M.1** QMS Properties Matrix: SEI Capability Maturity Model

| Base QMS Activities | Leadership | Information and Analysis | Strategic Planning | Human Resource Development and Management | Process Management | Business Results | Customer Focus and Satisfaction |
|---|---|---|---|---|---|---|---|
| | | | | Base QMS Elements | | | |
| Planning | | RM.AB.1, QP.GO.1, QP.GO.3, QP.AB.1, QP.AB.2, TM.GO.1, TM.AB.3, TM.AB.4 | | TP.GO.1, TP.GO.2, IC.AB.1 | RM.AB.1, RM.AB.2, RM.AB.3, PP.GO.1, PP.GO.2, PP.CO.1, PP.CO.2, PP.AB.1, PP.AB.2, PP.AB.3, PT.CO.1, PT.AB.1, PT.AB.2, PT.AB.3, SM.GO.1, SM.GO.2, SM.CO.2, SM.AB.1, QA.GO.1, QA.AB.1, QA.AB.2, CM.GO.1, CM.AB.1, CM.AB.2, CM.AB.3, IM.GO.1, IM.GO.2, IM.AB.1, | | RM.AB.1, RM.AB.2, RM.AB.3, PP.GO.1, PP.GO.2, PP.GO.3, PP.CO.1, PP.CO.2, PP.AB.1, PP.AB.2, PP.AB.3 |

**Table M.1** QMS Properties Matrix: SEI Capability Maturity Model (Continued)

| Base QMS Activities | Leadership | Information and Analysis | Strategic Planning | Human Resource Development and Management | Process Management | Business Results | Customer Focus and Satisfaction |
|---|---|---|---|---|---|---|---|
| Planning (Continued) | | | | | PE.GO.1, PE.AB.1, IC.AB.1, PR.GO.1, PR.AB.1, QP.GO.1, QP.GO.3, QP.AB.1, QP.AB.2, QP.AB.3, QM.GO.1, QM.GO.2, QM.AB.1, DP.GO.1, DP.AB.1, DP.AB.2, DP.AB.3, TM.GO.1, TM.AB.1, TM.AB.2, TM.AB.3, TM.AB.4 | | |
| Implementing | RM.AB.1, RM.AB.3, PP.GO.3, PP.CO.1, PP.AB.2, PP.AB.3, PP.AC.1, PP.AC.3, | PP.AC.15, PT.AC.11, CM.CO.1, IM.AC.5, PE.AC.2, PE.AC.9, PR.AC.3, QP.CO.1, | | TP.GO.2, TP.CO.1, IC.CO.1, IC.AC.1, IC.AC.2, IC.AC.3, IC.AC.4, IC.AC.5, | RM.CO.1, RM.AC.1, RM.AC.2, RM.AC.3, PP.AC.1, PP.AC.2, PP.AC.3, PP.AC.4, | | RM.CO.1, RM.AC.1, RM.AC.2, RM.AC.3, PP.AC.1, PP.AC.2, PP.AC.3, PP.AC.4, |

**Table M.1** QMS Properties Matrix: SEI Capability Maturity Model (Continued)

| Base QMS Activities | Leadership | Information and Analysis | Strategic Planning | Human Resource Development and Management | Process Management | Business Results | Customer Focus and Satisfaction |
|---|---|---|---|---|---|---|---|
| Implementing (Continued) | PP.AC.9, | QP.CO.2, | | IC.AC.6, | PP.AC.5, | | PP.AC.5, |
| | PP.AC.10, | QP.AB.3, | | IC.AC.7 | PP.AC.6, | | PP.AC.6, |
| | PP.AC.11, | QP.AC.1, | | | PP.AC.7, | | PP.AC.7, |
| | PT.GO.3, | QP.AC.2, | | | PP.AC.8, | | PP.AC.8, |
| | PT.CO.1, | QP.AC.3, | | | PP.AC.9, | | PP.AC.9, |
| | PT.AB.2, | QP.AC.4, | | | PP.AC.10, | | PP.AC.10, |
| | PT.AB.3, | QP.AC.5, | | | PP.AC.11, | | PP.AC.11, |
| | SM.CO.2, | QP.AC.6, | | | PP.AC.12, | | PP.AC.12, |
| | SM.AB.1, | QP.AC.7 | | | PP.AC.13, | | PP.AC.13, |
| | QA.CO.1, | QM.AC.3, | | | PP.AC.14, | | PP.AC.14, |
| | QA.AB.1, | QM.AC.4, | | | PP.AC.15, | | PP.AC.15, |
| | QA.AB.2, | DP.AC.3, | | | PT.AC.1, | | PP.ME.1, |
| | CM.AB.2, | TM.GO.2, | | | PT.AC.2, | | PP.VE.1, |
| | CM.AB.3, | TM.GO.3, | | | PT.AC.3, | | PP.VE.2, |
| | PF.AB.1, | TM.CO.1, | | | PT.AC.5, | | PP.VE.3, |
| | PF.AB.2, | TM.AB.3, | | | PT.AC.6, | | PT.AC.2, |
| | PD.AB.1, | TM.AC.1, | | | PT.AC.7, | | PT.AC.3 |
| | TP.AB.1, | TM.AC.2, | | | PT.AC.8, | | |
| | TP.AB.2, | TM.AC.4, | | | PT.AC.9, | | |
| | IM.AB.1, | TM.AC.5, | | | PT.AC.10, | | |
| | PE.AB.1, | TM.AC.6, | | | PT.AC.11, | | |
| | IC.GO.1, | TM.AC.7, | | | PT.AC.12, | | |
| | IC.GO.2, | TM.AC.8, | | | PT.AC.13, | | |
| | IC.GO.3, | TM.ME.1 | | | SM.AC.1, | | |
| | IC.CO.1, | | | | SM.AC.2, | | |
| | IC.AB.1, | | | | SM.AC.3, | | |
| | IC.AB.2, | | | | SM.AC.4, | | |
| | IC.AB.3, | | | | SM.AC.5, | | |
| | IC.AB.4, | | | | SM.AC.6, | | |
| | IC.AB.5, | | | | SM.AC.7, | | |
| | IC.AC.1, | | | | SM.AC.8, | | |

**Table M.1** QMS Properties Matrix: SEI Capability Maturity Model (Continued)

| | | | | Base QMS Elements | | | |
|---|---|---|---|---|---|---|---|
| Base QMS Activities | Leadership | Information and Analysis | Strategic Planning | Human Resource Development and Management | Process Management | Business Results | Customer Focus and Satisfaction |
| Implementing (Continued) | IC.AC.2, IC.AC.3, IC.AC.4, IC.AC.5, IC.AC.6, IC.AC.7, IC.ME.1, IC.VE.1, IC.VE.2, IC.VE.3, PR.AB.1, QP.AB.1, QP.AB.2, QM.CO.1, QM.AB.1, DP.AB.1, DP.AB.2, TM.AB.1, TM.AB.2, PC.AB.1 | | | | SM.AC.9, SM.AC.10, SM.AC.11, SM.AC.12, SM.AC.13, QA.CO.1, QA.AC.1, QA.AC.2, QA.AC.3, QA.AC.4, QA.AC.5, QA.AC.7, QA.AC.8, CM.GO.1, CM.AB.1, CM.AB.2, CM.AB.3, CM.CO.1, CM.AC.1, CM.AC.2, CM.AC.3, CM.AC.4, CM.AC.5, CM.AC.6, CM.AC.7, CM.AC.9, CM.AC.10, PD.GO.1, PD.GO.2, PD.CO.1, PD.AB.1, | | |

**Table M.1** QMS Properties Matrix: SEI Capability Maturity Model (Continued)

| Base QMS Activities | Leadership | Information and Analysis | Strategic Planning | Human Resource Development and Management | Process Management | Business Results | Customer Focus and Satisfaction |
|---|---|---|---|---|---|---|---|
| | | | | **Base QMS Elements** | | | |
| Implementing (Continued) | | | | | PD.AC.1, PD.AC.2, PD.AC.3, PD.AC.4, PD.AC.5, PD.AC.6, TP.AC.2, TP.AC.4, TP.AC.5, IM.CO.1, IM.AC.1, IM.AC.2, IM.AC.3, IM.AC.4, IM.AC.5, IM.AC.6, IM.AC.7, IM.AC.8, IM.AC.9, IM.AC.10, IM.AC.11, PE.GO.1, PE.GO.2, PE.CO.1, PE.AC.1, PE.AC.2, PE.AC.3, PE.AC.4, PE.AC.5, PE.AC.6, PE.AC.7, | | |

**Table M.1** QMS Properties Matrix: SEI Capability Maturity Model (Continued)

| Base QMS Activities | Base QMS Elements | | | | | | |
| --- | --- | --- | --- | --- | --- | --- | --- |
| | Leadership | Information and Analysis | Strategic Planning | Human Resource Development and Management | Process Management | Business Results | Customer Focus and Satisfaction |
| Implementing (Continued) | | | | | PE.AC.8, PE.AC.9, PE.AC.10, IC.GO.1, IC.GO.2, IC.CO.1, IC.AC.1, IC.AC.2, IC.AC.3, IC.AC.4, IC.AC.5, IC.AC.6, IC.AC.7, PR.GO.2, PR.CO.1, PR.AC.1, PR.AC.2, PR.AC.3, QP.CO.1, QP.CO.2, QP.AC.1, QP.AC.2, QP.AC.3, QP.AC.4, QP.AC.5, QP.AC.6, QP.AC.7, QM.CO.1, QM.AC.1, QM.AC.2, QM.AC.3, | | |

**Table M.1** QMS Properties Matrix: SEI Capability Maturity Model (Continued)

| Base QMS Activities | Base QMS Elements | | | | | | |
|---|---|---|---|---|---|---|---|
| | Leadership | Information and Analysis | Strategic Planning | Human Resource Development and Management | Process Management | Business Results | Customer Focus and Satisfaction |
| Implementing (Continued) | | | | | QM.AC.4, QM.AC.5, DP.GO.2, DP.GO.3, DP.CO.1, DP.CO.2, DP.AC.1, DP.AC.2, DP.AC.3, DP.AC.4, DP.AC.5, DP.AC.6, DP.AC.7, DP.AC.8, TM.GO.2, TM.GO.3, TM.CO.1, TM.AC.1, TM.AC.2, TM.AC.4, TM.AC.5, TM.AC.6, TM.AC.7, TM.AC.8, PC.AC.3, PC.AC.4, PC.AC.5, PC.AC.8 | | |
| Managing | RM.VE.1, RM.VE.2, | RM.ME.1, PP.AC.15, | | IC.GO.3, IC.ME.1, | RM.GO.1, RM.GO.2, | | RM.GO.1, RM.GO.2, |

**Table M.1** QMS Properties Matrix: SEI Capability Maturity Model (Continued)

| Base QMS Activities | Leadership | Information and Analysis | Strategic Planning | Human Resource Development and Management | Process Management | Business Results | Customer Focus and Satisfaction |
|---|---|---|---|---|---|---|---|
| Managing (Continued) | RM.VE.3, PP.AC.4, PP.VE.1, PP.VE.2, PP.VE.3, PT.AC.3, PT.AC.12, PT.AC.13, PT.VE.1, PT.VE.2, PT.VE.3, SM.VE.1, SM.VE.2, SM.VE.3, QA.AC.4, QA.AC.5, QA.AC.8, QA.VE.1, QA.VE.2, QA.VE.3, CM.VE.1, CM.VE.2, CM.VE.3, CM.VE.4, PF.CO.2, PF.CO.3, PF.VE.1, PD.VE.1, TP.VE.1, TP.VE.3, IM.VE.1, | PP.ME.1, PT.AC.11, PT.ME.1, SM.ME.1, QA.ME.1, CM.AC.8, CM.ME.1, IM.ME.1, PE.AC.9, PE.ME.1, PE.ME.2, IC.ME.1, PR.ME.1, QP.GO.2, QP.ME.1, QP.VE.1, QP.VE.2, QP.VE.3, QM.AC.4, QM.ME.1, DP.AC.5, DP.ME.1, TM.AB.4, TM.ME.1 | | IC.VE.1, IC.VE.2, IC.VE.3 | RM.ME.1, RM.VE.1, RM.VE.2, RM.VE.3, PP.GO.1, PP.GO.2, PP.GO.3, PP.CO.1, PP.CO.2, PP.AB.1, PP.AB.2, PP.AB.3, PP.AC.1, PP.AC.2, PP.AC.3, PP.AC.4, PP.AC.5, PP.AC.6, PP.AC.7, PP.AC.8, PP.AC.9, PP.AC.10, PP.AC.11, PT.ME.1, PT.VE.1, PT.VE.2, PT.VE.3, SM.GO.4, SM.CO.1, SM.AC.5, SM.ME.1, | | RM.ME.1, RM.VE.1, RM.VE.2, RM.VE.3, PP.ME.1, PP.VE.1, PP.VE.2, PP.VE.3 |

**Table M.1** QMS Properties Matrix: SEI Capability Maturity Model (Continued)

| Base QMS Activities | Base QMS Elements | | | | | | |
|---|---|---|---|---|---|---|---|
| | Leadership | Information and Analysis | Strategic Planning | Human Resource Development and Management | Process Management | Business Results | Customer Focus and Satisfaction |
| Managing (Continued) | IM.VE.2, IM.VE.3, PE.VE.1, PE.VE.2, PE.VE.3, IC.VE.1, IC.VE.2, IC.VE.3, PR.VE.1, QP.VE.1, QP.VE.2, QP.VE.3, QM.VE.1, QM.VE.2, QM.VE.3, DP.VE.1, DP.VE.2, DP.VE.3, TM.CO.2, TM.CO.3, TM.VE.1, TM.VE.2, PC.VE.1, PC.VE.2 | | | | SM.VE.1, SM.VE.2, SM.VE.3, QA.GO.2, QA.GO.4, QA.ME.1, QA.VE.1, QA.VE.2, QA.VE.3, CM.GO.2, CM.GO.3, CM.GO.4, CM.CO.1, CM.AC.4, CM.AC.5, CM.AC.6, CM.AC.7, CM.AC.8, CM.AC.9, CM.ME.1, CM.VE.1, CM.VE.2, CM.VE.3, CM.VE.4, PF.ME.1, PF.VE.1, PD.ME.1, PD.VE.1, TP.ME.1, TP.ME.2, TP.VE.1, | | |

**Table M.1** QMS Properties Matrix: SEI Capability Maturity Model (Continued)

| Base QMS Activities | Leadership | Information and Analysis | Strategic Planning | Human Resource Development and Management | Process Management | Business Results | Customer Focus and Satisfaction |
|---|---|---|---|---|---|---|---|
| | | | | **Base QMS Elements** | | | |
| Managing (Continued) | | | | | TP.VE.2, | | |
| | | | | | TP.VE.3, | | |
| | | | | | IM.GO.2, | | |
| | | | | | IM.ME.1, | | |
| | | | | | IM.VE.1, | | |
| | | | | | IM.VE.2, | | |
| | | | | | IM.VE.3, | | |
| | | | | | PE.ME.1, | | |
| | | | | | PE.ME.2, | | |
| | | | | | PE.VE.1, | | |
| | | | | | PE.VE.2, | | |
| | | | | | PE.VE.3, | | |
| | | | | | IC.GO.3, | | |
| | | | | | IC.ME.1, | | |
| | | | | | IC.VE.1, | | |
| | | | | | IC.VE.2, | | |
| | | | | | IC.VE.3, | | |
| | | | | | PR.ME.1, | | |
| | | | | | PR.VE.1, | | |
| | | | | | QP.GO.2, | | |
| | | | | | QP.ME.1, | | |
| | | | | | QP.VE.1, | | |
| | | | | | QP.VE.2, | | |
| | | | | | QP.VE.3, | | |
| | | | | | QM.GO.3, | | |
| | | | | | QM.ME.1, | | |
| | | | | | QM.VE.1, | | |
| | | | | | QM.VE.2, | | |
| | | | | | QM.VE.3, | | |
| | | | | | DP.ME.1, | | |
| | | | | | DP.VE.1, | | |

**Table M.1** QMS Properties Matrix: SEI Capability Maturity Model (Continued)

| Base QMS Activities | Base QMS Elements | | | | | | |
|---|---|---|---|---|---|---|---|
| | Leadership | Information and Analysis | Strategic Planning | Human Resource Development and Management | Process Management | Business Results | Customer Focus and Satisfaction |
| Managing (Continued) | | | | | DP.VE.2, DP.VE.3, TM.ME.1, TM.VE.1, TM.VE.2, PC.VE.1, PC.VE.2 | | |
| Improving | PC.CO.2, PF.CO.2, PF.CO.3, TM.CO.2, TM.CO.3 | PF.CO.2, PF.CO.3, PF.AC.4, PF.ME.1, PD.GO.2, PD.AC.5, PD.AC.6, PD.ME.1, TM.CO.2, TM.CO.3, PC.AC.9, PC.ME.1, PF.AC.4 | | | PF.GO.1, PF.GO.2, PF.GO.3, PF.CO.1, PF.AB.1, PF.AB.2, PF.AC.1, PF.AC.2, PF.AC.3, PF.AC.4, PF.AC.5, PF.AC.6, PF.ME.1, PF.VE.1, PD.GO.1, PD.GO.2, PD.CO.1, PD.AB.1, PD.AC.1, PD.AC.2, PD.AC.3, PD.AC.4, PD.AC.5 | | |

**Table M.1** QMS Properties Matrix: SEI Capability Maturity Model (Continued)

| Base QMS Activities | Base QMS Elements | | | | | | |
| --- | --- | --- | --- | --- | --- | --- | --- |
| | Leadership | Information and Analysis | Strategic Planning | Human Resource Development and Management | Process Management | Business Results | Customer Focus and Satisfaction |
| Improving (Continued) | | | | | PD.AC.6, PD.ME.1, PD.VE.1, PC.GO.1, PC.GO.2, PC.GO.3, PC.CO.1, PC.CO.2, PC.AB.1, PC.AC.1, PC.AC.2, PC.AC.3, PC.AC.4, PC.AC.5, PC.AC.6, PC.AC.7, PC.AC.8, PC.AC.9, PC.AC.10, PC.ME.1, PC.VE.1, PC.VE.2 | | |
| Communicating | | QP.VE.3 | | TP.VE.3, IC.GO.1, IC.GO.2, IC.AB.2, IC.AC.3, IC.VE.3 | RM.VE.3, PP.GO.3, PP.VE.3, PT.GO.3, PT.AC.1, PT.AC.4, PT.VE.3, SM.GO.3, | | PT.AC.4, CM.GO.4 |

**Table M.1** QMS Properties Matrix: SEI Capability Maturity Model (Continued)

| Base QMS Activities | Leadership | Information and Analysis | Strategic Planning | Base QMS Elements | | | |
|---|---|---|---|---|---|---|---|
| | | | | Human Resource Development and Management | Process Management | Business Results | Customer Focus and Satisfaction |
| Communicating (Continued) | | | | | SM.AC.5, SM.VE.3, QA.GO.3, QA.AC.6, CM.GO.4, CM.VE.4, PF.AC.7, PD.VE.1, IM.VE.3, PE.VE.3, IC.GO.1, IC.GO.2, IC.AB.2, IC.AC.3, IC.VE.3, PR.VE.1, QP.VE.3, QM.VE.3, DP.VE.3, TM.AC.3, TM.VE.2, PC.VE.2 | | |
| Training | | QP.AB.4, QP.AB.5, TP.AC.6, TP.ME.1, TP.ME.2 | | RM.AB.4, PP.AB.4, PT.AB.4, PT.AB.5, SM.AB.2, SM.AB.3, QA.AB.3, QA.AB.4, | RM.AB.4, PP.AB.4, PT.AB.4, PT.AB.5, SM.AB.2, SM.AB.3, QA.AB.3, QA.AB.4, | | |

**Table M.1** QMS Properties Matrix: SEI Capability Maturity Model (Continued)

| Base QMS Activities | Leadership | Information and Analysis | Strategic Planning | Human Resource Development and Management | Process Management | Business Results | Customer Focus and Satisfaction |
|---|---|---|---|---|---|---|---|
| Training (Continued) | | | | CM.AB.4, CM.AB.5, PF.AB.3, PF.AB.4, PD.AB.2, TP.GO.3, TP.AB.1, TP.AB.2, TP.AB.3, TP.AB.4, TP.AC.1, TP.AC.2, TP.AC.3, TP.AC.4, TP.AC.5, TP.AC.6, TP.ME.1, TP.ME.2, TP.VE.1, TP.VE.2, TP.VE.3, IM.AB.2, IM.AB.3, PE.AB.2, PE.AB.3, PE.AB.4, IC.AB.3, IC.AB.4, IC.AB.5, PR.AB.2, PR.AB.3, | CM.AB.4, CM.AB.5, PF.AB.3, PF.AB.4, PD.AB.2, IM.AB.2, IM.AB.3, PE.AB.2, PE.AB.3, PE.AB.4, IC.AB.3, IC.AB.4, IC.AB.5, PR.AB.2, PR.AB.3, QP.AB.4, QP.AB.5, QM.AB.2, QM.AB.3, DP.AB.4, TM.AB.5, PC.AB.2, PC.AB.3, PC.AB.4 | | |

**Table M.1** QMS Properties Matrix: SEI Capability Maturity Model (Continued)

| Base QMS Activities | Leadership | Information and Analysis | Strategic Planning | Human Resource Development and Management | Process Management | Business Results | Customer Focus and Satisfaction |
|---|---|---|---|---|---|---|---|
| | | | | **Base QMS Elements** | | | |
| Training (Continued) | | | | QP.AB.4, QM.AB.2, QM.AB.3, DP.AB.4, TM.AB.5, PC.AB.2, PC.AB.3, PC.AB.4 | | | |
| Motivating | | | | | | | |

**Table M.2** QMS Properties Matrix Summary: SEI CMM

| Base QMS Activities | Base QMS Elements | | | | | | | | |
|---|---|---|---|---|---|---|---|---|---|
| | E1 | E2 | E3 | E4 | E5 | E6 | E7 | Total | % |
| A1 | 0 | 8 | 0 | 3 | 50 | 0 | 11 | 72 | 9.7 |
| A2 | 59 | 32 | 0 | 10 | 160 | 0 | 25 | 286 | 38.4 |
| A3 | 57 | 26 | 0 | 5 | 102 | 0 | 10 | 200 | 26.9 |
| A4 | 5 | 13 | 0 | 0 | 45 | 0 | 0 | 63 | 8.5 |
| A5 | 0 | 1 | 0 | 6 | 30 | 0 | 2 | 39 | 5.2 |
| A6 | 0 | 5 | 0 | 47 | 32 | 0 | 0 | 84 | 11.3 |
| A7 | 0 | 0 | 0 | 0 | 0 | 0 | 0 | 0 | 0 |
| Total | 121 | 85 | 0 | 71 | 419 | 0 | 48 | 744 | |
| % | 16.3 | 11.4 | 0 | 9.5 | 56.3 | 0 | 6.5 | | |

**Note:**

A1 = Planning
A2 = Implementing
A3 = Managing
A4 = Improving
A5 = Communicating
A6 = Training
A7 = Motivating

E1 = Leadership
E2 = Information and Analysis
E3 = Strategic Planning
E4 = Human Resource Development and Management
E5 = Process Management
E6 = Business Results
E7 = Customer Focus and Satisfaction

# N

# Properties Matrix Summary

Table N.1 QMS Properties Matrix Summary Comparison

| Base QMS Activities | Base QMS Elements | | | | | | | MB (%) | ISO 9001 (%) | SEI CMM (%) |
|---|---|---|---|---|---|---|---|---|---|---|
| | E1 | E2 | E3 | E4 | E5 | E6 | E7 | | | |
| A1 | | | | | | | | 23.5 | 15.7 | 9.7 |
| A2 | | | | | | | | 19.9 | 32.2 | 38.4 |
| A3 | | | | | | | | 17.6 | 44.5 | 26.9 |
| A4 | | | | | | | | 30.9 | 0.7 | 8.5 |
| A5 | | | | | | | | 1.5 | 5.5 | 5.2 |
| A6 | | | | | | | | 2.2 | 1.4 | 11.3 |
| A7 | | | | | | | | 4.4 | 0 | 0 |
| MB (%) | 10.3 | 13.2 | 6.6 | 12.5 | 29.4 | 4.4 | 23.6 | | | |
| ISO 9001 (%) | 7.5 | 9.6 | 0.7 | 6.9 | 66.4 | 0 | 8.9 | | | |
| SEI CMM (%) | 16.3 | 11.4 | 0 | 9.5 | 56.3 | 0 | 6.5 | | | |
| MB points (%) | 9.0 | 7.5 | 5.5 | 14.0 | 14.0 | 25.0 | 25.0 | | | |

**Note:**

| | |
|---|---|
| A1 = Planning | E1 = Leadership |
| A2 = Implementing | E2 = Information and Analysis |
| A3 = Managing | E3 = Strategic Planning |
| A4 = Improving | E4 = Human Resource Development and Management |
| A5 = Communicating | E5 = Process Management |
| A6 = Training | E6 = Business Results |
| A7 = Motivating | E7 = Customer Focus and Satisfaction |

# A